John Courtney Murray and the
American Civil Conversation

John Courtney Murray and the American Civil Conversation

Edited by

Robert P. Hunt
and
Kenneth L. Grasso

William B. Eerdmans Publishing Company
Grand Rapids, Michigan

Copyright © 1992 by Wm. B. Eerdmans Publishing Co.
255 Jefferson Ave. S.E., Grand Rapids, Mich. 49503

Printed in the United States of America

Library of Congress Cataloging-in-Publication Data

John Courtney Murray and the American civil conversation / edited by
    Robert P. Hunt and Kenneth L. Grasso.
        p.   cm.
    Includes bibliographical references.
    ISBN 0-8028-0538-8 (pbk.)
    1. Murray, John Courtney.   I. Hunt, Robert P., 1955-   .
II. Grasso, Kenneth L.
    BX4705.M977J64   1992
    261.7′092 — dc20   92-4738
                                                            CIP

Contents

Introduction

IN HIS OWN LIFETIME, John Courtney Murray, S.J., was among America's best-known and most respected theologians. Murray's pathbreaking articles on church-state relations laid the intellectual groundwork for Vatican II's "Declaration on Religious Liberty" and what some have termed "the Catholic Human Rights Revolution" that followed in its wake. Simultaneously, Murray's innumerable articles, speeches, and lectures established him as perhaps the leading Catholic interpreter of the American democratic experiment and commentator on American public life. It was no accident that when, in 1960, *Time* magazine featured a lengthy article on "U.S. Catholics and the State," its cover featured a portrait of John Courtney Murray.

In the aftermath of his untimely death in 1967, Murray's work ceased to receive much serious and sustained attention. It even became fashionable in some circles to dismiss his work as hopelessly outdated and of little more than antiquarian interest. In recent years, however, Murray has been rediscovered. The occasion of this long-overdue rediscovery has been growing public debate about the proper role of religion in American public life and the moral foundations of American democracy. And, as the work of a confessionally and politically diverse array of scholars has established, Murray's work is relevant to us today precisely because it goes to the very heart of these contemporary debates. Robert W. McElroy is hardly alone in concluding that "the life-work of John Courtney Murray remains an unequaled starting point" for these discussions.

Recent scholarship has not only established Murray's relevance but has cast important new light on the nature and scope of his work. Although, as McElroy has pointed out, Murray was seldom a systematic writer, he was indeed a systematic thinker and was dedicated to a coherent intellectual project. George Weigel has pointed out that what he terms the John Courtney Murray Project consists of a number of distinct facets. The first of these was Murray's reexamination of the Catholic tradition of political and social thought as it related to the issue of church-state relations. This reexamination culminated in his developing a theory of religious freedom rooted not in religious in-differentism or subjectivism but in the exigencies of the objective moral order and Christian revelation. A second facet addressed the relation-ship of Catholicism to American democracy, to what Murray dubbed "the American Proposition." Murray concluded that the American experiment in self-government, properly understood, is fully compat-ible with Catholic teaching because that experiment in ordered liberty is rooted not in the secularistic rationalism of the Enlightenment but in "principles that are structural to the Western Christian political tradition." Finally, the Murray Project dealt with nothing less than the moral and philosophical foundation of democratic government. In opposition to the then-dominant proceduralist school, which grounded democratic government in the liberal individualist tradition, Murray sought to formulate a theory of democratic government rooted in "the Great Tradition" of Western constitutionalism and in the natural-law teaching that lies at the heart of that tradition.

Since Murray believed that democracy can flourish only where the natural-law tradition is held as patrimony, he was disposed to argue for the revival of a distinctively American public philosophy and theory of democratic government that fed off this patrimony. The essays contained in this volume reflect upon each of these aspects of Murray's political philosophy and, in the spirit of ecumenism and civil conver-sation that was dear to Murray's heart, arrive at some conclusions on the contemporary significance of the Murray Project.

The first three essays, by Richard John Neuhaus, William R. Luckey, and David Novak, provide three different theological perspec-tives on Murray's work. Neuhaus's essay, written shortly before his "ecclesial transition" to Roman Catholicism, stresses the areas of agree-ment between Murray's natural-law-based philosophy and the Lutheran perspective grounded in the orders of creation. He applauds Murray's careful appreciation of the essential moral purpose of, and intrinsic limits on, political life. Luckey explores Murray's impact on the development of Catholic doctrine as it relates to democratic government, and he finds Murray to be a faithful progenitor of the *philosophia perennis*. Novak, while finding parallels between his own and Murray's efforts to connect reason and revelation, questions whether Murray's particular brand of Thomism can truly effect a revival of natural law.

Murray's analysis of the American experiment in self-government is the organizing theme of the second set of essays. Robert F. Cuervo connects Murray's call for a public philosophy to the broader historical movement in the 1950s and 1960s to develop a viable philosophical foundation for democratic society in the face of the totalitarian threat. In light of Murray's concept of the nature and purpose of the public philosophy, Kenneth L. Grasso explores the implications for American democracy of the changing character of American pluralism. Murray's interpretation of the founding of America and the nature of the American proposition is the subject of Peter A. Lawler's essay. He asks whether Murray's natural-law philosophy, grounded in the harmony of faith and reason, does full justice to the views of the framers of the Constitution. David T. Mason asks whether the dualistic nature of Murray's philosophical and political enterprise, applauded by several other contributors, accords sufficient dignity to political life.

As was mentioned earlier, contemporary public debate over the proper relationship between religion, morality, and politics (as evidenced, for example, in the abortion controversy and the various efforts to apply Christian principles to contemporary economic life) has led to a Murray revival. The continuing relevance of the Murray Project is brought home in the third set of essays, which explore contemporary public arguments in light of Murray's work. Francis Canavan, S.J., discusses Murray's philosophy of religious liberty and its implications for contemporary America. Gerard V. Bradley applies Murray's analysis of the religion clauses of the First Amendment to the modern Supreme Court's interpretation of those clauses. He argues that Murray's religious "articles of peace" are in fact based upon particularly Christian principles and cannot be fully understood apart from those principles. Situating Murray within the contemporary Catholic debate over the economic implications of Catholic social teaching is the task undertaken by John C. Cort in his essay. Mary C. Segers uses Murray's distinction between public and private morality and his argument for a limited state to arrive at some tentative conclusions about where Murray might situate himself in the contemporary abortion debate. On the other hand, Robert P. Hunt uses Murray's account of the moral foundation of democratic government and his critique of continental laicism to suggest that various attempts to appropriate Murray as a defender of liberal neutralism are misconceived.

In a fitting epilogue for the volume, George Weigel explores the significance of Murray's thought for America today and suggests possible lines of development for the John Courtney Murray Project.

It was never presumed that these essays would provide the last word on Murray or the implications of his thought. Murray himself noted that "civility dies with the death of the dialogue," and the editors hope that these essays foster civil conversation about the relevance of the John Courtney Murray Project to the American experiment in ordered liberty.

The editors would particularly like to thank the Reverend Francis Canavan for his gentle yet persistent guidance and encouragement of their reflections on the great issues of political philosophy. And we would like to thank Father Richard John Neuhaus and George Weigel for their invaluable assistance in bringing this volume to fruition, and Timothy Straayer, our editor at Eerdmans, for his work in preparing the manuscript for publication. Thanks must also be extended to Kean College of New Jersey and St. Peter's College for their support of our research efforts, and to Karin Korb and James Mazzouccolo for providing the capable clerical assistance needed to bring the manuscript to completion.

I. CONFESSIONAL PERSPECTIVES ON THE MURRAY PROJECT

Democracy, Desperately Dry

Richard John Neuhaus

IN THE LAST FEW YEARS before his death in 1967, John Courtney
Murray was widely viewed as a known quantity, a spent force, a
venerable figure to whom gratitude was due for his past contributions,
but not as someone pertinent to the configuration of a radically new
future. This is the perspective on Murray conveyed by Garry Wills's
intriguing *Bare Ruined Choirs*, written in 1972. According to Wills (and
others), Murray had become something of a curmudgeon in those last
years. Amid the revolutionary heavy breathing of younger Jesuits,
Murray was the "old man" who could be counted on to put in a word
for "realism" at a time when talk about realism was derided as "defending the status quo."

If, in the latter half of the 1960s, one were looking for a Jesuit who
read prophetically "the signs of the times" and represented the putative
wave of the future, he was surely to be found in poet-polemicist Daniel
Berrigan. Temperamentally and substantively, the contrast between
Murray and Berrigan could hardly have been more dramatic. There was
the sharpest of differences between Murray's understanding of politics
and the political excitations of what we now call "the sixties." In 1960 he
wrote in *We Hold These Truths*,

> hence the climate of the City [of Man] is likewise distinctive. It is not
> feral or familial but forensic. It is not hot and humid, like the climate
> of the animal kingdom. It lacks the cordial warmth of love and
> unreasoning loyalty that pervades the family. It is cool and dry, with

3

the coolness and dryness that characterize good argument among
informed and responsible men. Civic amity gives to this climate its
vital quality. This form of friendship is a special kind of moral virtue,
a thing of reason and intelligence, laboriously cultivated by the
discipline of passion, prejudice, and narrow self-interest. It is the
sentiment proper to the City. It has nothing to do with the cleavage
of a David to a Jonathan, or with the kinship of the clan, or with the
charity, *fortis ut mors,* that makes the solidarity of the Church.[1]

In almost every specific, Murray's description of what politics in
the City of Man should not be is precisely what the politics of "The
Movement" of the sixties claimed to be. For many of its adherents, The
Movement was comparable to, often in competition with, and sometimes a replacement for "the solidarity of the Church." In the Roman
Catholic and other churches, superannuated refugees from radicalisms
past still have a palpable and poignant yearning for the feral and
familial solidarity of The Movement that was. As the old Old Left of
the 1930s comforted itself with the thought of what would be "Come
the revolution," so the new Old Left of the sixties dreams of the revival
of The Movement for "radical and systemic change" — a movement
that, in its view, has been temporarily blocked by the aberrant conser-
vatisms of the past twenty years.

Those born since, say, 1950 find it hard to appreciate the more
recent provenance of terms such as *liberal, conservative,* and *radical.* At
the end of the sixties, I tried to describe the curious convulsions of
ideological alignments in *Movement and Revolution;* I have more recently
described how my own mind has changed since then.[2] The point
pertinent to Murray is that, against the grain of the time, he remained,
most determinedly, a liberal. He refused to be "radicalized," the term
favored back then by the young and even by many, if not most, of his
contemporaries. Today it is frequently said that liberalism became a
term of opprobrium, "the *L* word," in the 1980s. But the *L* word was
in deepest disfavor also in the sixties. Among those associated with
"progressive" politics, it was *de rigueur* to declare oneself a "radical" of

1. Murray, *We Hold These Truths: Catholic Reflections on the American Proposition*
(New York: Sheed & Ward, 1960), pp. 7-8.
2. Peter Berger and Richard John Neuhaus, *Movement and Revolution* (Garden
City, N.Y.: Doubleday, 1969); Neuhaus, "Religion and Public Life: The Continuing
Conversation," in *How My Mind Has Changed,* ed. James M. Wall and David Heim
(Grand Rapids: William B. Eerdmans, 1991), pp. 52-62.

one sort or another. People disagreed about what kind of revolution was needed, but there was no doubt about the need for revolution. John Courtney Murray didn't want a revolution. Put differently, he thought we had had one in 1776, and he was exceedingly fond of it. With Lincoln, he thought that, among the political choices available, the American order was something like "the last, best hope of earth." Which is another way of saying that John Courtney Murray was a liberal.

As a liberal, he was very much opposed to illiberalism, whether of attitude or regime. He had no use for the "participatory democracy" of radicalisms that ran roughshod over rules, traditions, and nuanced argument. Passion was to be disciplined, not indulged, and certainly not celebrated. He understood that political excitements become institutionalized in oppression. The enemies of liberalism, whether domestic or foreign, were his enemies. Therefore Murray was, among other things, an anticommunist — and without apology, although not without nuance. Here, too, care must be exercised lest the rush of events overwhelm our remembrance of how the great contests were framed in still recent history.

Those born since 1950 typically think the label "liberal anticommunist" curious, if not an oxymoron. Anticommunism, they were taught to believe, was the specialty of conservatives, even of right-wingers. One expects that those, still younger, who come to political awareness after the great crumblings of Communist regimes that became manifest in 1989 will find it at least equally curious that anybody could not have been anticommunist. So rapidly do events transform political perceptions and vocabularies. To understand Murray, however, we must keep a firm fix on the arguments of his time.

Although Murray's thought was distinctive in many respects, he was very much at home in the 1950s "liberal consensus" notably described by Daniel Bell in *The End of Ideology* (1962). In this respect, Murray was regularly and rightly associated with Reinhold Niebuhr, and it is no accident (as Marxists used to say) that both of them graced the cover of *Time* as paladins of "The American Century" championed by that magazine's publisher, Henry Luce. Murray's "at homeness" with the liberal establishment can be interpreted as a sign of his facile accommodation to the powers that be, as was brilliantly, albeit wrong-headedly, argued by John Murray Cuddihy in *No Offense: Civil Religion and Protestant Taste* in 1978. But it is both more charitable and more accurate to recognize that, among intellectuals in post–World War II

America, it seemed to be a settled belief that liberal democracy had been vindicated in its victory over National Socialism and had to be defended with the firmest resolve in the face of its only globally ambitious and ideologically driven enemy — namely, communism.

The liberal consensus of the 1950s rested on three pillars, embodied in three iconic figures: Franklin D. Roosevelt, Reinhold Niebuhr, and Joseph Stalin. The Roosevelt tradition represented liberal social progress, Niebuhr kept liberals alert to the limits and imperatives of political morality, and Stalin represented the enemy of all that liberals held dear. In this scheme of things, we might place Murray alongside Niebuhr. Certainly, for many Roman Catholics he was a larger figure than Niebuhr. And one could argue that, by virtue of his influence through the Second Vatican Council, Murray will, in the long term, turn out to be the larger figure. This may be true at least in the sense that he helped to position by far the largest Christian community in support of religious freedom and democratic governance. By contrast, it is doubtful that Niebuhr, for all his personal and intellectual greatness, has had a similarly lasting influence upon Protestantism in America, never mind world Christianity.

In any event, by the latter half of the sixties all three pillars seemed to be losing their force to define the liberal consensus. The Roosevelt era's confidence in social progress was eroded by domestic challenges. Notably, the "black power" leadership that set itself in opposition to the civil rights movement led by Martin Luther King, Jr., persuaded many blacks and whites alike that "racist oppression" is not an aberration but is endemic to the American order. In addition, under Lyndon Johnson, we had discovered what Michael Harrington called "the other America." While there was euphoria about Johnson's War on Poverty, there was also a growing suspicion that the enemy, poverty, was the inevitable creation of our capitalist ways. From a revived Old Left, and from many who had formerly belonged to the liberal consensus, the word went out that something more radical was called for.

But of course the most important factor in the undermining of liberal confidence was Vietnam. In the fall of 1964, Clergy Concerned About Vietnam (later, Clergy and Laity Concerned) was formed. I recall being somewhat jolted at one of its rallies, in 1966, when Harvey Cox of Harvard Divinity School issued a rousing call for a "post-Niebuhrian ethic." Mr. Cox, unlike most others in what was becoming The Movement, was at least aware of the limiting ordinances of the Niebuhrian tradition. A growing number of Christians felt that those limiting ordinances could no longer be tolerated. It was becoming obvious that liberals were inviting political utopianism in from the cold to which it had been consigned by such as Niebuhr and Murray.

As for the third iconic figure, the icon of evil, Stalin's Soviet Union no longer served the liberal faith the way it used to. Khrushchev had attacked "Stalinism," and intellectuals in the West eagerly wanted to believe that he and his colleagues were "reformers." More important, "Amerika" (as some radicals spelled it) was in no moral position to criticize Soviet oppression, we were told, since the United States itself was guilty of perpetrating horrors such as its war in Vietnam. Even so moderate a figure as Martin Luther King, Jr., declared at a rally organized by Clergy Concerned on April 4, 1967 (exactly one year before his death), that "America is the greatest purveyor of violence in the world today."

This was the context in which liberals stopped saying they were anticommunist. Anticommunism came to be understood as the property of the Right. To be anticommunist was to support U.S. policy in Vietnam; anticommunism was a hypocritical denial of the systemic injustices of American society; anticommunism was a distraction from the real struggle between the poor of the world, represented by the valiant freedom fighters backed by Hanoi, and the oppressive forces of imperialist capitalism, represented by the United States. By the latter part of the sixties, all three pillars of an earlier liberalism seemed to have lost their defining force. Most liberals were as determinedly anti-anticommunist as they had been determinedly anticommunist before. But John Courtney Murray was having none of it.

II

Father Walter Burghardt, S.J., preached the homily at Murray's funeral in 1967. He talked about Murray's contributions to democratic theory and practice and, most particularly, to the Roman Catholic understanding of religious freedom. "With the mind went the manner," said Burghardt. "What John Murray said or did, he said or did with 'style.' I mean, the how was perfectly proportioned to the what. . . . How natural it sounded when he ordered a 'Beefeater martini desperately dry.' How uplifted you felt when he left you with, 'Courage, Walter! It's far more important than intelligence.' "[3]

Murray took his politics, like his Beefeater, desperately dry. In this respect he was going against the current of the political culture and was also encountering difficulties with the apparent direction of church teaching. He was less than enthusiastic about the grand moral (moralistic?) sweep of John XXIII's encyclical *Pacem in Terris* ("Peace on Earth"), and Paul VI's *Populorum Progressio* ("The Development of Peoples"), issued in the year of Murray's death, was likewise not in the Murray "style." Yet it was surely more than a matter of style, more than a matter of the "how" not being proportioned properly to the "what." In such papal pronouncements, and especially in the way they were politically deployed, one suspects that Murray would find much of the "what" missing.

It is not enough for Christians to cry, "let justice roll down like waters, and righteousness like an ever-flowing stream" (Amos 5). Murray insisted that a decent respect be paid to available irrigation systems. More specifically, Murray called attention to the irrigation system of truths and embodying institutions that is liberal democracy. To this day, it must be noted, pronouncements by Rome typically fail to take account of the American experiment in liberal democracy in the manner that it deserves, and in the manner that Murray so persistently recommended. (The Roman propensity to associate liberalism and democracy with the botched French Revolution of 1789 is due also, of course, to the continuing dominance of Continental thinkers on Roman Catholicism.)

It is a grave disservice to Murray to depict him as an uncritical celebrant of the American experiment. Self-criticism is at the heart of the liberalism that Murray represented. But, unlike more recent varieties of liberalism, Murray's liberalism was not an exercise in self-flagellation. It did not result in the paralysis of will that comes from blinding ourselves to what is worthy and important — maybe even of universal importance — in the experiment of which we are part. There was no hint of triumphalism or chauvinism in Murray's affirmation of the American experiment. There was, rather, a sense of humble wonder, of gratitude, of the awesome responsibility to

3. See George Weigel, *Tranquillitas Ordinis: The Present Failure and Future Promise of American Catholic Thought on War and Peace* (New York: Oxford University Press, 1987), p. 108.

preserve and transmit an achievement that is at once noble, fragile, and manifestly imperfect. Murray refused to become embroiled in subjective questions of whether "we" were better than "they" or whether our practice lived up to our moral claims. As lucidly and calmly as possible — that is to say, in a manner desperately dry — he contended for certain truths and the genius with which those truths have been institutionalized, however imperfectly, in the American experiment.

There are clear alternatives to the democratic "proposition," and judgments must be made. The judgment called for is not, first of all, a judgment about which social or political system is preferable: Is the United States superior to the Soviet Union, or Sweden superior to China? Rather, the judgment is, first and most importantly, between rival truths or propositions, between radically different concepts of how the earthly city is to be ordered. Murray was most particularly struck by the perennial temptations to "monism" in political thought and practice. Murray described with compelling clarity what he meant by monism:

> [the totalitarian's] cardinal assertion is a thoroughgoing monism, political, social, juridical, religious: there is only one Sovereign, one society, one law, one faith. And the cardinal denial is of the Christian dualism of powers, societies, and laws — spiritual and temporal, divine and human. Upon this denial follows the absorption of the Church in the community, the absorption of the community in the state, the absorption of the state in the party, and the assertion that the party-state is the supreme spiritual and moral, as well as political authority and reality. It has its own absolutely autonomous ideological substance and its own absolutely independent purpose: it is the ultimate bearer of human destiny. Outside of this One Sovereign there is nothing. Or rather, what presumes to stand outside is "the enemy."[4]

Of course the two great examples of such totalitarian monism in this century were National Socialism in Germany and Marxist Leninism. The latter held much of the world captive for decades, and also held in thrall some of the best minds in the West. In the early

4. Murray, "The Church and Totalitarian Democracy," *Theological Studies* 18 (December 1952): 531.

1980s, before the transformations of the Gorbachev era, President Ronald Reagan famously — or, as some say, notoriously — referred to the Soviet Union as an "evil empire." This provoked enormous criticism, and it is interesting to ask why that should be. That the Soviet Union was an empire, holding nations and peoples subject against their will, can hardly be disputed. The more fervent objections were undoubtedly to the adjective "evil." Some said the employment of such weighty language was tantamount to a call for holy war. Others protested that it got in the way of "improved relations" between "the superpowers." Yet others complained that it was a self-righteous assertion of America's moral superiority. And of course some raised all of these objections and more.

Prescinding as best we can from the partisan passions of the animus toward Reagan that animated much of our intellectual and journalistic leadership, it is useful to inquire into the antimoralistic moralism evident in the protest against the reference to an "evil empire." Among the truths proposed by that species of moralism is that there are no truths in the political realm, or at least no truths by which opposing political claims can be condemned as false. But Murray very unfashionably believed that politics deals in truths and falsehoods. The founders of the American experiment, he insisted, did not merely have "values" or "interests." They declared "we hold these truths." To be sure, truth and falsehood are not always self-evident, nor is there universal agreement about what constitutes truth. Distinctions and judgments must be made, and arguments must be not only conducted but also encouraged.

From the indisputable fact that there is no universal agreement on truth and falsehood some draw the conclusion that everything is relative. Murray drew a quite different conclusion. The fact of disagreement and confusion (and he liked to point out that most of what we call disagreement is really confusion) does not mean that civil argument about truth and falsehood is futile but that continuing the argument is ever more urgent. Democratic dispositions, habits, and institutions are essential to the continuing civil argument. Yet the very obligation to continue the argument is itself dependent upon truth claims that prevent premature closure, that keep us from coming to conclusions that end the argument.

This does not mean that Murray was committed to what is dismissively called "merely procedural democracy." Murray did embrace procedural democracy, but there was nothing "mere" about that procedure. Such procedure does not preclude understandings of what is true and false; to the contrary it assumes such understandings. Greater than any external threat to the American experiment is a proceduralism that denies the need to give foundational reasons for maintaining the procedure. Murray detected this danger in the kind of "secular technological reason" that views the ensemble of democratic institutions as a machine that will run of itself, requiring only the maintenance of engineers, without recourse to philosophical or theological justifications. Against that view, Murray contended that the truths held by the founders must be reexamined and reappropriated by each generation so that, in Lincoln's magisterial language, a nation so conceived and so dedicated can undergo a new birth of freedom. Murray wrote that

> if this country is to be overthrown from within or from without, I would suggest that it will not be overthrown by Communism. It will be overthrown because it will have made an impossible experiment. It will have undertaken to establish a technological order of most marvelous intricacy, which will have been constructed and will operate without relations to true political ends: and this technological order will hang, as it were, suspended over a moral confusion; and this moral confusion will itself be suspended over a spiritual vacuum. This would be the real danger resulting from a type of fallacious, fictitious, fragile unity that could be created among us.[5]

The monist and the technocrat, then, stood in sharpest contradiction to Murray's understanding of the democratic project. In both religious and secular garb, both are still very much with us today. Although critical of technocracy, Murray was by no means disdainful of the technical aspects of good governance. His understanding of natural reason and natural law required a recognition of the moral integrity of the "ordinary" tasks that are built into the orders of creation and preservation. Such tasks did not require an explicitly sacral or ecclesiastical benediction external to themselves in order to possess moral integrity. It has frequently been argued that recognition of the integrity of the secular was a distinctive achievement of the Reformation. Murray had no doubt that he came to an appreciation of the secular by a thoroughly Catholic route. The integrity of the secular

5. Murray, "Return to Tribalism," *Catholic Mind* 60 (January 1962): 7.

does not mean the complete autonomy of the secular — not by any means. In the Christian view there is an ontological unity that, however broken now by sin, is secured in God's self-revelation in Israel and the Christ and will one day be evident to all when history is consummated in the kingdom of God.

III

For Reformation thinkers, especially Lutherans, and for Murray, secular tasks possess an integrity that Christians are bound to affirm. One might debate whether Murray's thought in this connection was definitively shaped by a cultural milieu formed by the Reformation tradition or whether, as he appeared to think, it was drawn from Thomas and distinctively Catholic teaching. That is a debate of particular interest to those better schooled in Thomistic thought. I suspect that Murray, both self-consciously and by cultural osmosis, drew on diverse sources and very self-consciously presented his argument in a distinctively Catholic form. Contrary to his traditionalist critics, I take this to be a measure of Murray's greatness and not evidence that he was trying to smuggle the "Americanist heresy" into the Catholic mainstream. In any event, what Murray frankly termed "dualism" is very sympathetic to a Lutheran understanding of the relationship between secular and sacred, law and grace, creation and redemption — and, by extension, the relationship between state and church.

A brief aside on "dualism" may be in order. Dualism, of course, is a term very much out of favor in current discussions on many fronts. It is thought to be a virtue of almost any approach to almost anything that it is integrated, harmonious, and "wholistic" (or "holistic," as in holy). This may be taken as further evidence of the perduring monism in our culture and habits of thought. Most views that boast of being "holistic," one suspects, have achieved that status by leaving out arguments and evidences that do not fit in the scheme being advanced. At the same time, while dualism is thought to be a very bad thing, the same odium is not attached to the term *dialectic*. In discussing Murray's argument, one might therefore be inclined to substitute *dialectic* for *dualism*. The risk, of course, is that *dialectic* suggests existentialist presuppositions or the kind of "dialectical theology" associated with Karl Barth, and both of those are alien to Murray's thought. The better part of wisdom, it might be argued, is to bite the bullet and stick with *dualism*. After all, that is the unfashionable term that Murray employed to posit his challenge to ever fashionable monisms.

Murray's criticism of a wet, steamy, and religiously impassioned ("holistic") approach to politics in no way put him in the camp of reductionist rationalists or of those who think the question of politics is exhausted by procedural and technical considerations. Politics is a discrete task among many human tasks. Its dignity does not depend on its claiming to be everything. Indeed, it is among the chief of political tasks to restrain the hubris of the political. That task cannot be achieved, however, by reference to the political alone.

While politics definitely is not everything, it is just as definitely part of everything. Other sources of authority, other gifts of discernment are required to keep politics in its place. The political enterprise itself, and warrants for political judgment, must be justified by reference to that which is beyond politics, or at least beyond what is ordinarily meant by politics. As this is true of politics in general, it is most particularly true of democratic politics. The attempt to untether democratic politics from its justifying foundations is what Murray described as an "impossible experiment." That impossible experiment has been essayed many times in the two-hundred-year history of the secular Enlightenment and is today exemplified in, for instance, Richard Rorty's *Contingency, Irony, and Solidarity* (1989). This kind of radically antifoundational "pragmatism" with respect to democratic governance represents a frankly nihilistic stance that was not a significant factor in the intellectual context in which Murray worked. Murray argued against constructions of the democratic argument that he thought undeveloped or wrongheaded, but he did not encounter "deconstructionists" who insist that justifying reasons for democracy are neither necessary nor possible. This is a complicating factor in continuing the Murray Project in our time.

The proceduralists and technocrats sometimes advanced a rigorous line of argument in excluding consideration of the "truths" that Murray believed to be at the heart of the democratic proposition. More often, however, they were simply unreflective philosophically, and Murray saw it as his task to help them recognize the presuppositions that they were so cavalierly taking for granted. He warned his contemporaries against the dangers of a technological order "suspended over a moral confusion," and that confusion "suspended over a spiritual vacuum." Today's nihilists respond that of course Murray was right, but the confusion and vacuum are unavoidable. They would further agree with Murray that this is an exceedingly dangerous state of affairs, for it invites a filling of the vacuum with belief systems that satisfy our hunger for comprehensive meaning. In other words, it makes the attractions of totalitarianism extremely seductive. But this, they respond, is the situation in which we find ourselves. There is no alternative. The best we can do is to maintain a posture of "irony" toward all pretensions to provide justifying reasons for democracy and hope that enough people will, for their self-interested reasons, find this kind of polity attractive enough to keep it going.

Facing his secular critics, Murray would today find his argument with the technocrats and proceduralists dramatically sharpened by the new ascendancy of the nihilists. They would greet his dire warnings about the yawning abyss of meaninglessness with a yawn. As their master Nietzsche well understood, thoroughgoing nihilism has anticipated the criticisms raised to nihilism. For the serious-minded nihilist, only madness or death remains. For those who, like Rorty, eschew seriousness and cultivate a deliberate light-headedness about our situation, there is sophisticated irony and the wan hope that the worst will be delayed for a while. In short, the intellectual situation has changed significantly in the last twenty years.

Many who think about these matters have come to agree with Murray that the democratic project probably cannot be sustained without justifying reasons, without reference to truths that we hold in common. They move on from there, however, to claim that since there can be no such reasons or truths, we are in a new situation, a situation in which Murray's appeal to justifying truths reflects nothing more than a yearning for an innocence irretrievably lost. There is no reason to doubt that, were he working today, Murray would be up to contending with a different intellectual situation in which less and less can be taken for granted as a starting point for reasonable argument.

Facing his religious critics, Murray would also find a different situation, although he would undoubtedly be struck by the ironic twists in which old arguments are advanced under new auspices. Among his religious critics we must include the Marxists who, Murray rightly saw, offer a functionally *religious* solution to the crisis posed by a vacuum of public meaning. Today the militant monism of Marxism is in rapid decline and seems destined to be consigned, as Marxists used to say, to the dustbin of history. While Murray would no doubt be greatly encouraged by this development, he would not likely have any illusions that it meant the end of the monist impulse in human history.

Similarly, one expects that Murray would continue to be encouraged, as he was encouraged in his lifetime, by the end of ecclesiastical ambitions to incorporate the entirety of the social order under the church's sacred hegemony. Here too, however, he would surely insist that the victory over sacred "triumphalisms" is never secure. The monist impulse is vibrantly alive in sundry and steamy "liberation theologies" that promise to effect a synthesis of the sacred and profane, of eschatological hope and temporal order, of the City of God and the city of man. And, usually appearing on the Right of the political spectrum, we witness among some Catholic traditionalists and Protestant fundamentalists a monist longing for a coherently "Christian" social order. Monists on the Right and monists on the Left cannot make their peace with liberal democracy. For them, Murray's talk of "dualism" cannot help but smack of compromise, of settling for less.

Although I am not aware that he wrote about it, I imagine Murray would agree that there is something admirable in some forms of Christian monism. One can sympathize with the adamant insistence that, if Christ is Lord at all, he must be Lord of all. One can further understand the insistence that Christians should not just sit back waiting for a divine intervention but work now to actualize that lordship in history. Christians have at times been guilty of passivity and "quietism" with respect to the political task. As much as he might sympathize, however, Murray would no doubt argue today, as he argued then, that the monist ambition to establish a coherent or "integral" Christian social order is dangerously misguided. Although the eschatological note was not prominent in Murray's writing, the limits and imperatives derived from eschatological hope are entirely consonant with his political expectations.

His "dryness" on these subjects did not reflect resignation or cynicism but the courage that recognizes the tasks that are appropriately ours at this provisional moment in the unfolding of God's purposes. In addition to that courage, he had the wisdom that recognizes the hubris, albeit pious hubris, of the monist ambition. Duality and dialectic mark the Christian way of being in the world *for the duration*. The second-century *Epistle to Diognetus* aptly describes the Christian circumstance: "Though they are residents at home in their own countries, their behavior there is more like that of transients; they take their full part as citizens, but they also submit to anything and everything as if they were aliens. For them, any foreign country is a homeland, and any homeland a foreign country."[6] Murray understood that the Christian is always an alien citizen and that it is precisely as an alien that the Christian citizen can affirm the democratic form of governance that makes no claim to being a satisfactory or permanent home.

For the Lutheran Christian, Murray's keen appreciation of the duality and dialectic of Christian existence has obvious connections with the theological construct of the "two kingdoms." (Two kingdoms, it should be noted, is better expressed as the twofold rule of God.) To be sure, Murray was not a Lutheran. His understandings of natural law and the capacities of reason, never mind issues of ecclesiastical authority, would be hard to square with Lutheran theology. In addition, living as he did before the Lutheran–Roman Catholic theological dialogues demonstrated their full fruitfulness, Murray would no doubt have great difficulties with a Lutheran understanding of the gospel (salvation by grace through faith) as the "meta-dogma" by which all Christian teaching is to be judged. All that said, however, there are notable parallels between Murray and a Lutheran understanding of the political task.

With respect to the political task, there is striking similarity, if not identity, between Murray's view of natural law and the Lutheran view of the "orders of creation and preservation." I emphasize *with respect to the political task*. What St. Paul says in Romans 1 about the knowledge to be discerned from nature, or creation, is by no means denied by Lutherans: "Ever since the creation of the world his invisible nature, namely, his eternal power and deity, has been clearly perceived in the things that have been made." The Lutheran point is that what can be known from nature — God's power and deity — is not good news (gospel) for sinful human beings concerned about how they stand before God. Indeed, it is unremittingly bad news (law), for, as the apostle says in the same passage, it leaves us "without excuse."

However, the orders of creation and preservation — carefully distinguished from the orders of redemption and salvation — provide normative guidance for the right ordering of the earthly *polis*. These orders, with their "offices" and "vocations," uphold the basic institutions of ordinary life, such as family, state, and economy. Thus in the

6. Rowan Greer, *Broken Lights and Mended Lives: Theology and Common Life in the Early Church* (University Park, PA: Pennsylvania State University Press, 1986), p. 141.

Lutheran view, as in Murray's, these institutions are not merely associations of convenience contrived in the self-interest of contracting individuals. What Peter Berger and I have discussed as the "mediating structures" in society have their appropriate "mandates" that are finally grounded in God's creating and preserving purposes. (I would note in passing that the phrase "creating and preserving" may be misleading, since everything is preserved by God's continuous, as opposed to once-and-for-all, creation.)

The Lutheran tradition also shares Murray's high estimate of the role of reason *in the civil realm*. Luther was emphatic in asserting that the secularly wise unbeliever makes a better ruler than the piously foolish Christian. Murray and the Lutheran tradition are at one in unyielding opposition to salvific politics, in warning against the siren songs of any proposed New Order that can satisfy the human yearning for fulfillment or the requirements of the divine will. Both Murray and Luther recognized that there are spheres of obligation and aspiration that are appropriate to the life of the church and that these are both qualitatively different from and superior to the obligations and aspirations appropriate to the political task. (Casting the ecumenical net somewhat more broadly, the same recognition is well expressed also in the concept of "sphere sovereignty" as set forth by the Dutch Calvinist Abraham Kuyper.)

Here again we encounter a necessary "dualism." The civil order must not be conceived according to the nature and mandates of the Church, nor should the Church recast its life in terms of any political order, whether that order be democracy, absolute monarchy, or something else. If the Church is to render its appropriate service to the civil community, it must make clear the ways in which it is different from that community. The civil community and the faith community are constituted and ordered by different, but not conflicting, truths. When church and state come into conflict, it is because one or the other or both have forgotten the truths appropriate to their constitution. The abiding temptation is to avoid such conflict by conflating what is distinctive about each community. The church-as-state and the state-as-church are monisms to be rejected for the sake of both the church and the civil order.

Murray's sensibilities with respect to the political project — but not only his sensibilities — can readily be affirmed by Christians in the Reformation traditions, and especially by Lutherans. To be sure, there are Reformation traditions, notably those associated with what is usually called the Radical Reformation, that vigorously reject both Murray's and Luther's view of Christian responsibility in the civil realm. There is no question but that Murray would be on Luther's side in contending against Anabaptists such as Thomas Müntzer and the "Zwickau prophets" who violently struggled to establish "the rule of the righteous" in a political order for which they claimed a special inspiration from God. The millenarian tradition dating back to Joachim of Fiore (d. 1202) was well known to both Luther and Murray, and both recognized its perennial eruptions in the monist political impulse. It might be said that Murray fought monism primarily because it endangered the political order, and Luther fought it primarily because it obscured the gospel. On second thought, however, and given the dramatic differences in their historical situations, those two concerns may be more closely and necessarily related than at first appears.

Admittedly, it is hard to imagine Martin Luther ordering a Beefeater martini desperately dry. He took his Wittenberg beer very wet. Yet I expect that both Luther and Murray drank with the serious light-heartedness that comes with knowing that we are all alien citizens. The legacy of both for Christian political thought is a powerfully cautionary appreciation of the fragility and ambiguity of all political achievements. That will be mistaken as an essentially negative legacy by those who do not understand that it is premised upon prior allegiance to, and robust confidence in, the genuinely new politics of a rightly ordered *polis* that is not of this world.

*   *   *   *   *

The above essay was written in the final stages of a journey that led the author into full communion and ordination as a priest in the Roman Catholic Church. To the discerning reader, the dynmics of that transition are perhaps evident in the essay itself. Suffice it that subsequent developments require no substantive changes in the argument offered. In my judgment, what was authentic in the Lutheran Reformation is fulfilled and what was lacking is remedied in becoming a Roman Catholic. Then and now, I understand myself to be in communion with both Luther and Murray. Admittedly, I am more disposed to martinis desperately dry than to beer. But then, living when he did, some choices were not available to Luther. — RJN

The Contribution of
John Courtney Murray, S.J.:
A Catholic Perspective

William R. Luckey

CATHOLICS IN THE UNITED STATES have frequently found themselves in a peculiar position regarding their relationship with both
their non-Catholic neighbors and the theory and practice of American
government. Some, such as myself, who were born into the faith and
who lived in almost completely Catholic neighborhoods, were insulated
from most of the conflict. The most experience we had of the fact that
not all people agreed with our beliefs was the basic "apologetics" we
received in Catholic school. This part of our training taught us to
explain and defend our beliefs and practices to those who either asked
about them or attacked them. Other Catholics were not so fortunate,
either living in environments openly hostile to the faith or at least
attending public schools in which there was no presumption in favor
of Catholicism.

In addition to the personal aspect of living in a religiously pluralist society, there was the problem of the government. While neither
my family nor the families of any of my friends saw any real conflict
between the essential principles of the United States government and
the teachings of Catholicism, later on in my education, I noticed that
many Catholics did. Questions arose in the minds of devout students
of Church history that can be phrased as follows: If Catholicism is the
true faith, would not an ostensibly Catholic state be the best state? If
that were to be the case, what should be the attitude of loyal Catholics
to their nonconfessional state?

It is my purpose in this essay to discuss the thought of a person

19

who, probably more than any other writer, has successfully clarified the issues involved in the religion-state question as well as the question of the role of Catholicism in a pluralist society. That writer is John Courtney Murray.

Fr. John Courtney Murray of the Society of Jesus, whose thought has long been neglected by Catholics (among others), was a professor of theology at Woodstock Theological College, an institution of advanced theological studies for Jesuits. But while he was a professor of theology, his own research and professional development led him into the world of political philosophy and political theology, and ultimately he came to be the moving force behind, and intellectual architect of, the document *Dignitatis Humanae* of the Second Vatican Council. This document had a most profound influence on the world because it radically altered the way the Catholic Church, long itself a profound influence on the governments of the world, looked at and dealt with the modern state.

Despite this fact, most Catholics, if they are familiar with Murray's work at all, are acquainted only with his book *We Hold These Truths: Catholic Reflections on the American Proposition*. While this is a well-reasoned book, it is merely a culmination of some serious reflections on a number of major questions involving theology, history, and politics. Probably the major reason for the widespread unfamiliarity with Murray's work is the fact that most of it appeared in such theological journals as *American Ecclesiastical Review, Proceedings of the Catholic Theological Society of America,* and *Theological Studies,* although he also made some contributions to such more widely distributed periodicals as *The Catholic Lawyer* and *Modern Age.* A few of these were incorporated into *We Hold These Truths,* but this by no means gives the interested reader a complete perspective on Murray's thought. Those who get a broader taste of Murray's work cannot help but be impressed with his erudition and his command of and insight into law, philosophy, medieval history, and education.

The Background of Murray's Thought

Most people over forty can remember a time when children could safely leave their bicycles outside their homes, when we did not have to keep the doors to our homes locked all the time, when children could walk to school without fear of violence or kidnapping. We may debate why this situation no longer obtains ad nauseam, but most people would agree that the immediate post–World War II period was a watershed era for the change in popular mores and morals responsible for these and other problems.

It is into this milieu that God put Fr. John Courtney Murray. His career was almost mysteriously guided along paths different from what he probably anticipated because of his prophetic vision of an impending moral and religious crisis in the West, a crisis not necessarily restricted to intellectual circles alone.

Born in 1903, Murray received bachelor's and master's degrees from Boston College. He then joined the Society of Jesus, received the Licentiate in Sacred Theology from the Jesuit theologiate at Woodstock College, and attended the Pontifical Gregorian University in Rome, where he received his doctorate in Sacred Theology in 1943.

Though educated as a dogmatic theologian, Murray noticed that while the church had been fixing its attention on World War II, totalitarianism, and associated problems, another menace had arisen of which Catholic Church and most other religions took virtually no notice. The startling truth was that there was a rising tide of a virulent anti-Catholicism and antitheism in Europe. Murray wrote in 1944 that

> to the modern Christian the world is not his father's house. In fact it represents more closely the "the strong man's house" (Mark 3:27) with the strong man not yet bound. For decades, as Pius XII recently pointed out, "the progress of mankind has been without God, indeed against God, without Christ, indeed against Christ." The world today is alienated from the Church. It stands over against the Church, as a closed system of life. And the faith of the ordinary Christian gets hardly any support from his environment. On the contrary, his greatest temptation is to live in the world, over against the Church.[1]

So that no one could misunderstand, Murray insisted that Nazism and fascism were not merely the accession to power by force and cunning of a small minority of totalitarian ideologues. This accession to power was made possible by the wholesale European abandonment of Christianity. Hence, argued Murray, every human being was being crucified on a cross — not merely the cross of the total war

---

1. Murray, "Towards a Theology for the Layman," *Jesuit Educational Quarterly* 11 (1949): 349.

of World War II but the cross of a de-Christianized and therefore dehumanized life.[2]

Upon returning to the United States, Murray did not find the situation to be much better. In a number of perceptive articles, he sounded the warning that a similar situation was surfacing here, albeit in a different form and structure. In "Christian Humanism in America: Lines of Inquiry," Murray first noted that the United States had enjoyed a unique situation in the world whereby the things of God *(res sacra)* and the things of man *(res humana)* were somewhat integrated because the American system has generally removed a number of historical barriers to such integration — not the least of which were fear of physical deprivation and fear of religious persecution. The Church itself had, if you will, made an alliance with the *res sacra* and the *res humana* and had thereby gotten the resources and the freedom to perform its task. But, according to Murray, this relationship was fraught with danger.

> Lengthy and deliberate cultivation of a *mystique de la terre* has tended to paralyze the action of any specifically Christian mystique. Affirmation of the *res humana*, once made in the context of belief in God and an all ruling moral order, has gone over into exclusive affirmation of the *res huius saeculi* under ignorance or denial of the transcendent.[3]

This obscuring of the transcendent has had the effect of throwing out of balance the traditional "grace perfects nature" relationship. Hence in the United States, where technology has been the subject of endless worshipful statements, Murray contended that "belief in man has proved, with some groups, to be the enemy of belief in God, so that to many, all values are simply immanent in man and have no transcendent reference."[4]

The major source of this rejection of God in the United States has been the emergence of a materialist ethos and the tendency to rely on scientific and technological genius. According to Murray, the enemy of this country today is the "technological secularist" — the

2. See Murray, "The Pattern for Peace and the Papal Peace Program" (Washington: Paulist Press, 1944), pp. 4-5.
3. Murray, "Christian Humanism in America," *Social Order* 3 (1953): 236-37.
4. Murray, "Christian Humanism in America," p. 237.

person who "knows everything about all the instruments and techniques of power that are available in the world and who, at the same time, understands nothing about the nature of man or about the nature of true civilization."[5]

The cause of this ignorance concerning the nature of man and civilization is associated with acceptance of the epistemological and methodological presuppositions of modern natural science as the exclusive means to and form of truth. Modern America has the tendency to raise scientific method and technological innovation to the level of an all-encompassing ideology: "the betrayal began when modernity, having divorced faith and reason, went on to decide that there is only one form of rational truth, one method for its pursuit, one measure of the certitudes attained."[6]

"In this decision," Murray continues, "the modern will to atheism is more clearly discernible." Rationalism evolved into scientism, and all truths not derived from empirical methodology came to be ignored. It became axiomatic that "God can have nothing to do with the order of intelligence. He is therefore to be relegated to the order of fantasy. Religion is the work of imagination," and "Christianity is a religion of myths."[7] In this context it seems as though the soul has been taken out of American society: "the realization has struck home to many that in the course of all our furious building we have succeeded in erecting an immense structure that encloses — a vacuum."[8]

Unfortunately, society abhors a vacuum as much as nature does. People always act for a reason, and in the post–World War II context the question became which set of ideas would be motivating them. Murray argued that modern man had boiled the alternatives down to a false dichotomy: either only God exists, or only the world exists. We reached this conclusion because we rejected the assertion that the eternal (i.e., God) and the finite and contingent (i.e., man) could exist in the same universe. Murray poses the question in this way: "If God is, and if he is what he is, how can anything else be?" The question had been answered very well by the Scholastic thinkers, but posed in the modern context, it constitutes an invitation to a betrayal of the

5. Murray, "The Return to Tribalism," *Catholic Mind* 60 (1962): 6-7.

6. Murray, *The Problem of God* (New Haven: Yale University Press, 1964), p. 90.

7. Murray, *The Problem of God*, p. 90.

8. Murray, "Reversing the Secularist Drift," *Thought* 24 (March 1949): 37.

whole Western philosophical and theological tradition, a tradition that views Creator and creature not as opposites but as poles. To make either choice in the dichotomy is to choose choose *atheism,* said Murray.[9]

While the assertion that man alone exists obviously indicates a choice in favor of atheism, the implications of the assertion that God alone exists are less immediately clear. Does this assertion make any sense? Does it not deny *man's* existence? Murray explains that since man and the world obviously exist, the assertion that God alone exists automatically identifies the world with God. In other words, this assertion indicates a choice in favor of pantheism. But Murray contends that to choose pantheism is in fact to choose atheism: "if everything is God, nothing is God. . . . Pantheism is a denial of God as creator, and, if God is not the creator, he is not God."[10] Moreover, the indictment extends to all varieties of pantheism, from more traditional older forms such as that found in Hinduism to more modern forms of nontheistic gnosticism. As Eric Voegelin so accurately characterizes it, these latter forms immanentize the eschaton — which is to say, nontheistic gnostic movements generally claim that the world is progressing toward a paradise on earth. Hence, in the modern context, the choice that God alone exists typically leads to utopian ideologies, which more often than not have resulted in totalitarianism.[11]

So, early in his academic career, Murray sounded a very serious, prophetic warning: the post–World War II chips are stacked against God and against the Judeo-Christian revelatory tradition, as well as classical Western philosophy, in favor of theoretical and practical atheism. His prophetic warning led Cardinal Wright to congratulate Murray along with two other Jesuits, Fr. Vincent Miceli and Fr. Henri de Lubac, for work in exposing the atheist threat.[12]

The Need for Interfaith Cooperation

It was this serious cultural drift toward atheism that opened up another probably unanticipated aspect of Murray's career, and one

---

9. Murray, *The Problem of God,* p. 92.

10. Murray, *The Problem of God,* pp. 92-93. Cf. chap. 5 of Thomas Molnar's *Theists and Atheists: A Typology of Unbelief* (The Hague: Mouton, 1980).

11. See chap. 6 of Voegelin, *The New Science of Politics* (Chicago: University of Chicago Press, 1950).

12. See Miceli, *The Gods of Atheism* (New York: Arlington House, 1973), p. xi.

that would not be recognized as universally mandated by the Church until Vatican II. This new facet of Murray's career was that of ecumenism.

While many Catholics suspect that ecumenism entails the rejection of Catholic teaching in order to reach theological agreement with other faiths, the Church in the Second Vatican Council defined it as "those activities and enterprises which, according to the needs of the Church and opportune occasions, are started and organized for the fostering of unity among Christians." This "unity" includes respect for the beliefs of other communions and may include "dialogue" among experts from the various churches, and "co-operation in whatever projects a Christian conscience demands for the common good."[13]

Although Murray seems to have been the most intent of the postwar theologians in warning the West of the demise of Christian belief and the *philosophia perennis,* he was of course not the only one pointing to such a problem in this era. For instance, he pointed to W. Butterfield, an English writer who argued strongly that at least in England the establishment of a postwar order based on Christian principles could never be the work of Catholics alone.[14] Murray agreed that some form of united effort among Christians was necessary. He felt that Christian cooperation could best be focused on concerns that Catholics and Protestants shared. "On the basis of this common interest we may co-operate to promote a more perfect observance of the natural law and to preserve certain Christian ideas, principles, institutions beneficial to Catholic and non-Catholic alike."[15] Murray quotes Jacques Maritain's *Ransoming the Time* to the effect that in order to achieve common political and social goals, Catholics and Protestants should establish mutual respect and understanding, and he warns us against any form of indifferentism by reminding us that this cooperation has its basis in the heart and in love, not in the intellect or on the basis of ideas.[16]

Murray believed that ecumenical cooperation was not only nec-

13. *The Documents of Vatican II: The Message and Meaning of the Council,* ed. Walter M. Abbott, S.J. (New York: Guild, 1962), p. 347.
14. See Murray, "Current Theology: Christian Co-operation," *Theological Studies* 3 (1942): 418. The reference is to Butterfield's article "Co-operation with Non-Catholics," *Clergy Review* 22 (1942): 660.
15. Murray, "Current Theology: Christian Co-operation," p. 418.
16. Murray, "Current Theology: Christian Co-operation," pp. 422-23.

essary but urgent in the face of the postwar atheistic enemy: "In the presence of this enemy, I consider the Catholic-Protestant polemic to be an irrelevance."[17] He quotes an earlier writing of Pope Pius XII, notable for its prescience, to the same effect:

> It will be a triumph indeed if the American people, with its genius for splendid and unselfish action, should thus lay the foundation for a better world, solving once and for all this old and thorny [social] question, and still keeping to the safe paths which the light of the gospel reveals to us. If this fortunate result is to be achieved, our forces must not be weakened by disunion; we must join them, and so to add to their effectiveness. It is only by united and concerted action that we can foster great schemes. For that reason we are impelled by charity to invite here the co-operation of those whom the Church mourns as separated from her communion.[18]

And Murray insisted that both Catholics and Protestants have an interest in this cooperation:

> There is a stand to be made against secularism, which makes freedom of religion mean freedom *from* religion, and which is particularly dangerous in its denial of the relevance of religion to social order and public life. The stand against this enemy can be made on the ground of human reason and the natural law, that define the nature of the human conscience and the nature of the State. On this ground, therefore, Catholics and Protestants can make a common stand, as an act of good will — a will that has for its object a common good.[19]

17. Murray, quoted by Robert W. McElroy in *The Search for an American Public Theology: The Contribution of John Courtney Murray* (New York: Paulist Press, 1989), p. 18.

18. Pius XII, *Sertum Laetitiae*, quoted by Murray in "Current Theology: Christian Co-operation," p. 427n.15.

19. Murray, quoted by McElroy in *The Search for an American Public Theology*, p. 19. The failure of the American citizenry to grapple with the issues Murray raised here has had at least two major effects: the destruction of Christian belief and the death of natural-law thinking among American youth. This loss is ably discussed by Allan Bloom in *The Closing of the American Mind* (New York: Simon & Schuster, 1987), pp. 62-137; and John Senior in *The Death of Christian Culture* (New York: Arlington House, 1978).

Murray's Intellectual Development on the Question of the Relationship between Church and State

The context in which Murray wrote on the controversial subject of church and state was that of papal utterances on the topic over the centuries. In Roman Catholic tradition, papal utterances — even when popes are not using their extraordinary power to declare certain doctrines infallibly true and binding — can develop into a corpus of binding doctrine if the same teaching is consistently reiterated over time.[20] The task of the Catholic theologian is, among other things, to seek to determine the certitude of papal pronouncements by ascertaining how well such pronouncements are grounded in the sources of sacred Tradition, which includes the Scriptures, apostolic practice, the writings of the early Church Fathers, and the decrees of the early church councils. The level of authority of papal pronouncements is determined on the basis of such sources. Hence, a papal teaching that clearly echoes the commonly understood scriptural notions and the teaching of the apostles and early fathers and appears in, say, the decrees of the Council of Nicea, binds the Catholic conscience much more strictly than a thirteenth-century papal pronouncement for which no previous tradition can be found. In such determinations, questions of what may be called "pure dogma" (i.e., creedal truths) present less of a problem than questions relating to the relation of church and state, because of the tenuous and historically contingent nature of the latter. Ironically, such matters as the progression of persons in the Trinity are much more susceptible to final statement than the question of the authority of the pope over a secular ruler or a secular state. It was exactly this type of question that was at the core of Murray's theological and philosophical reflection.

The Basic Catholic Teaching on Church and State

The proper relationship between the church and the state was stated authoritatively by Pope Gelasius I (A.D. 492-496). Addressing Emperor Anastasius, he wrote,

> two there are, august emperor, by which this world is chiefly ruled,
> the sacred authority [*auctoritas*] of the priesthood and the royal power

20. See Ludwig Ott, *Fundamentals of Catholic Dogma* (Rockford, Ill.: TAN, 1974), pp. 4-5.

[*potestas*]. Of these the responsibility of the priesthood is more weighty in so far as they will answer for the kings of men themselves at the divine judgment. You know, most clement son, that, that although you take precedence of all mankind in dignity, nevertheless you piously bow the neck to those who have divine affairs and seek from them the means of your salvation, and hence you realize that, in the order of religion, in matters concerning the reception and right administration of the sacraments, you ought to submit yourself rather than rule. . . . For if the bishops themselves, recognizing that the imperial office was conferred on you by divine disposition, obey your laws so far as the sphere of public order is concerned lest they seem to obstruct your decrees in mundane matters, with what zeal, I ask you, ought you to obey those who have been charged with administering the sacred mysteries?[21]

Explaining the proper spheres further in a document entitled *On the Bond of Anathema,* Gelasius wrote that before the coming of Christ, rulers assumed the functions of divine worship, but after his coming, "he distinguished between the offices of both [sacred and secular] powers according to their own proper activities and separate dignities . . . so that Christian emperors would need priests for attaining eternal life and priests would avail themselves of imperial regulations in the conduct of temporal affairs."[22]

It is not a matter of debate that church and state both exercised influence over moral, legal, and even military spheres of medieval European society. Nor does anyone deny that Gelasius viewed the spiritual as being the superior of the two. But the major question to which Murray addressed himself was the relationship of that *auctoritas* to that *potestas* in the modern, pluralistic democratic state. He examined that relationship both in terms of Catholic teaching and in terms of the right order of political things philosophically considered.

The difficulty in interpreting Gelasius hinges on his use of such terms and phrases as "authority," "power," and "sphere of public order." What precisely did he mean when he said to the emperor that "although you take precedence over all mankind in dignity you piously

21. Gelasius I, "Letter to Emperor Anastasius," in *The Crisis of Church and State, 1050-1300,* ed. Brien Tierney (Englewood Cliffs, N.J.: Prentice, 1964), pp. 13-14.

22. Gelasius I, "Letter to Emperor Anastasius," p. 14.

bow the neck to those who who have charge of divine affairs"? What precisely did he mean when he said that bishops must obey the state in all "mundane matters"?

Murray argues that although Gelasius's pronouncement could have served as the basis for theologically sound teaching, it was completely misinterpreted when it was initially delivered. Modern Roman Catholic teaching is formulated on the basis of principle — theory precedes practice. But during the Middle Ages, the process of formulating teaching regarding the proper relationship of both powers more characteristically involved moving in the opposite direction — from practice (specifically papal practice) to theory. In this case, says Murray, the meaning of Gelasius's statements was determined on the basis of a consideration of how the popes (especially the medieval popes) acted on specific occasions. This approach, which Murray describes as "hierocratic," was developed primarily by the canon lawyers and also by John of Salisbury and Giles of Rome. Murray terms this position "political Augustinism" and argues that it "blurs the distinction between the two powers by attributing to the civil power an excessively religious function, making it a disciplinary agent for the restraint of concupiscence and an instrument of man's supernatural redemption."[23]

To put it another way, hierocratic theory views the state as the arm of the church in the world. In terms of the much-discussed "two swords" of the gospel (Luke 22:38), the church (i.e., the pope) holds both swords and gives the temporal one to the secular ruler to use it as he, the pope, commands. If the temporal sword is misused, it is taken back and given to another — the ruler is declared deposed, or is actually deposed, and a new one is set in his place.

According to Murray, this political Augustinism and its practice culminated in Pope Boniface VIII's bull *Unam Sanctam* (1302), which clearly reflects the thinking of Giles of Rome:

> certainly anyone who denies that the temporal sword is in the power of Peter has not paid heed to the words of the Lord when he said, "Put up thy sword into its sheath" (Matthew 26:52). Both then are in the power of the church, the one by the hand of the priest, the

23. Murray, "Governmental Repression of Heresy," *Proceedings of the Catholic Theological Society of America* (1948): 62.

other by the hand of kings and soldiers, though at the will and sufferance of the priest.[24]

This thinking of Boniface VIII later became enshrined in the canons of the church and various commentaries on the subject.[25] This process was reinforced by the erroneous reaction to political Augustinism of the lawyers of Philip the Fair, who asserted that the secular ruler is completely free from the spiritual *auctoritas* — a position clearly evident in Dante's *De Monarchia* and Machiavelli's *Prince*. The widespread acceptance of this position culminated in Gallicanism, caesaropapism, the anticlerical violence of the French Revolution, and the modern laicized (as distinct from "lay") state.

Murray's Teaching on Church and State

The root of Murray's position on the role of religion in the modern, pluralistic democracies may come as a surprise to those of the Catholic "right" who, while never having read him, nevertheless accept a caricature of him as a "liberal" (whatever that means) on the basis of common characterizations.[26] However shocking it might be to those who claim Catholic orthodoxy and yet reject Murray out of hand, the foundation of his thought is the teaching of Aristotle and Aquinas.

Murray correctly shows that the middle position between the extremes of the hierocratic ideas of Giles and Boniface and the secularizing of Philip and Dante is the natural-law idea that both the *auctoritas* and the *potestas* are constituted, defined, and *limited* by their ends, which is to say, the purposes for which each exists. Murray argues that the concepts of the power of both state and church rest on a basic notion that there is a hierarchy of ends in human life, a hierarchy of orders directed to those ends, and a hierarchy of powers governing these orders. The orders are the ecclesiastical and the civil. Explaining two variations of what he considers the true position on the relationship between church and state, Murray writes that both

---

24. Boniface VIII, *Unam Sanctam,* in *The Crisis of Church and State, 1050-1300,* p. 189.

25. Pope Gregory VII shared the views of Boniface VIII; see *Dictatus Papae* (March 1075), in *The Crisis of Church and State, 1050-1300,* pp. 48-50.

26. On this, see Michael Davies, *Apologia Marcel Lefebvre: Part I, 1905-1976* (Dickenson, Tex.: Angelus, 1979), pp. 425-44.

proceed from the principle of the primacy of the spiritual end, therefore of the spiritual order, therefore of the spiritual power. On the other hand, both admit the principle of the relative autonomy of the temporal end and order of human life (the state) and consequently the sovereignty of the civil power in that order. Therefore both admit that the power of the church in the temporal order can only be indirect (to say that it is an indirect power is the same as saying that it is a *spiritual* power, competent to judge, direct and correct only the spiritual life of a man, unto the end which is eternal life).[27]

Hence, although the spiritual power is supreme, as Gelasius states, the spheres themselves are autonomous, and the state is not an arm of the church. "The finality of the temporal power, though inferior, is a generic finality in its own right," says Murray, and that finality is the basis of the idea of the autonomy of the state.[28]

This assertion of Murray gives us an indication of why there was so much opposition to his writing, as for example in articles written by Msgr. George W. Shea, and Fr. Joseph Clifford Fenton.[29] Shea, Fenton, and a large segment of conservative Catholics and Catholic admirers of Franco's Spain were willing to accept Aquinas's teaching on purely dogmatic matters and matters of individual morality, but they never accepted or comprehended his teaching on law and government, despite the fact that even the old Code of Canon Law demanded such adherence (Canon 1366).

Thomas Gilby ably summarizes Aquinas's teaching on the matter in four main principles:

> first, that the right of political authority to command derived from social needs inherent in human nature as such, and was not postulated because of corrupt proclivities due to original sin. Law was not restricted to the criminal code; power had the positive function of

27. Murray, "Governmental Repression of Heresy," p. 69. See Aquinas, *Summa Theologica*, II-II, q.147, a.3.

28. Murray, "St. Robert Bellarmine on the Indirect Power," *Theological Studies* 9 (1948): 504. Cf. Jacques Maritain, *Man and the State* (Chicago: University of Chicago Press, 1951), 152ff. Maritain acknowledges his debt to Murray for this section of his book on p. 157n.11.

29. See Fenton, "The Theology of the Church and the State," *Proceedings of the Catholic Theological Society of America* (1947): 15-46.

encouraging virtue as well as the negative function of checking vice. . . . Secondly, this authority, at least in the abstract, was distinct from and not of itself beholden to the authority of the church. . . . Third, . . . that temporal power was immediately concerned only with temporal affairs although its purpose was to promote social virtue and its just commands obliged in conscience. . . . Fourth . . . government and legislation were more directly functions of art than of ethics.[30]

Aquinas and Murray accept two other principles that must be mentioned here. Gilby correctly states that it was Aquinas's view that the just commands of the state are binding for the individual conscience. The reason this is so leads us to Murray's justification for the binding power of *both* the church *and* the state and establishes the basis of their relative autonomy. The key, according to Murray, lies in an oft-discussed passage from Paul's epistle to the Romans:

Let every soul be subject to higher powers: for there is no power but from God: and those that are, are ordained of God. Therefore, he that resisteth the power, resisteth the ordinance of God. And they that resist, purchase to themselves damnation. For princes are not a terror to the good work, but to the evil. Wilt thou then not be afraid of the power? Do that which is good: and thou shalt have praise from the same. For he is God's minister to thee, for good. But if thou do that which is evil, fear: for he beareth not the sword in vain. For he is God's minister: an avenger to execute wrath upon him that doeth evil. (Rom. 13:1-4)

It should be noted here that, according to Murray's interpretation, St. Paul is speaking of the ruler or government as receiving his or its power *directly* from God. Murray writes very approvingly in a number of places of the theory of John of Paris that "the prince is not *minister ecclesiae*, but *minister Dei*. The finality of his power is determined by its origin; it is of the natural moral order."[31] That is to say, Murray asserts that the government receives its authority directly from God,

30. Gilby, *The Political Thought of Thomas Aquinas* (Chicago: University of Chicago Press, 1958), xxi-iv.

31. See, e.g., Murray, "Governmental Repression of Heresy," p. 56. Cf. John of Paris, *On Royal and Papal Power,* especially chap. 13.

without the mediation of the Church, for purposes that are natural and moral. Of course Murray cautions that this does not sanction excesses on the part of the ruler, such as one sees in the theory of the "Divine Right of Kings." The truth is that the power of the ruler is limited by the natural ends of the state; hence, the ruler can rightfully do only that which honestly contributes to those ends: "the limits of his [the ruler's] direct power are set by natural law; he is to ordain what the common good, the exigencies of a humanly virtuous life in common demand."[32]

The second additional principle that Aquinas and Murray lay down is related to the assertion that politics is more a function of art than of ethics. This principle requires that political decisions ought not to be conceived as deductions from clear natural-law principles but rather as choices "between alternatives both of which may have good moral reasons in their favor": political decisions are arrived at by a "kind of poetic freedom, not by determinism proper to the deductive sciences."[33] Murray's endorsement of this sort of freedom to arrive at political decisions is based on two foundational ideas. The first is human dignity, which appears as a central theme in the Vatican II document on religious liberty *Dignitatis Humanae* more than in Murray's own writings. In his introduction to the document in the Abbott edition of 1966, Murray states that "the dignity of man consists in his responsible use of freedom." If man has dignity, as Vatican II and Murray affirmed, then man must have freedom. Therefore, says Murray,

> an exigence for immunity from coercion is resident in the human person as such. It is an exigence of his dignity as a moral subject. This exigence is the source of the fundamental rights of the person — those political-civil rights concerning the search for truth, artistic creation, scientific discovery, and the development of man's political views, moral convictions and religious beliefs.[34]

32. Murray, "Governmental Repression of Heresy," p. 56. Cf. Aquinas, *Summa Theologica*, II-II, q.47, a.3.

33. Gilby, *The Political Thought of Thomas Aquinas*, p. xxiv. Cf. James V. Schall, S.J., *Christianity and Politics* (Boston: St. Paul, 1981), pp. 83-84.

34. "The Declaration on Religious Freedom: A Moment in Its Legislative History," in *Religious Liberty: An End and a Beginning*, ed. John Courtney Murray, S.J. (New York: Macmillan, 1966), p. 40. Cf. Francis P. Canavan, S.J., *Freedom of Expression: Purpose as Limit* (Durham, N.C.: Carolina Academic Press, 1984), especially chap. 1.

Murray on Religion and Democracy

It is here that our own discussion of Murray's views of the role of religion in modern democracy really begins. Traditional Catholic teaching asserts that human beings have a free will — this because they are created in the image and likeness of God and therefore possess qualities similar to those of God, though obviously not as extensively. God has a free will, and so does his human creature. Since God does not want slaves as followers, he allows human beings to use their free will to choose between good and evil — evil that usually comes disguised as good. The choices are difficult at times because of the effects of original sin, which, the Catholic Church teaches, has not perverted human nature but has darkened our intellect and weakened our will.[35] This complicates our ability to choose the good, but certainly it does not make it impossible. Human nature is still a reflection of God's nature and still possesses the free will God gave it. But this free will, Murray asserts, gives us the capability but not the right to choose evil. Citing Acton's phrase, Murray states that "freedom is not the power of doing what we like, but the right of being able to do what we ought."[36] It is in this light that Murray argues that human dignity demands a commensurate "poetic freedom" to achieve the common good. The freedom goes hand-in-hand with responsibility to render politics an ethical and moral activity. "Part of the inner architecture of the American ideal of freedom has been the profound conviction that only a virtuous people can be free" (p. 47).

Free government is not inevitable in Murray's eyes: it is merely *possible,* and "its possibility can be realized only when the people as a whole are inwardly governed by the recognized imperatives of the universal moral law" (p. 47). That is why the American Constitution has two aspects. First, it is a charter of freedom, recognizing human dignity and the right to choose what one ought. Second, it is a plan for political order, a plan based on these recognized principles of "a universal moral law" (p. 24).

It is clear that Murray considers the contemporary emphasis on the individual to be a great advance in both political thinking and

35. See Ott, *Fundamentals of Catholic Dogma,* pp. 106ff.
36. Murray, *We Hold These Truths: Catholic Reflections on the American Experience* (Garden City, N.Y.: Doubleday Image Books, 1964), p. 47. Subsequent references to this volume will be made parenthetically in the text.

Church teaching. But how does he account for this point of view given the Church's tendency to constrain the authority of the individual in past teaching and practice on the one hand, and the evident dangers of radical individualism stemming from the Enlightenment on the other (as in the excesses of the French Revolution)? Murray argues that the focus upon the individual person came about in reaction to the authoritarianism of the divine-right monarchies in general and the *ancien régime* in particular — and he grants that this reaction produced some very evil consequences indeed (p. 297).[37] His chronology of events leading to this reaction is as follows: in the Middle Ages there was one Christian-Catholic commonwealth with the pope as its head. With the advent of Protestantism and the nation-state system came the age of the "confessional state," a context in which each state was a microcosm of medieval Europe, except that the religion of each state was chosen by its ruler. Murray points to France as the type of the Catholic state. There the antipapal, promonarchical thinking promulgated by Philip the Fair gradually reduced French Catholicism to an appendage of the state — which is to say, it produced Gallicanism. The relationship between church and state in France was thus similar to that in the Protestant countries and the caesaropapist states of the East.[38] As the movement of thought during the Enlightenment turned the "subject" into the "citizen," the various confessional states were unable to cope with the changes. This movement of thought "was destructive of course, as the rise of the nation-state had been, but it too bore in its depths an *intention of nature* . . . to situate the human person at the center of the whole social order, and make him the temporal element of the dyarchy whereby society is to be ruled." Murray goes on to explain that this "dyarchy" was no longer "church and state" but rather "church and society; or perhaps more exactly . . . 'the freedom of the Church and the freedom of the citizen.'"[39]

But what then is the Church free to do, and what is the citizen free to do? Affirming Gelasius's distinctions, Murray argued that the Church is above the state, but he insisted that that does not make the state the arm of the Church. The Church, founded by Christ, is limited

37. Cf. Murray, "Contemporary Orientations of Catholic Thought on Church and State in the Light of History," *Theological Studies* 10 (1949): 213-24.
38. Murray, "Governmental Repression of Heresy," p. 62.
39. Murray, "Contemporary Orientations of Catholic Thought on Church and State in the Light of History," p. 23.

by its ends — the salvation of mankind. Though it is a true society, its powers are purely spiritual. If the church does engage political life, it does so through its teachings on faith and/or morals, which affect (or should affect) the behavior of individuals. Hence, this power of the Church is "indirect."[40] On the other hand, since the Church is above the state, and its ends are supernatural, it has the right to act in its own spiritual sphere without interference from the state. Murray states his position as follows:

> as the human person is free in society when all his inalienable rights are juridically guaranteed immunity from inhibition and provided with the due conditions of their exercise, so also the Church is free in society when her intrinsic dignity, her unique juridical personality as the visible and only Church of Christ is recognized, and her independently sovereign powers to teach, rule and sanctify are guaranteed immunity from inhibition and provided with the due conditions of their exercise. The basic right of the Church, as of the human person, is the right to be recognized for what she *is:* this is a right that she can no more renounce than the human person can abdicate his essential dignity.[41]

So, in any society that sees the Church for what it is — a vehicle of salvation — it is free to present the gospel to individuals for their voluntary assent. In an article entitled "For the Freedom and Transcendence of the Church," Murray summarizes this view:

> endowed with a freedom that is a prolongation of the freedom of the Incarnate Word Himself, the Church proposes herself to all men, for their free acceptance by faith, a gift of grace, but she does not submit herself to judgment by the civil power as such nor does she admit any empowerment of the civil ruler as such to enter into judgment upon her claims.[42]

Here lies the genius of the American system and especially the First Amendment. While the courts and various advocacy groups are con-

40. Murray, "St. Robert Bellarmine on the Indirect Power," p. 496.
41. Murray, "Governmental Repression of Heresy," pp. 76-77.
42. Murray, "For the Freedom and Transcendence of the Church," *The American Ecclesiastical Review* 126 (1952): 31.

stantly concerned with violations of the establishment clause of the
First Amendment, Murray located the foundation of religious freedom
in the free exercise clause, not in the establishment clause, which he
characterized as merely the means to the end of free exercise.[43]

On this point, it is interesting to note that Murray viewed the
religion clauses of the First Amendment as "articles of peace" (p. 57).
The Constitution is not the work of theologians, he says, and contrary
to the claims of some critics the First Amendment establishment and
free exercise clauses are not dogmatic expressions of indifferentism.
The Bill of Rights was produced by lawyers who made good law,
respecting the intent of the founding fathers, who held that the government should not wield any authority over the establishment of religion
or its free exercise (pp. 65, 57). The primary reason they established
this restriction, says Murray, is that the government *is not competent in
these matters*. It has no divine commission over dogma or worship.[44]
This conclusion follows clearly from Murray's interpretation of the
Gelasian text and his teaching on the freedom of the church.

It is also worth noting that these "articles of peace" have basically
solved, at least in theory, the problem created by the plurality of beliefs
present in the United States, and they hold promise for solving similar
problems in other countries (p. 57). Human dignity and freedom
encompass the specific freedom to pursue truths, religious and otherwise, on one's own. Government has no authority to pass judgment
on religious dogma or matters of worship either on its own or as a tool
of a religious body (p. 49).

The foundation of Murray's approach to religious freedom is
fundamentally different from that of either traditional social-contract
theory (e.g., Locke's *Letter concerning Toleration*) or more recent versions
of this orientation (e.g., that which came to expression after Murray's
death in John Rawls's *Theory of Justice*). The reason for this is that
social-contract thinking is based on a nominalist epistemology that
denies human beings possess a true, common nature and views the
individual as an atom completely motivated by self-interest, for whom
all relationships and even obedience to law must be voluntary.[45] Mur-

43. See Francis P. Canavan, S.J., "Religious Freedom: John Courtney Murray,
S.J. and Vatican II," *Faith and Reason* 13 (1987): 324.

44. Murray, "The Declaration on Religious Freedom," p. 37.

45. See Francis P. Canavan, S.J., "Liberalism in Root and Flower," in *The
Ethical Dimension of Political Life: Essays in Honor of John H. Hallowell*, ed. Francis P.
Canavan, S.J. (Durham, N.C.: Duke University Press, 1983), p. 47.

ray rejects this approach to religious liberty not only because of its denial of a true, common human nature but also because of its destructive implications.

> The eighteenth century gospel, based on the individualistic law of nature, could not at the time [of the French Revolution] fail to be popular. For the primary drive then was toward destruction, and the law of nature concept of human rights was an appropriate dynamism of destruction, precisely because of the philosophical nonsense it enshrined. I mean that its individualistic rationalistic nominalism, precisely because it disregarded the organic character of society, and precisely because its concept of "progress" entailed a complete denial of the past and of the continuity of human effort, was an effective solvent of the corporate institutional structure of society as it then was. (P. 299)[46]

Murray concurred with Aquinas that when a civil order grants citizens freedom and rights in accord with true human nature, they love, cherish, and respect that civil order.[47] Thus Murray consistently accepts the traditional Thomistic notion of the common good. In a religiously diverse society, the "articles of peace" (in the American context, the religion clauses of the First Amendment) are necessary for the maintenance of that common good because, Murray asserts, social peace is the highest integrating element of that common good (p. 67).

The wisdom of this argument is readily apparent. The common good of any social body, whether a family, a bridge club, a lodge, a corporation, or a state, has a certain content defined by its nature and its ends. If such a body is torn by strife, it will not find it easy to realize its characteristic content, since it will be expending all its energies on trying to work out some minimal terms for maintaining the peace. In a religiously pluralistic state, the higher levels of the common good can be sought only if the various sects "agree to disagree" on dogmatic questions and get on with the business at hand.

But once religious strife is quelled and free exercise is a reality, where do the reconciled parties turn to establish a social bond and define the common good? How is the specific content of the common

---

46. For Murray's complete critique of nominalism, see *We Hold These Truths*, pp. 298-99.

47. See Aquinas, *Summa Theologica*, II-II, q.95, a.3.

good defined? Catholic thinking on the common good has both a static and a variable aspect. These two aspects can be summed up by saying that the common good is anything that benefits the generality of society in terms of its moral and material well-being, provided that the laws encouraging that common good are not themselves intrinsically immoral and remain in keeping with the true ends of both the individual and the state. Aquinas quotes Isidore of Seville on this point: "law [relating to the common good] should be 'possible both according to nature *and* according to the customs of the country.'" Hence, the common good does not consist in enforcing *all* virtue and/or repressing *all* vice. Nor does it consist in structuring the country according to some preconceived rationalistic or ideological scheme.[48]

Religion, Democracy and the Consensus

Murray's application of the common good to modern pluralistic society comprises the development and maintenance of what he terms a consensus. Clearly Murray does not locate the source of the social bond and fabric in the tenets of any particular religious body.

Normally when we speak of a consensus we mean the views that most people of a community can agree upon. So, for example, it might be the consensus among the members of a gang of outlaws that it would be more profitable to rob an armored car than a bank. The point is that the common idea of consensus does not include an objective evaluation of the rightness or wrongness of the object of the consensus.

Murray held that the common notion of consensus is deficient. At least in the case of the sort of consensus signified by the title of his major work *We Hold These Truths*, the consensus consists not in mere agreement on any set of principles at all but in a public philosophy, and as such it is based on an objective, knowable set of norms. As Robert Cuervo has noted, "citing Cicero's *De Re Publica*, Murray says that a true republic is not just any association but is a people *juris consensu et utilitatis communione sociatus* — a people united by a common agreement about law and rights and a desire for mutual (not just selfish) advantage."[49] As Murray himself puts it, "the truths we hold as a people belong to the order of philosophi-

48. Aquinas, *Summa Theologica*, II-II, q.95, aa.2, 3.

49. Cuervo, "Public Philosophy in a Democracy: Transcendent Values and Free Society in the Political Thought of John H. Hallowell and Irving Kristol," Ph.D. diss., Fordham University, 1980, p. 8.

cal and political truth. . . . The truths are a product of reason reflecting on human experience. They are not simply a codification or registration of experience" (p. 87).

These truths contain "universal validity": "not only do *we* hold these truths; they are human truths of a sort that man as such is bound to hold" (p. 87). Moreover, Murray expands the common meaning of consensus to allow for dissent as well as agreement. The purpose of such dissent is not to undermine the consensus but to "solidify it and make it more conscious and articulate" (p. 88). This allowance for dissent keeps the consensus from petrifying, which is essential if it is to engage the new questions that naturally surface in a dynamic political system.

It is here that we arrive at the hub of the question of what Murray conceives to be the role of religion in a modern, pluralist democracy. In brief, he believes that since the state is a natural institution, the function of religion within it is to bolster and encourage obedience to the natural law. Murray follows the reasoning of St. Thomas very closely on this point. Aquinas asks whether all the *moral* principles of the Old Testament belong to the natural law. After distinguishing the moral teachings of the Old Testament from the mere ceremonial precepts, Aquinas says that

> the moral precepts . . . are about things pertaining of their very nature to good morals. Now since human morals depend on their relation to reason, which is the proper principle of human acts, those morals are called good which accord with reason, and those are called bad which are discordant from reason. . . . It is, therefore, evident that, since the moral precepts are about matters which concern good morals, and since good morals are those which are in accord with reason, and since also every judgment of human reason must needs be derived in some way from natural reason, it follows of necessity that all the moral precepts [of the Old Testament] belong to the law of nature.[50]

Murray holds that the natural law has no specifically Catholic presuppositions. It assumes only that man's knowledge of reality reveals a moral order inherent in the structure of the universe. Since God is the author of that universe, and it is not possible that God could

---

50. Aquinas, *Summa Theologica*, I-II, q.100, a.1.

create a universe contrary to his nature, it follows that *to obey the natural law is to obey God himself.* Says Murray, "here is the basic natural law assertion, *that the dictates of common human reason are the dictates of God,* who is eternal Reason, the Logos. This is the final explanation of their obligatory character. Their ultimate origin is divine, though the mode of their knowing is human and rational" (p. 119; italics mine).

In a very real sense, according to Murray, an established religion is not a necessary precondition for a just state *provided* there is a consensus that adheres to the natural law and the law of that nation adheres to that consensus. Religion in the state, as opposed to religion in the life of the individual (where it is the major vehicle of salvation), is ancillary to a good order — for the natural law and the Decalogue are congruent. Following on this point, Murray elaborates on the role of the Church in the state:

> it is not the function of the Church as such to elaborate the public consensus, which is a body of rational knowledge, a structure of rational imperatives, that sustain and direct the action of the People Temporal and of their secular rulers. The proper task of the Church is the custody and development of the deposit of faith which is a body of revealed truth, a structure of mystery, that sustains and directs the action of the People Spiritual. (P. 124)

Interestingly enough, Murray places the primary responsibility for the care and elaboration of the public consensus in the *studium,* the university: "this is the institution that together with the Church, stood between the people and the princes, the men of power, who bore the responsibility of using their power in that high service of justice and the freedom of the people" (p. 124). It is the task of the university to ensure that the rulers perform their duties wisely, by defining justice and elucidating what the freedom of the people requires in different circumstances.

Evaluation and Critique

Among Murray's many contributions to our understanding of political philosophy and political theology, two stand out specially. First, he clarified for Catholics and non-Catholics alike the actions of the medieval Catholic Church in the political realm — an understanding that only began to become clear to the hierarchy, and especially Leo XIII, at the end of the nineteenth century. This clarification culminated in the document *Dignitatis Humanae* of Vatican II. It appears now that a fuller comprehension and dissemination of Murray's writings will help bring about further steps toward the religious peace Murray felt was so necessary in the modern democratic state. This process is especially beneficial for Catholics, who have been the victims of nativism, "know-nothingism" and the continuing bias of intellectuals and the media.

Murray is accused by some of his coreligionists of merely trying to "make Catholicism more acceptable to Protestants." This charge is quite erroneous, as will be evident to anyone who reads his many writings with an open mind. Murray was a brilliant and original thinker, and his command of so many materials is astounding. Yet he was a thoroughly orthodox Catholic — no liberal (in any sense of the term) and certainly no indifferentist. The Church seems to have vindicated Murray's work in its decrees on religious liberty *(Dignitatis Humanae)* and the Church in the modern world *(Gaudium et Spes)*.

More apropos to our task here is the second great contribution of Murray, a contribution that has particular importance in the age of the omnipotent state, to use Pius XII's phrase. In 1951 Eric Voegelin presented this major point in a different way: "the spiritual destiny of man in the Christian sense cannot be represented on earth by the power organization of a political society; it can be represented only by the church. The sphere of power is radically de-divinized; it has become temporal."[51] Murray has succeeded in reminding all those who would redivinize the state, from whatever point of view, that the moral foundation of the modern, pluralistic democratic state is natural law, stemming from the very nature of man and the mind of his Creator, rather than from the particular doctrines of an established religious body. Murray's "theology of the Bill of Rights," if you will, counsels us against any mere libertine reaction, so common today, among those who see religion and politics as somehow directly related in some plot to overturn our freedoms. Instead, he helps us to see that religion — true revelation, grace — does not eradicate nature but perfects it. The Decalogue does not contradict the natural law; it helps us remember its principles.

It seems that Murray did not fully anticipate the soul-closing effects of ideology operative in the media and education. He did

51. Voegelin, *The New Science of Politics,* p. 106.

acknowledge the possibility of the death of the consensus, however. In a chilling passage, he points out that

> perhaps one day the noble many storeyed mansion of democracy will be dismantled, leveled to the dimensions of a flat majoritarianism, which is no mansion but a barn, perhaps even a tool shed in which the weapons of tyranny may be forged. Perhaps there will one day be wide dissent even from the political principles which emerge from the natural law, as well as dissent from the constellation of ideas that historically undergirded these principles — the idea that government has a moral basis; that the universal moral law is the foundation of society; that the legal order of society . . . is subject to judgment by a law that is not statistical but inherent in the nature of man; that the eternal reason of God is the ultimate origin of all law; that this nation in all its aspects — as a society, a state, an ordered and free relationship between governors and governed — is under God. The possibility that widespread dissent from these principles should develop is not foreclosed. (P. 53)

But what happens if that occurs? Regrettably, we can answer that question from our own experience. Murray himself lived long enough to see only the beginning stages of this dissolution, but the process gathered strength during the late 1960s and the 1970s.

In any event, Murray ultimately answered the question in this way: in times when the consensus is dissolved, the onus of preserving and reinvigorating the consensus — specifically, the Western, natural-law tradition — will devolve on the Catholic Church. In the event of the dissolution of the consensus of the people at large, its guardianship will have to be "passed to the Catholic community, within which the heritage was elaborated long before America was" (p. 53).

John Courtney Murray, S.J.: A Jewish Appraisal

David Novak

John Courtney Murray as Philosophical Model

I DID NOT HAVE THE PRIVILEGE of knowing the late Fr. John Courtney Murray personally, but he did, nevertheless, play an important role in my own intellectual development. I read his book *We Hold These Truths* one year after its initial publication, just after I was graduated from the University of Chicago in 1961, and just before I was to enter the Jewish Theological Seminary of America in New York to begin my studies for rabbinical ordination. That was a point of crucial transition in my life.

The University of Chicago in the late 1950s and early 1960s was still very much under the influence of the Aristotelian educational philosophy of its legendary former chancellor Robert Maynard Hutchins. In that supportive atmosphere I discovered the tradition of natural law. This tradition, it seemed to me then, presented the bridge I very much needed to interrelate my Jewish faith with my commitment to reason. All other intellectual traditions to which I had been exposed seemed to affirm faith but deny reason, affirm reason but deny faith, or deny both faith and reason. The tradition of natural law, though, asserted that there is an intelligible order in the universe and that by intelligent inquiry a human intelligence could discover his or her consistent place in that universal order. Moreover, that recognition of an intelligibility beyond mere human invention also entailed, at least for most of those who considered themselves to be the perpetuators of this tradition, the further recognition that this universal intelligible order is ultimately dependent upon God. Of course, this recognition alone could not constitute the far more dense content of Jewish faith (or Christian or Muslim faith), but it could at least make the connection between faith and reason possible. At that time and for a time afterward, it seemed to provide me with what was intellectually necessary, although never what was spiritually sufficient. Even then, however, I was left with this gnawing question: If natural law as a bridge between faith and reason is appealing in theory, can it still have any practical significance in our society, which was where I was to live and work at my vocation?

During that transitional summer of 1961, when this question was very much on my mind, I discovered Murray's work. It was an important discovery because Murray as a Catholic had virtually the same problem I as a Jew had. And he, being older and wiser than I, seemed to be far ahead of me in dealing with it.

Both Catholicism and Judaism were regarded as outside the mainstream of American thought, indeed outside the mainstream of modern Western thought altogether. In the eyes of many, intelligent Catholics and intelligent Jews were faced with one of two options: either opt for the integrity of their own faith tradition and thus remove themselves from present intellectual discourse, or opt for the present realm and thus bracket their faith tradition if not leave it altogether. The latter, more radical step was, of course, the one taken by many of the best and the brightest. The intellectual landscape, then and now, is filled with former Catholic and former Jewish (and former Protestant, especially evangelical) believers. But Murray suggested a third way in sharp contrast to both of these options, which, culturally at least, was more radical than both of them. It is boldly expressed in a passage from his book that to this day is still quite vivid in my mind:

a Catholic . . . knows that the principles of Catholic faith and morality stand superior to, and in control of, the whole order of civil life. The question is sometimes raised, whether Catholicism is compatible with American democracy. The question is invalid as well as impertinent; for the manner of its position inverts the order of values. It must, of course, be turned round to read, whether American democracy is compatible with Catholicism.[1]

1. Murray, *We Hold These Truths: Catholic Reflections on the American Proposition* (New York: Sheed & Ward, 1960), pp. ix-x. Subsequent references to this volume will be made parenthetically in the text.

One must remember, furthermore, that the book in which these lines were written was published in 1960, the very year when, for the first time in American history, a Catholic candidate for president, John F. Kennedy, had a real chance to win.

In the American Catholic community at the time there was an understandable attempt to show how thoroughly American Catholicism really is. The attempt was understandably largely polemical in intent, formulated and presented to counter the aspersions that had long been cast on the patriotism of all Catholic Americans, aspersions coming from certain Protestant circles and drawing upon the whole history of anti-Catholicism in America.

On the other hand, there were elements in the American Catholic community that were highly suspicious of this easy marriage between their God and this new American version of Caesar. They were drawing upon an older type of European Catholic suspicion about the whole American democratic proposition, this *novus ordo seclorum*, especially its pluralism, which would never afford the Church the place of political or even cultural preeminence it still enjoyed in some older European societies. For them, anything but an explicitly pragmatic modus vivendi with America would surely prove to be dangerous to the faith of Catholics in America before long. Murray's voice provided a way out of this impasse for Catholics and, by analogy, for other religious believers as well.[2]

At the time I first read Murray, virtually all the rabbinical statements I had read or heard that dealt with the role of Judaism in America were of two kinds.

On the one hand, the statements of the more liberal rabbis were almost always attempts to show how thoroughly American Judaism really is. The conclusion that could be drawn from their statements was, however (whether or not consciously intended), that Judaism had done a fine job in providing historical precedent for American democracy and that America should be grateful for these past services. Nevertheless, since the contribution had already been made, American thought could now suffice on its own — even for Jews.

On the other hand, the statements of the more traditional rabbis

---

2. For a thorough discussion of this whole situation in American Catholic thought, as well as a thorough analysis of Murray's role in it, see George S. Weigel, *Tranquillitas Ordinis: The Present Failure and Future Promise of American Catholic Thought on War and Peace* (New York: Oxford University Press, 1987), pp. 107ff.

usually were an attempt to show how subtly dangerous American culture and thought really are to the survival of Jewish faith and observance. To be sure, these rabbis were grateful that Jews were not being murdered and persecuted in America as they had been in the countries most of them had personally fled, such as Czarist Russia or, more recently, Nazi Germany. However, anything more than an explicitly pragmatic modus vivendi with America would surely prove to be dangerous to traditional Jewish life in America before long. And unlike the more liberal rabbinical statements about Judaism and America, whose assimilationist conclusions were mostly implicit and perhaps even unconscious, the statements of these more traditional rabbis included quite explicit conclusions (as, indeed, did most everything else they taught). As one who was exposed to the teaching of these rabbis during his impressionable adolescence, I can attest that nothing was left to the imagination or powers of inference of those who sat at their feet.

The parallels between the American Catholic and American Jewish situations in America in the mid-twentieth century are indeed striking. (The fact, moreover, that both communities then were still composed mostly of immigrants or their children explains the further similarity that, like most more recent arrivals here, many Catholics and Jews were either too enchanted or too frightened by this radically new society to be quite rational about it yet.) Nevertheless, despite these similarities, there was an important difference (at least for me). No one in the American Jewish community was offering the alternative John Courtney Murray was offering in the American Catholic community.

As time went on, it became increasingly evident to me that the reason the Murray Project (as it has now come to be called) was not finding an analogue in the American Jewish community was not because of the very fundamental differences between Judaism and Catholicism. For, although Murray was a distinguished Catholic theologian, his political thought was not formulated with the christological or ecclesiological doctrines of Christianity in general or Roman Catholicism in particular, doctrines that make the differences between Judaism and any form of Christianity *toto caelo*. Rather, Murray's political thought was formulated with the doctrines of the natural-law tradition. And he himself made a point of this tradition's independence.

It is sometimes said that one cannot accept the doctrine of natural law unless one has antecedently accepted "its Roman Catholic presuppositions." This, of course, is quite wrong. The doctrine of natural law has no Roman Catholic presuppositions. Its only presupposition is threefold: that man is intelligent; that reality is intelligible; and that reality, as grasped by intelligence, imposes on the will the obligation that it be obeyed in its demands for action or abstention. (P. 109)

The reason for the absence of a Jewish project like the Murray project lay not in what differentiates Judaism from Catholicism. Rather, the reason lay in the fact that Jewish natural-law theory was mostly unknown to Jews themselves, let alone non-Jews. And this is not because of any intellectual inferiority of Judaism in comparison to Catholicism but, rather, because Judaism's presence in the intellectual discourse of the non-Jewish world is much newer than that of Catholicism, even though it is the older faith. Surely, this has been so for the past fifteen hundred years, But, because of the new pluralistic cultural climate that has slowly been developing in America, the voice of Judaism — and not just the voice of dejudaized Jews — is being actively sought, especially in the area of public moral discourse. This being the case, I gradually resolved (beginning with my graduate work at Georgetown University with the Thomistic philosophers Germain Grisez and the late Heinrich Rommen) to expose Jewish natural-law theory to my fellow Jews and then beyond.[3] The task has not been easy. There are still many in both worlds who are incredulous about the whole project. But I must thank John Courtney Murray for providing me with a powerful intellectual model. And, although Murray was a Catholic theologian, he was relevant to my project because he was a Catholic philosopher as well.

The Philosophical Problem of Natural Law

So far I have tried to show the desirability of an appropriation of the natural-law tradition for a Jewish or Christian believer who is also convinced that there is a connection between faith and reason as two independent but mutually related spheres of human activity in the

---

3. For my main work on this whole subject, see Novak, *The Image of the Non-Jew in Judaism: An Historical and Constructive Study of the Noahide Laws* (New York: Edwin Mellen Press, 1983).

world. There remains, however, the issue of the current plausibility of this tradition, let alone the issue of its truth. Even the plausibility of the assertions of the natural-law tradition requires more than just the type of historical research that uncovers a history of Catholic or Jewish (or Protestant or Muslim) recognition and development of it. Natural law as *law* has always proclaimed itself to be normative, not just descriptive. Although history certainly plays a role in any normative system, history alone, as the record of the past, cannot make a primary normative claim on the present. Even when history functions normatively, it does so only because present criteria have been constituted that indicate why those who are present ought to listen to voices from the past. That is why the problem of law — natural law or any other kind — is a philosophical problem before it is a historical one. To deal with this philosophical problem comprehensively would require far more space than the confines of this essay. Therefore, I shall concentrate on Thomistic natural-law theory as it is found in Murray's *We Hold These Truths*.

In speaking of the premises of natural law, Murray states,

> it supposes a metaphysic of nature, especially the idea that nature is a teleological concept, that the "form" of a thing is its "final cause," the goal of its beginning; in this case, that there is a natural inclination in man to become what in nature and destination he is — to achieve the fullness of his own being. . . . It supposes a natural theology, asserting that there is a God, who is eternal Reason, *Nous*, at the summit of the order of being. (Pp. 327-28)

Clearly, he is affirming Thomistic natural-law theory in a most explicitly Aristotelian way. However, here is where a number of astute philosophical commentators, even some who are themselves wholly sympathetic with the project of natural law in the contemporary world, have found a major obstacle. That major obstacle is Aristotelian metaphysics.

The very term *metaphysic(s)* admits of several meanings as it is first used to designate Aristotle's chief work on ontology. *Meta* means "that which follows," and it can signify nothing more profound than the literary fact that Aristotle's work on ontology follows his chief work on natural science in the *oeuvre* — it is *meta ta physika*. Although this is certainly so, the term has also been seen as having conceptual significance. It can also mean that Aristotle conceived of ontology as that which goes beyond what is physical, moving from the physical up to that which is beyond it, as a cause is beyond its effect by being its ground.[4] Both cause and effect are related in a hierarchical order — Nature (*physis*, in this context more broadly conceived than the sum of *ta physika* — "physical entities"). Metaphysics constitutes those first principles (*archai*) that the full functionality of physics calls for.[5] And even though in the ontological order metaphysics precedes physics, in the epistemological order (i.e., the way we learn these truths) physics precedes metaphysics. Metaphysics is the expansion of physics to what must be finally seen as its epistemological conclusion, or to what must originally be seen as its ontological foundation. That ontological foundation, as Murray correctly represented it, is teleological.

Physical teleology, the type that leads directly into metaphysical teleology, is normative in the Aristotelian system because it is primarily seen in astrophysics. Aristotelian astrophysics deals with a higher form of entity, one that is both superior in intelligibility and superior in intelligence. The very matter of the heavens is different in kind from earthly matter. As such, and only as such, can the heavenly bodies function as exemplars for the lower human intelligences. Human intelligences can view these bodies only from afar, from the earth, and yet they desire to be like them as much as is possible for their limited intelligence. The summit of the intelligent and intelligible heavenly realm is God. God is so intelligible that everything else in nature is intelligible in relation to him in a descending order. God is so intelligent that he (actually, "it" is the more appropriate pronoun to be used for this intransitive God) is interested in nothing but himself. Thus, in their striving to order their lives intelligently, humans are to look to those higher beings that are already functioning with this desired excellence. Being intelligible, these higher beings can be the objects of human intelligence. Being intelligent, they can be exemplary for human intelligence as subject.[6]

What Galileo and Newton did to make this system lose its key physical point of reference was to show that heavenly matter, like earthly matter, is only intelligible, not intelligent. As such, it has no exemplary status, leaving man as the only intelligent being whom we can identify in ordinary experience or in any valid abstraction from

4. See J. Ritter and K. Gruender, *Historisches Wörterbuch der Philosophie* (Basel: Schwabe, 1980), 5: 1186, 1197.

5. See Aristotle, *Metaphysics* 981b25-30.

6. See Aristotle, *Nicomachean Ethics* 1141a34ff.; *Metaphysics* 1026a20ff.

it. Thus, the whole system requires the acceptance of a physical paradigm that has been consistently inoperative in physical science since the Renaissance. Final causes are simply no longer part of the world of discourse in physics, and it is physics that still largely determines the parameters of discourse for all the other natural sciences. Without physics, there is no meta-physics in the Aristotelian sense. One of the obvious facts of modernity (and postmodernity, where many believe our culture is now located) is not that metaphysics has died (as only the Logical Positivists once thought) but that metaphysics has never again been able to display the same self-confident hegemony it once displayed when Aristotle was *the Philosopher.*

One can see an admission of the fundamental impediment to the philosophical reintroduction of traditional Aristotelianism, however desirable that might be, in the work of the contemporary philosopher Alasdair MacIntyre. MacIntyre himself is not only sympathetic to the comprehensiveness of Aristotelianism but has even attempted to reintroduce Thomistic Aristotelianism into current philosophical discourse. Nevertheless, he is certainly aware that he can do so only through a method radically different from that of traditional Thomists such as Murray. Hence, MacIntyre admits that "what is clear is that the Aristotelian scheme provides a link between science and the type of ultimate explanation provided by rational theology and that this kind of link, although far from absent in the science of Galileo and Newton, has disappeared in nineteenth- and twentieth-century science."[7] However, even in Galileo and Newton, the link between the two is not teleological.

One sees this post-Renaissance lack of any similar relation between metaphysics and ethics in the work of all the major modern philosophers. Thus, for example, even though Kant could devise a "metaphysic of morals," he did not present it as an ontology, a science of being that underlies both physical and moral reality.[8] And even though Whitehead did devise such a metaphysics as an ontology, it seems to function only as a ground for physical reality. Whitehead himself did not use his ontology to ground any kind of ethical system, and it is doubtful that his contemporary disciples could do so follow-

7. MacIntyre, *Whose Justice? Which Rationality?* (Notre Dame, Ind.: University of Notre Dame Press, 1988), p. 101.
8. See Kant, *Groundwork of the Metaphysic of Morals,* trans. H. J. Paton (New York: Harper Torchbooks, 1964), p. 94.

ing from his metaphysics alone.[9] As for Heidegger's ontology, it should be recalled that he never constituted being per se *(Sein)* but only being-as-manifest-in-human-consciousness *(Dasein)*. In other words, his phenomenology never led into the ontology he himself originally promised in his magnum opus, *Being and Time*.[10] And Heidegger, like Whitehead, also failed to ground anything like an ethical system.

Now some Aristotelians, both Thomistic and non-Thomistic, have attempted to get themselves out of this impasse by asserting that the teleology of human life, upon which Aristotelian ethics is based, does not need the kind of ontological grounding that traditional, pre-Galilean and pre-Newtonian physics-cum-metaphysics formerly provided. However, without this ontological grounding, or at least some other ontological grounding, it is hard to see how this can lead to anything more than Kantianism. In Kantianism we do see teleology, but the only *telos* turns out to be human reason itself as it constructs its own universe *by and for* itself. The human actor in this system actually projects his or her own ends based on self-knowledge as a first cause: we become makers of a world rather than participants in one already there. This is essentially different from Aristotelianism, certainly from that of the Thomistic variety. Here human reason can effectively order natural inclination to do good only because the seeker of the goods and the goods being sought are already present to each other in a larger reality: Nature. That is why these goods can be achieved by the human actor: we know ourselves in essentially the same way we know the rest of nature. Thus, neither human nor nonhuman nature is a *de novo* construction or projection of *homo faber*. Murray himself emphasized this distinction when he wrote that

> reason does not create its own laws, any more than man creates himself. Man has the laws of his nature given to him, as nature itself is given . . . and so his reason reflects a higher reason; therein consists its rightness and its power to oblige. . . . It appoints an order of nature — an order of beings, each of which carries in its very nature also its end and purposes. (P. 330)

9. See Alfred North Whitehead, *Process and Reality* (New York: Macmillan, 1929), p. 405.
10. See Martin Heidegger, *Being and Time*, trans. J. Macquarrie and E. Robinson (New York: Harper & Row, 1962), pp. 32-35.

Whether or not one agrees with Murray's particularly Thomistic presentation of the relation between human reason and what lies beyond it, one can generally agree with him that human reason cannot sustain itself unless it is located in a larger context of some kind. The question is what that larger context might be if Aristotelian metaphysical nature can no longer perform the comprehensive function.[11]

The Theological Problem of Natural Law

There are also theological problems facing Murray and other traditional Thomists in their natural-law theory. The usual complaint raised against them (and their counterparts in Judaism and Islam) comes from fideists. They argue that humans are simply unable to perceive clearly what is good for themselves in any unambiguous sense. It is only through revelation pointing to salvation by God that humans can hope for any true fulfillment at all. This complaint is best known in the form raised by Protestants heavily influenced by Luther. Nevertheless, this sort of complaint, *mutatis mutandis,* is raised by Jewish and Muslim fideists against those who are the equivalents of the Thomists in their respective traditions.[12]

Theologians who also affirm the reality of natural law have an answer to this sort of challenge to the validity of their position. Murray himself expresses it quite cogently.

> The Christian call is to transcend nature, notably to transcend what is noblest in nature, the faculty of reason. But it is not a call to escape from nature, or to dismantle nature's own structure. . . . In so far as they touch the moral life, the energies of grace . . . quicken to new and fuller life the dynamisms of nature, which are resident in reason. Were it otherwise, grace would not be supernatural but only miraculous. (P. 298)

Here again, it is not only Christianity that sees itself as the divinely

---

11. The current inappropriateness of Aristotelian teleology in both philosophy and theology does not mean that all teleology need be abandoned, therefore. For its continued theological use, see Novak, "Theonomous Ethics: A Defense and a Critique of Tillich," *Soundings* 49 (Winter 1986): 448-50.

12. See Marvin Fox, "Maimonides and Aquinas on Natural Law," *Dine Israel* 3 (1972): v.

given means for transcending the limitations of nature. Judaism and Christianity (and Islam) simply differ on the specific content of this divine grace. The formal theological problem of nature and grace is virtually the same in the various faith traditions, even if the real differences as to what this grace consists of are *toto caelo*. Jews and Christians (and Muslims) have enough resources in their respective traditions at least to counter effectively if not actually to refute the antirational fideism also present in their traditions.

The more difficult theological problem comes not from the outside, from those who deny the legitimacy of any theological affirmation of natural law, but rather from the inside. The question here is: If teleological metaphysics and its natural theology can no longer cogently ground natural law by connecting it to God, what can reestablish that grounding connection? Metaphysics and theology are no longer part of the same order. And if metaphysics is the only link between ethics (pertaining to what is between humans) and theology (pertaining to what is between humans and God), we seem to be left with three alternatives.

First, believers from the various faith traditions can confine *their* ethics to the specific content of *their* own revelations. All ethics, then, can be divine positive law only as interpreted and applied by the authority structures in each of the traditions. Ethics in this view is possible only when it has a direct theological grounding. It follows from this, of course, that ethics thereby ceases to be an area in which adherents of the different faith traditions can intelligently interact with each other, let alone with American society as a whole, in which theology — anybody's theology — has no such immediate authority. And those who persist in talking this kind of theological language in public discourse are rightly suspected of being religious imperialists who are attempting to force *their* religious ethics down *everyone else's* throat. This objection comes from the adherents of the other religious traditions in our pluralistic society just as fast and just as vehemently as it does from avowed secularists. (This should offer some small comfort to those secularists who worry that more religion in public discourse will lead to some kind of official state religion in America.)

Second, one can accept the kind of spiritual schizophrenia I described at the beginning of this essay, and simply separate one's religious thinking and acting from one's thinking and acting in regard to everything not directly involving God. This, of course, leaves one's religion an ever-shrinking role in one's life as the secular world claims more and more of one's time and energy, intellectual as well as physical.

Finally, one can adopt a Kantian-type approach and argue for an ethical metaphysics rather than a metaphysical ethics of the Aristotelian type. This approach is attractive to philosophers because it can produce at least a minimal natural-law theory — something most ably shown of late by the influential philosopher John Rawls. The question is, though, whether such philosophical attractiveness can still be integrated with religious faith.

This approach, when more strictly Kantian, is based on the idea that man is the autonomous creator of a universal morality *(causa noumenon)*. We have already seen why on Aristotelian grounds alone a Thomist such as Murray rejects this approach philosophically. However, its rejection on theological grounds by a Jewish or Christian believer (and Murray was a Catholic before he was an Aristotelian) must be even stronger. For any connection between ethics and God as either *arche* or *telos* of the moral life is ruled out by this approach in principle. It can accept only human transcendence; God becomes a postulate at best. I do not see how any Jewish or Christian believer, however much he or she might want to construct a natural-law theory, could possibly accept with any kind of theological consistency an approach to ethics the very *conditio per quam* of which is that man is the measure of all things.[13]

Another approach, however, more neo-Kantian than strictly Kantian, is based on the idea that a finite number of humanly sought values or goods are simply given and that practical reason can determine an ordered relationship with them — a rational ethical system. However, for this approach, the human relationship with God is either irrelevant or merely one good among others. But surely no Jewish or Christian believer could with any theological integrity accept an approach (let alone actually devise it) in which God is neither *origo* of nor *summum bonum* for what humans are to do with their lives.[14]

The revival of natural law can be a cogent option only if these

---

13. See Kant, *Critique of Pure Reason*, trans. N. Kemp Smith (New York: Macmillan, 1929), B819; and *Critique of Practical Reason*, trans. L. W. Beck (Chicago: University of Chicago Press, 1949), pp. 234ff. See also John Rawls, *A Theory of Justice* (Cambridge: Harvard University Press, 1971), pp. 252ff.

14. For an insightful critique of these Kantian-type natural-law theories adopted by some religiously committed philosophers, including neo-Kantian versions (whether so named by their authors or not), see Russell Hittinger, "Varieties of Minimalist Natural Law Theory," *American Journal of Jurisprudence* 34 (1989): 155ff.

extremes can be successfully avoided. Without that it cannot amount to more than nostalgia. I have tried to show that the metaphysically constituted theology of Aristotelian Thomism proposed by Murray cannot effect this revival (nor, certainly, can a Kantian or even a Neo-Kantian approach). In other words, while I agree with Murray's overall project, I do not agree with the way he attempts to argue for it at this point in history.

A Philosophical Alternative

The assumption held by traditional Thomists such as Murray is that there is a definable human nature to which everyone can refer without prior allegiance to any religious tradition and that natural-law precepts can be derived from this human nature. However, this assumption is philosophically unconvincing at the present time because it invokes a correspondence theory of truth when there is no longer any commonly accepted object of correspondence. If "truth is the agreement of thinking with reality" *(veritas est adaequatio intellectus ad rem)*, the statement has a noetic function only when there is some agreement about what "reality" is the criterion of what is true, as opposed to false thinking about "it." Only when this is the case does truth follow being *(veritas sequitur esse rerum)*. Only when there is a common acceptance of a "nature" can "natural" law be rationally persuasive. When that is not the case, however, it might still be instructive to consider the result if one views natural law as it has been affirmed by Jews, Christians, and Muslims as *part of their* traditional teaching about and to the world at large rather than as an independent tradition of its own. If we do this, a different theory of truth is clearly called for.

Within the covenantal communities of faith themselves a correspondence theory of truth is still valid. The community acknowledges a body of normative revelation from God. It is itself the criterion of what is true as opposed to what is false thinking about it. Thus, one could say that truth is the agreement of thinking with the word of God *(veritas est adaequatio intellectus ad verbum Dei)*. The word of God as the criterion of truth cannot be established on the basis of any external criterion and still retain the absolute primacy the religious traditions claim for it. Thus, Jews praise God as the giver of *torat 'emet*, which means "the doctrine of truth," the corollary of which is that nothing else can be true if it is inconsistent with it.[15] That is why Judaism and Christianity call their unique truths *mysteries*.[16] They are inaccessible to outside judgment or appropriation.

Despite the necessity for a correspondence theory of truth in the internal discourse of a covenantal community, the community also has something to say beyond its own borders. Here a correspondence theory of truth, at least at this point in history, cannot be employed for the reasons we have already seen. That is why the Thomistic version of natural law as presented by a theologian such as Murray cannot have enough plausibility to be convincing in social discourse outside the Catholic world in which it has been traditionally developed. (And even there its theory is hardly *philosophia perennis* anymore.) *Ius naturale* will have to give way to *ius gentium* — namely, not what the community accepts as a priori universal truth but only what it itself constitutes as generally normative in and for the world beyond the immediate pale of its own adherents.[17] Here one will have to

---

15. For Jews, the truth of the Torah is the truth of God's own revelation. Thus the *Palestinian Talmud: Sanhedrin* 1.1/18a notes that "the seal of God is truth *('emet)*." A homily that follows this dictum sees it based on Isaiah 44:6 — "I am the first and I am the last, and besides Me there is no god." Hence, the Torah is Truth per se, to which all that is true must correspond; that is why *'emet* essentially means "being faithful" — the consistency of God's word to those to whom it is addressed (see, e.g., Ps. 111:8) and the requirement of consistency from those to whom that word is addressed (see, e.g., Ps. 15:2). In rabbinic theology the Torah is the *hagia sophia* wherewith God creatively orders the world. See *Midrash Bereshit Rabbah*, beg. re Prov. 8:30.

16. For rabbinic emphasis on the oral tradition as being more mysterious and, therefore, holier than even the written Torah (Scripture), see *Midrash Shemot Rabbah* 46.1 re Hos. 8:12; *Midrash Tanhuma:* Ki Tissa, 34; and *Babylonian Talmud: Gittin* 60b re Exod. 34:27.

17. On the complex relationships between the concepts of *ius gentium* and *ius naturale* as used in Roman law, see A. P. d'Entreves, *Natural Law: An Historical Survey* (New York: Harper Torchbooks, 1965), pp. 17-32. Some Roman legal thinkers (e.g., Ulpian) maintain that *ius naturale* is based on a simple empirical observation of what is common to all animals, man included. In this view, then, *ius gentium* stands above *ius naturale* as intellect stands above instinct. But other Roman legal thinkers, largely influenced by Stoic philosophy, hold that *ius naturale* stands above *ius gentium* as a higher intellect stands above a lower intellect, it being the criterion of *quod semper aequum ac bonum est*. In the Muslim, Jewish, and Christian natural-law tradition, which has accepted the second view and discarded the first, the vague Stoic idea of nature was replaced by the more precise Aristotelian idea of nature when the Aristotelian corpus came to be translated into Arabic, then Hebrew, and then Latin in the twelfth and thirteenth centuries. Nevertheless, since one cannot go back to the Aristotelian idea (nor, a fortiori, to the Stoic idea) of

appeal to historically evident data rather than to the type of metaphysics Murray suggested.

This broader teaching about the world contains the minimal constituents of the fuller revelation proclaimed by Judaism and Christianity
respectively. This point comes out in the works of both Maimonides and
Aquinas, each of whom based his work on earlier sources in his religious
tradition.[18] If we now remove the added Aristotelian metaphysics of
nature from both of their formulations of earlier Jewish and Christian
tradition, we will need a coherence theory of truth to talk about this
teaching in the world beyond the faith communities. This world is the
secular world as it has been with us since the dawn of modernity.

A coherence theory of truth says that one explanation of a problematic situation is better than another if it offers a more coherent and
economic reconstitution of its elements and thereby leads to a more
comprehensive solution. Say there are three possible explanations of
a given situation, the first of which reconstitutes some aspects of the
problem, the second of which reconstitutes more of the aspects of the
problem, and the third of which reconstitutes even more of the aspects
of the problem but requires the acceptance of more new assumptions
than the second explanation. The coherence theory of truth dictates
that the explanation that reconstitutes the most aspects of the problem
with the fewest assumptions is the best explanation now available for
our use, and hence it would indicate that truth is to be found in the
second explanation. The first explanation is less plausible because it
has not gotten as strong a handle on the situation as the second
explanation has; the situation is still too far ahead of this explanation.
Conversely, the third explanation is less plausible because it has gotten

---

nature, it would seem that the relation between *ius gentium* and *ius naturale* of Ulpian
et al. comes closer to the modern emphasis on the more empirical meaning of
"nature" and the greater emphasis on historical reality (of which *ius gentium* has
always been explicitly seen as a part). It would seem that we must seek to satisfy
the human desire for *quod semper aequum ac bonum est* in the revelations proclaimed
in and by the covenantal traditions.

18. Maimonides views the minimal seven Noahide laws, which the rabbis
considered binding on all humankind, as included in the larger and the deeper
Mosaic Torah. See *Mishneh Torah: Laws of Kings* 9.1; and *Guide of the Perplexed* 2.40;
see also *Babylonian Talmud: Sanhedrin* 59a. Aquinas, *mutatis mutandis*, makes the same
point regarding the relation between natural law and revealed law. "[It] is not that
whatever is contained in the Law and the Gospel belongs to the natural law, since
they contain many things that are above nature; but what belongs to the natural
law is fully contained in them" (*Summa Theologica*, I-II, q.94, a.4 ad 1).

too strong a hold on the situation. It holds the situation to be an expendable example of its own preconceived idea; the situation has fallen too far behind it. This third explanation is usually seen as being insuperably vulnerable to the refutation known as Ockham's Razor. The second explanation avoids the pitfalls of these two extremes. Nevertheless, even it cannot presume to offer up eternal truth, since every explanation is inherently surmountable at some later time.[19] It is necessarily a pragmatic theory of truth, since truth is judged by the criterion of temporal value, not by that of everlasting being.[20]

This is precisely how the broader teachings of the religious traditions, which pertain to the world beyond their respective covenants, can speak to, in, and about that world with more persuasiveness than Murray's type of natural-law theory. Being partially in the same world as the adherents of secularist traditions, they are faced with certain common problematic situations — situations that call for normative answers. Furthermore, there is now the recognition that all our positions are tradition-bound, that there is no nature standing over and above the traditions that can be invoked as a transcendent criterion of truth to which the true answer must ultimately correspond. This being the case, we are left either to find certain common substantive over-

---

19. See Karl Popper, *Popper Selections,* ed. D. Miller (Princeton: Princeton University Press, 1985), pp. 133ff., 179.

20. Within Judaism, Christianity, and Islam, on the other hand, the word of God functions as that criterion of everlasting truth to which everything that is true must correspond. "The grass withers, the flower fades; but the word of our God endures forever *(l'olam)*" (Isa. 40:8). Nevertheless, this does not mean that there is no employment of the coherence theory of truth in theological reasoning. Theological problems frequently require the same problem-solving techniques that we have seen operating according to the coherence theory. Such is often the case when the desired correspondence is neither apparent nor direct. Indeed, the greater gap between the reader and the text that results when critical historical scholarship is used by theologians makes this situation of less apparentness and directness more prevalent now than it was before this method of scholarship became unavoidable in our culture. Even so, this situation does not preclude use of the correspondence theory, since theological reasoning must always include an ongoing hermeneutic of commonly accepted revelation the truth of which transcends both the particular theological problem that is being worked on (whatever it might be) and the community of discourse that is working on it. For any attempt to solve such a problem must be conducted with revelation in the background and redemption on the horizon. In relation to the former it must always see itself as originally derivative; in relation to the latter it must always see itself as ultimately tentative. On the use of the coherence theory in theology, see Novak, "The Role of Dogma in Judaism," *Theology Today* 45 (1988): 54ff.

lappings between traditions or to show that one tradition has superior resources for dealing with a problem facing all the traditions, religious or secular, represented in that society at that time. Alasdair MacIntyre shows quite astutely how this latter case of interaction between traditions takes place: "the achievement of the understanding of one tradition by the adherents of another . . . in certainly rare but crucial types of cases . . . may lead to a judgment that by the standards of one's own tradition the standpoint of another tradition offers superior resources for understanding the problems and issues which confront one's own tradition."[21]

This is where Jewish-Christian dialogue, which has long been an important component in my own experience and theological reflection, plays a key role in the process of dialogue between religious communities and the secular world.[22] In the old Aristotelian model, the one accepted by such premodern theologians as Maimonides and Aquinas and the Muslim Avicenna, metaphysics supplied the medium needed for that dialogue.[23] Following this model, these religious thinkers thought they could reach beyond their immediate religious traditions and speak both to each other and even to that which was not specifically religious at all ("the philosophers") in the *same* way. That medium, as we have seen, is no longer available.

Based on the model of the overlapping of traditions I have tried to present briefly here, Jews and Christians must first be able to talk to each other *before* they can talk to the secular world, which is farther removed from both of them. Discourse must begin between those whose traditions overlap most. Surely in the history of the West, no two religious traditions have overlapped more than Judaism and Christianity.[24]

At those points of mutually identifiable overlapping, discourse can still, to a certain extent, be structured by a correspondence theory of truth. In the case of Jews and Christians, the common acceptance of the Hebrew Bible as the word of God, as preserved in its present text, provides the needed transcendent object: discourse can be judged

21. MacIntyre, *Whose Justice? Which Rationality?* p. 370.

22. See Novak, *Jewish-Christian Dialogue: A Jewish Justification* (New York: Oxford University Press, 1989), especially pp. 114ff.

23. See Harry A. Wolfson, *Spinoza* (Cambridge: Harvard University Press, 1934), pp. 10-11.

24. See Ludwig Wittgenstein, *Philosophical Investigations*, 2d ed., trans. G. E. M. Anscombe (New York: Macmillan, 1967), pp. 31-32 (§§ 66-67).

true or false depending on its correspondence or lack of correspondence with the text as the basic normative datum. Now, in fact, Jews and Christians have disagreed about more in the Hebrew Bible than they have agreed about. For example, one community says that the Sabbath is perpetually binding on all members of the covenant; the other says that "the Son of man is the lord of the Sabbath" (Matt. 12:8). Nevertheless, on the doctrinal level there remains essential agreement about God as creator and revealer and about the still unredeemed condition of this world, and on the practical level there remains agreement about the sanctity of human life, the integrity of the family, and the right to a variety of individual and cooperative achievements. This is the Judeo-Christian tradition, one shared by both communities without at all compromising their respective covenants with God.

In the secular world there is much less commonality because there is much less of substance held in common. Therefore, Jews and Christians, largely in concert, will have to employ a coherence theory of truth in their discourse with the secular world. In doing so they will come closest to the issues of the natural-law project, if not the theory, of a Thomistic thinker such as Murray.

This theory will work quite well when dealing with an issue such as ecology.[25] Virtually everyone is now agreed that the modern technological relationship between humans and their nonhuman surroundings is becoming more and more unacceptable for both physical and spiritual reasons. There are some — even some theologians — who blame the problem of technology on the biblical teaching about humans having dominion over the earth (à la Gen. 1:26).[26] The fact is, however, that biblical teaching in its normative thrust (which is the most immediate aspect of that teaching) structures, guides, and limits the human relationship with the environment without reducing humans to the level of all other nonspiritual parts of that environment. It does so by means of an elaborate system of norms of responsibility — responsibility *to* God, *with* one another, and *for* the world. What Jews and Christians have to do in regard to this common problem, a problem recognized by secularists as keenly as by themselves, is to constitute a more coherent solution than that which secularists can provide out

25. See Novak, "Technology and Its Ultimate Threat: A Jewish Meditation," *Research in Philosophy and Technology* 10 (1989): 43ff.

26. See Gordon Kaufman, *Theology for a Nuclear Age* (Philadelphia: Westminster Press, 1985), p. 31.

of their traditions. By "more coherent" I do not mean "final" or "unfalsifiable." A coherence theory of truth cannot make any such absolute claims for any conclusion it reaches. This is only one important example. Here I can only obliquely suggest the possibility of constituting a better solution, not what the content of that solution is actually to be or how it is specifically to be argued.

Conclusion

I have tried to show in this essay that the universal truth assumed by a Thomist such as Murray to correspond with nature as a transcendent object cannot be constituted. For it requires a transcendence of traditions that is simply untenable for both philosophical and theological reasons. Surely this does not mean, however, that transcendence cannot be affirmed or that a correspondence theory of truth ought never to be employed. Both are indeed possible — but they are possible plurally, not singularly. Each tradition constitutes its *own* relationship with its *own* respective transcendent object. Judaism and Christianity each constitute their respective transcendent objects as the word of God. There are some areas of substantive overlapping; there are more and deeper areas where there is none. In the case of the secular world, there is much less overlapping with Judaism or Christianity. But when there is overlapping between the secular and religious worlds, it is almost always at the point where the two religious traditions themselves overlap. Thus, there are only more specific truths and more general truths. Aside from some basic logical truths, universal truth, in theology or even philosophy, will have to wait for the final redemption of the world.[27] In the meantime, rationalities function within their respective traditions, a point Alasdair MacIntyre has helped us to understand better.

Yet, it would seem, reason has the best chance of surviving and persisting in such traditions as Judaism and Christianity that are grounded in the affirmation of a divine creative wisdom who governs the whole universe, albeit in ways known only very partially and dis-

---

27. Ultimately, this *lex divina* is seen by each covenantal community as being universal law; but it cannot be considered intelligible either immediately *(ratio quoad nos)* or even by inference *(ratio per se)* without historical revelation. See Job 38:1ff.; *Babylonian Talmud: Pesahim* 68b; and *Niddah* 73a re Habakkuk 3:6.

junctively by created minds. Reason does not seem to be capable of surviving and persisting in an otherwise absurd universe and in an otherwise meaningless process of history. Even when Judaism and Christianity become antirational, which they too often do, the very sources of their respective traditions provide the means for correcting this error. In other words, reason needs faith as much as faith needs reason. (It is *intellectus quarens fidem* as much as *fides quarens intellectum.*) And so, despite our fundamental philosophical differences over metaphysics and natural law, let alone our even more fundamental religious differences, I am convinced that the late John Courtney Murray and I, as both believers and thinkers, could agree on this last point. In the light of that agreement, and considering how many in the world would surely disagree with us, our differences do not seem overwhelming after all.

II. MURRAY AND THE AMERICAN EXPERIMENT

John Courtney Murray and the Public Philosophy

Robert F. Cuervo

1945-1964: "Believing Skepticism" vs. the Revival of Natural Law

THE MOOD THAT DOMINATED American political thought and intellectual life in the first two decades after World War II was one of
skepticism, particularly toward the self-assured, allegedly scientific, militant ideologies of fascism, Nazism, and communism that threatened
American freedom. The skepticism of the liberal intellectuals of the early
postwar period also extended to developments at home that threatened
to become ideological, such as the anticommunism of Sen. Joseph
McCarthy and the revival of American conservatism. This is the thesis
advanced by Robert Booth Fowler in *Believing Skeptics: American Political
Intellectuals, 1945-1964.*

While skepticism and antirationalism were the main intellectual
currents of this period, other Americans (e.g., Walter Lippmann, John
Hallowell, and John Courtney Murray) opposed ideology by trying to
revive the idea of a natural moral law that both governments and
citizens are obliged to obey. While just as opposed to ideology as their
mainstream brethren, they refused to fight ideology by denying the
existence of objective truths or absolutes. Rather, these public philosophers opposed ideology with a body of natural-law doctrine that they
claimed was part of the Great Tradition of Western civilization.

Hatred of ideology was a dominant liberal theme in the postwar
period and can be found in the writings of Arthur Schlesinger, Jr.,

67

Sidney Hook, Edward Shils, Clinton Rossiter, and Daniel Bell. Schlesinger, in his famous *The Vital Center*, was so confidently anti-ideological that it is difficult to call him a skeptic. Ideologies were supported by "true believers," to use Eric Hoffer's popular term.[1] Thus, a position of skepticism about absolutes and ideals became the liberal weapon of choice against ideologies.

According to the skeptics, "fanatics felt impelled to change the world to make it conform to the truth they 'knew' to be true."[2] According to Daniel Bell, "the tendency to convert concrete issues into ideological problems, to invest them with moral color and highly emotional charge, is to invite conflicts which can only damage a society."[3] The obvious implication is that the pursuit and implementation of absolute truth raises the specter of conflict and totalitarianism.

Foreign ideologues were not the only targets of post–World War II intellectuals. According to Fowler, America's past and present were examined for traces of ideology and fanaticism. Daniel Boorstin singled out Quakers, Puritans, and both sides of the pre–Civil War slavery debate as ideological. At various points during the 1950s, Thomas Jefferson, William Jennings Bryan, and the leaders of the Populist movement were denounced as "true believers." Richard Hofstadter claimed that "both Populism and Progressivism were addicted to a 'moral absolutism' that inevitably leads to 'ruthlessness in political life.'"[4] While Roosevelt's New Deal was spared the ideological label, many intellectuals of the 1930s were reviled as "literary Stalinoids." In short, the critique of American "ideology" was both pervasive and comprehensive.

The American Right also was targeted by the believing skeptics, whether it was the militant John Birch Society or the more moderate conservatism of William F. Buckley, Jr., and his *National Review*. However, the chief ideologue of the right, in the opinion of liberal intellectuals, was Sen. Joseph McCarthy. Then as now, it was common to regard McCarthyism as a threat to civil liberties. For believing skeptics, McCarthy, though fighting against communist ideology, was a fanatic, ideologue, and demagogue in his own right. He became a

1. See Robert Booth Fowler, *Believing Skeptics: American Political Intellectuals, 1945-1964* (Westport, Conn.: Greenwood Press, 1978), p. 10.
2. Fowler, *Believing Skeptics*, p. 10.
3. Bell, *The End of Ideology* (New York: Free Press, 1962), p. 121.
4. Fowler, *Believing Skeptics*, pp. 29-32.

permanent negative symbol for the believing skeptics, even though "he was dead by 1957 and destroyed politically well before then."[5]

The era of believing skepticism was also the period in which behavioral political science and its "new" democratic theory achieved prominence. According to Fowler, liberal intellectuals of this period distrusted human nature, popular rationality, and utopianism. Some historians (e.g., Richard Hofstadter) warned that ideological fanatics would not get very far in the absence of "a great number of unexceptional citizens who possessed 'the one-hundred per cent mentality.' "[6] In the face of potentially irrational and ideological citizens, the new democratic theory deemphasized the majoritarian aspects of democracy in favor of constitutionalism and checks and balances. Such authors as Joseph A. Schumpeter and Robert A. Dahl tried to recast elections as polyarchy — the choice between competing elites rather than contests to determine the majority will in an abstract sense. Even pluralist theory, which holds that politics and policy-making result from the struggle between selfish interest groups, was advocated as offering a solution to the problem of fanatical majorities while still preserving a reasonable amount of democracy.

In framing the new democratic theory, political scientists tried to avoid moral "absolutes" and defended the empirical scientific method as a universal solution. Robert A. Dahl, for instance, made clear that he "rejected any political theory that claimed to deduce its principles from natural rights."[7] This is very different from traditional political theory, for which "there were certain true principles, natural laws, divine laws, or basic normative axioms of one sort or another, which people could discover by reason, and from which one could deduce the proper political values." Not only Plato and Aristotle but also the "entire natural rights tradition of liberalism" operated on such assumptions.[8]

This was not the case for the new political science, which "tended more and more to take as its standard of meaning the empirical world and to insist that one must produce empirical [i.e., sensible] verifications for assertions of fact." Natural laws and rights did not meet these standards and could not be considered "scientific." Thus, Fowler

---

5. Fowler, *Believing Skeptics*, pp. 23-25.
6. Fowler, *Believing Skeptics*, p. 11.
7. Fowler, *Believing Skeptics*, p. 45. See Dahl, *A Preface to Democratic Theory* (Chicago: University of Chicago Press, 1956), p. 45.
8. Fowler, *Believing Skeptics*, p. 41.

writes, "many social scientists insisted that questions of fact and matters of value were two distinct realms and no fact could justify a value and vice versa. The result was further skepticism about the possibility of providing any absolute justification for political norms."[9]

Before turning to the revival of natural law, let us clarify why Fowler called liberal intellectuals "believing" skeptics. However skeptical and relativistic their epistemology seemed, early postwar intellectuals had little difficulty accepting American liberal democracy as a positive good. They also counseled avoidance of absolutes and ideologies as if this were a positive doctrine, and, accordingly, they emphasized openness and tolerance. They also believed that the economic system of the time created economic growth without inflation and that the surpluses of this growth could be used to fund social programs for the poor. They also believed in a bipartisan foreign policy of containing communism.[10]

The skeptics believed that it was not necessary to employ ideology to defend these goods. Liberal intellectuals emphasized problem-solving instead of dogmatism, interests rather than ideology, compromise rather than conflict. They perceived, in their day, a general consensus about procedural and substantive values, an "end of ideology."[11]

But one group of reflective scholars of the early postwar period viewed believing skepticism as an unacceptable alternative to ideology. These writers maintained that civility (and stability) is ultimately guaranteed by something more than the policy consensus of the day or mere skepticism about ideology.[12] The democratic community must depend upon a more fundamental set of truths — the public consensus — which, given the transcendent nature of the truths involved, has come to be called the public philosophy.

How can we define this public philosophy? Let us turn to the founders of the public philosophy movement for an answer. The journalist Walter Lippmann defined the public philosophy as "a body of positive principles which a good citizen cannot deny or ignore."[13]

9. Fowler, *Believing Skeptics,* pp. 41-42.

10. See Godfrey Hodgson, *America in Our Time* (New York: Vintage Books, 1978), pp. 67-98.

11. See Fowler, *Believing Skeptics,* pp. 15-16, 48-50.

12. For a more extended treatment of this thesis, see Cuervo, "Public Philosophy in a Democracy: Transcendental Values and Free Society in the Political Thought of John H. Hallowell and Irving Kristol," Ph.D. diss., Fordham University, 1980, pp. 7-20.

13. Lippmann, *Essays in the Public Philosophy* (New York: Mentor Books, 1955), p. 79.

John Courtney Murray stated that the public consensus is "an ensemble of substantive truths, a structure of basic knowledge, an order of elementary affirmations that reflect realities inherent in the order of existence."[14] Citing Cicero's *De Re Publica*, Murray said that a true republic is not just any association of people but is a people *juris consensu et utilitatis communione sociatus* — a people united by a common agreement about laws and rights and a common desire for mutual, not just selfish, advantage. And John H. Hallowell argued that government truly based on the consent of the governed "is found . . . only in those nations where there is a community of values and interests, where there is a positive affirmation of certain fundamental values common to the large majority of individuals and groups within the nation."[15]

The first principle of the public philosophy is that human reason is capable of discovering valid principles about the common good and about the natural moral law. The common good entails, among other things, the state's duty to ensure peace, order, and justice so that citizens can pursue good lives — specifically, lives of moral self-improvement and personal religious salvation. It also means that both government and citizens, in their political behavior, seek the good of society as a whole instead of personal self-interest. In addition to its specific content, the common good serves as a standard both for evaluating new proposals and for dealing with changes in the political environment.

Human reason can also recognize valid principles of natural law. By reflecting on the ends appropriate to human nature, human reason transcends the statutory or positive law of the state and discovers binding moral principles in the nature of things. Cicero called this law "right reason in agreement with nature." It is a universal moral law that binds all people in all places and that may not rightly be altered by human beings. The author of the natural law is God himself, who is the author of nature.

As a universal, fundamental, or "higher" law, natural law is a standard by which positive law should be made and judged. For Lippmann, Murray, and other public philosophers, natural law serves as

---

14. Murray, *We Hold These Truths: Catholic Reflections on the American Proposition* (New York: Sheed & Ward, 1960), p. 9. Subsequent references to this volume will be made parenthetically in the text.

15. Hallowell, *The Moral Foundation of Democracy* (Chicago: University of Chicago Press, 1954), pp. 35-36.

the cornerstone of the public philosophy because it places moral limits on the actions of both rulers and citizens. For the public philosophers, the natural law of reason "fixed the boundaries beyond which the Sovereign — the King, the Parliament, the voters — were forbidden to go." Natural law civilizes democracy, because a law "above the ruler and the sovereign people, above the whole community of mortals" restricts arbitrary government and dictatorship on the one hand, and popular license and tyranny of the majority on the other.[16]

To whose reason is the public philosophy made clear? First of all, we must follow Aquinas in distinguishing between the wise and the many. The primary or elementary principles of the natural law (e.g., prohibitions of murder, theft, and lying) are self-evident to the reason of the many — which is to say, to everyone. The secondary, more complicated principles of the moral law are self-evident only to the wise, who have studied the moral law in great detail, and it is these more elaborate principles that constitute the public philosophy (pp. 117-18).

Additionally, the ability to discover the principles of the public philosophy requires an intellect that is free from selfishness or excessive emotion. In Lippmann's words, "the public interest is mixed with, and is often at odds with, . . . private and special interests. Put this way, we can say, I suggest, that the public interest may be presumed to be what men would choose if they saw clearly, thought rationally, acted disinterestedly and benevolently."[17] Or, as Murray wrote, the "elaboration [of the public consensus] is the task of the wise and honest" (p. 118).

The public philosophers feared that the Western world, including America, was losing its public philosophy. Lippmann argued that liberalism was trying to preserve the public philosophy while attacking the classical metaphysics and Christian theology that had supported it. The result was a gradual weakening of democratic man's "capacity to believe." By the twentieth century, modern man "had a low capacity

16. Lippmann, *Essays in the Public Philosophy*, pp. 76-77. In varying degrees, public philosophers note that the natural law, a product of reason, has been supplemented by religious insights derived from revelation, which has strengthened the insights of reason concerning human dignity, man's unique nature, human rights and duties, and the limits of the state's authority over citizens. John H. Hallowell, for instance, emphasizes the dual role played by reason and revelation in discovering the public philosophy. However, this should not lead us to misconstrue natural law or the public philosophy as religious rather than political.

17. Lippmann, *Essays in the Public Philosophy*, p. 40.

to believe the invisible, the intangible, the imponderable," including the very possibility of a natural moral law. Accordingly, "in the prevailing popular culture, all philosophies are the instrument of some man's purpose, all truths are self-centered and self-regarding, and all principles are the rationalization of some special interest. There is no public criterion of the true and false."[18]

Public philosophers argue that the loss of transcendent values causes dysfunctions of varying severity in the body politic. Some of these dysfunctions are dangerous in themselves. Others are not immediately dangerous, but they could combine with other factors to weaken the state in time of crisis.[19]

In the absence of a public philosophy, politicians will tend to flatter the citizenry rather than risk their jobs by being candid. Such a tendency, historically, has been a liability of democracy, but the public philosophy can restrain such behavior by providing a sense of republican self-discipline that limits the demagoguery of the politician and the popular passions that political rhetoric can stir. Irving Kristol has noted that some demagogic American politicians have championed utopian programs and promised to abolish poverty, attempting to convince the poor that such a goal is actually achievable. When their expectations are inevitably disappointed, the result is disillusionment, recrimination, and occasionally even violence.[20]

The loss of the transcendent values that limited democratic rulers, majorities, and pressure groups resulted in the theory that democracy is no more than a set of procedures for enacting the will of the most powerful interest groups. Contemporary political scientists tell us that democracy is not based on a consensus about moral values but is sustained by a consensus to play politics by the "rules of the game." Of this view, Kristol (in the spirit of the public philosophers) has written that "democracy, like any other political order, rests upon a consensus, and . . . this consensus cannot — as contemporary political science seems to assume — be merely procedural. . . . Unless one is going to

18. Lippmann, *Essays in the Public Philosophy,* pp. 88, 89.

19. The public philosophers of the immediate postwar period did not include in this list of dysfunctions some of the issues debated rather strenuously today, particularly those related to sexual privacy, but that is simply because they were engaging the issues of special concern in their own time. This is not to say that issues at the forefront of public debate today have no place on the list.

20. Kristol, *On the Democratic Idea in America* (New York: Harper & Row, 1972), pp. 139-41.

set up as an idol the brassy machinery of democratic politics, one must ask: democracy for what? There needs to be a transcending standard by which the 'national interest' can define itself, and by which the popular will can judge and correct itself."[21]

Without this transcending standard — that is to say, without the public philosophy — democratic politics is simply a battle of lobbyists, access peddlers, and political action committees in which money rather than justice becomes the key factor in policy making. Of itself, this is not a fatal flaw, but it does lead to injustices, contributes to a selfish approach to politics, and, most importantly, gives rise to feelings of insignificance, helplessness, and cynicism on the part of average citizens.

The loss of the public philosophy also erodes the idea of law. According to Murray, "for a variety of reasons, the intellectualist idea of law as reason had begun to cede to the voluntarist idea of law as will" (p. 41). The public philosopher argues that law is a product of human reason, restraining the arbitrary wills of both rulers and citizens by means of a natural moral law. Voluntarists reject this approach, defining law simply as the will of the official, legislature, or government that makes the laws. Voluntarists maintain that the rational moral standards proposed by the natural law are subjective value judgments that are irrelevant to the actual law-making process. All that remains for the voluntarist is the positive law of the state, which, freed from the restraint of the public philosophy, is often redefined as the arbitrary will of the state. John Hallowell has concluded that the voluntarist (or legal positivist) idea of law as an empty form to be filled in with any content willed by the state was the perfect recipe for the German Enabling Act of 1933, which conferred dictatorial powers on Adolf Hitler.[22]

Another consequence of the abandonment of the public philosophy of reason and natural law is the tendency toward social engineering, especially grandiose schemes of social and biological control based on natural science. The Nazi regime was a practical example of this. When man's unique nature as a rational being and a child of God is disregarded, schemes like those found in Aldous Huxley's *Brave New World* come to be advocated seriously in the name of "science," includ-

21. Kristol, "The New Books: Democracy and Its Discontents," *Harper's*, September 1961, p. 99.
22. See Hallowell, *The Decline of Liberalism as an Ideology: With Particular Reference to German Politico-Legal Thought* (New York: Howard Fertig, 1971).

ing such horrors as the laboratory breeding of children and the psychological conditioning of entire populations. Indeed, the prospect begins to approach the cynical characterization of Thurman Arnold, who compares the democratic state to an insane asylum run by politician-therapists.[23] As C. S. Lewis noted darkly, "the power of man to make himself what he pleases . . . [ultimately] means the power of some men to make other men what they please."[24] The consequence is not utopia but technocratic tyranny.

Now that we have discussed the dysfunctions that accompany the loss of the public philosophy, let us explore the possibility of its restoration. To do this, we must remind ourselves of the senses in which the public philosophy is public. We find two such senses in the public philosophers' writings.

In the first sense, the public philosophy is public because it deserves to be held by the public. It deserves to be held because its teachings are principles of the right order of a democratic society, principles self-evident to the reason of those trained in the study of the common good. These principles are then presented, through education, to the general public so that they, too, will accept the public philosophy.

Even if the public fails to accept its principles, the public philosophy would still be binding on a given society. This does not mean that the people will govern themselves by a philosophy they do not accept or that such a philosophy should be forced upon them. The assertion that the public philosophy binds even a reluctant community means that since that philosophy contains necessary civilizing truths, the rejection of the public philosophy entails the consequences of ignoring those truths. "I would maintain," says Murray, ". . . that the public consensus of the West, and of the United States as an historic participant in the Western style of civilization, would remain the public consensus, even if it were held, as perhaps it is held, only by a minority within the West" (p. 98) He believed this to be case because the principles involved are both right and reasonable.

The second sense in which the public philosophy is public flows from the obvious dilemma posed by the first sense. Even if it is true that, as Richard Bishirjian has put it, "at the center of the public philosophy is a moral consensus which does not depend on popular

23. Hallowell, *The Moral Foundation of Democracy*, pp. 10-11.
24. Lewis, *The Abolition of Man* (New York: Macmillan, 1947), p. 72.

opinion at any given moment,"[25] it remains the case that the public philosophy does need popular support in some sense. As Murray notes, "the American Proposition rests on the . . . traditional conviction that there are truths; that they can be known; that they must be held; for, if they are not held, assented to, consented to, worked into the texture of institutions, there can be no hope of founding a true City, in which men dwell in dignity, peace, unity, justice, well-being, freedom" (p. ix). In other words, if the public philosophy is actually to civilize us and produce the good society, it must be held or at least assented to by the vast majority of citizens.

How will the public philosophy be reestablished among the people once it has been lost? As a rule, the public philosophers look to the educational process for an answer to this question.

Murray's version of this educational process is perhaps the best example. He accepted the idea that the principles of the public philosophy are secondary or "remote" tenets of natural law. As such, these principles are most readily apparent to the wise, who teach them to the many. Murray quotes Aquinas on this point:

> There are certain things which the natural reason of every man, immediately and of itself, discerns and judges, as to be done or not done; for instance, honor your father and mother, do not kill, do not steal. . . . There are, however, other matters which those who are wise judge, after rather subtle reflection, to be matters of necessary observance. These things are of the natural law indeed, but in such a way that they are matters for instruction. The wise teach them to those of lesser reflectiveness; for instance, come to your feet at the presence of white hair, honor the prerogatives of age, and such other things.[26]

It is obvious that this will appear paternalistic and undemocratic to some, since the transmission of the public philosophy is placed in the custody of the minority that is teaching it. We must, however, acknowledge the true nature of this venture. The teaching of the public philosophy requires the willingness of the many to be taught by the few. But since the vitality of the public philosophy depends upon the

25. Bishirjian, in *A Public Philosophy Reader*, ed. Richard J. Bishirjian (New Rochelle, N.Y.: Arlington House, 1978), p. 20.

26. Aquinas, *Summa Theologica*, cited by Murray in *We Hold These Truths*, p. 115.

acceptance of the teaching offered, the transmission of the public philosophy is in reality an exhortation aimed at producing an enlightened, civic-minded public opinion, something that is democratic in the best sense of the term.

In this spirit, Murray tells us that the true forum for restoring the public philosophy is the university. In America, the public philosopher does not seek the philosopher-king but the philosopher-teacher as the means of restoring the public consensus, though the nonacademic intellectual (e.g., Walter Lippmann) can also contribute to this end (pp. 121-23).

This overview of public philosophy demonstrates that there is a consensus more fundamental to democracy than the kind of policy consensus on mainly practical questions (e.g., Keynesian economics, welfare state programs, the containment of communism) that the "believing" skeptics of the 1950s accepted. Totalitarianism is not prevented by a relativism that abandons the public philosophy along with feared ideologies. Conviction, not doubt, is the necessary means of discovering and defending a good society.

Murray's Notion of the American Public Consensus

Let us now examine the basic contents of the public philosophy as Murray understood it. He spoke of an American public consensus, but he did not intend to relativize or nationalize the public philosophy. Rather, he simply endorsed the idea that certain conditions in a country's culture and history might require that some aspects of the public philosophy take on greater importance in that nation's circumstances.

For Murray, the basic fact about America was its heritage of religious pluralism. Accordingly, the American public consensus, while sharing in the larger public philosophy of Western civilization, has been focused on the problem of maintaining political unity amid this religious pluralism. There are five basic tenets in the traditional American consensus, according to Murray, that have supplied this unity: (1) the conviction that the United States is a nation under God, (2) the tradition of natural law, (3) the principle of consent, (4) the idea of a virtuous people, and (5) the vindication of human and historical rights. Let us now briefly examine each of these.

1. Murray believed that the opening remarks of the Declaration of Independence ("the Laws of Nature and of Nature's God") affirm

the sovereignty of God over all nations. This "radically distinguishes the conservative Christian tradition of America from the Jacobin laicist [i.e., secularist] tradition of Continental Europe" (p. 28). Though America has always had her share of agnostics and unbelievers, "it has never known [at least not as of 1960] organized militant atheism on the Jacobin, doctrinaire Socialist, or Communist model" (p. 29).

Murray mentions several presidents (John Adams, Abraham Lincoln, Dwight Eisenhower) who emphasized the sovereignty of God in their proclamations. He also quotes an atypical remark of Justice William O. Douglas from *Zorach vs. Clauson* — "we are a religious people whose institutions presuppose a Supreme Being" (pp. 29-30). It is true that there is a secularist dissenting rejoinder to such invocations, but in 1960 it was clearly a dissent and not a view held by a majority of the people. And some view of the sovereignty of God is still alive in America, and can potentially serve as a restraint on political action.

2. Murray states that "the American political community was organized in an era when the tradition of natural law and natural rights was still vigorous" (p. 30). Subscribing to the doctrine of natural law, especially during our formative period, had certain advantages. First, it prevented the emergence of "two Americas" (one religious and one anticlerical) in contrast to Europe, where two mutually hostile camps arose in a number of countries. If members of different religions, along with freethinkers and agnostics, accept natural-law morality, then there will be less potential for conflict over basic moral issues (p. 31). Second, the tradition of natural law, along with the doctrine of the sovereignty of God and the medieval English legal tradition, has given America a strong sense of constitutionalism. The positivist idea that government is a "phenomenon of force" never really found general acceptance in America. Government in America is based on the concept of authority, not force alone, and it is limited by law and morality (p. 32).

Murray, it should be noted, does not draw a strong distinction between preliberal natural-law theories and liberal natural rights theory as do Leo Strauss and John Hallowell. Strauss, for example, has argued that emphasizing rights as the content of natural law can lead to irresponsibility in the absence of corresponding duties — duties that had been emphasized by preliberal natural law.[27] Murray's principle of the virtuous people, however, makes clear that his (and the

---

27. Strauss, *Natural Right and History* (Chicago: University of Chicago Press, 1953), pp. 226-27.

traditional American) reading of natural rights does not authorize popular license.

3. Murray's third tenet is the principle of consent in the making of laws. He points out that this idea of consent goes back to the medieval English idea of kingship and was not invented by such later liberals as Locke or Jefferson. For instance, the late medieval jurist Sir John Fortescue distinguished between absolute and constitutional monarchs on the basis of whether the king allowed his people to consent to the laws he proposed (p. 33).

America has a strong tradition of government by consent, as is evident in its principled dedication to representation, free elections, and frequent changes of administrations. The American consensus is that the people can govern themselves and that they have a sense of justice. The rights of free speech and press, for example, have a social purpose — to direct citizens, through argument and open political discussion, to justice. They are not the product of abstract individualist thought (pp. 33-34).

In America, Murray notes, "the state is distinct from society and limited in its offices toward society." Government is not the judge of truth in society; to the contrary, it submits itself to the truth of society (p. 35). Some conservatives read a relativist implication into this statement and fear that Murray is giving aid to contemporary advocates of government neutrality on moral questions. This is not the case; he argues that society discovers truth and then, by means of government, enacts its judgments into policy. The principle of consent and the state-society distinction do not produce a state-sanctioned morality; they are grounded in the nature of politics and are essential attributes of moral self-governance.

4. Murray asserted that the American people have not "pursued this ideal [of liberty] so madly as to rush over the edge of the abyss, into sheer libertarianism" (p. 36). An integral part of the American public philosophy is that Americans must be a virtuous people exercising moral self-restraint. "Only a virtuous people can be free." Free government is possible only for those who recognize the imperatives of the universal moral law and understand the ethical nature of political freedom. "In any phase civil society demands order. In its highest phase of freedom it demands that order should not be imposed from the top down, as it were, but should spontaneously flower outward from the free obedience to the restraints and imperatives that stem from inwardly possessed moral principle. . . . Men who would be politi-

cally free must discipline themselves" (pp. 36-37). America's founders did not seek to protect America's freedoms by mechanical checks and balances alone. They relied on the civic-mindedness and self-restraint of the country's citizens. Without republican virtue, disorder would arise, and people would use their elected institutions to promote injustice.[28]

It is this tenet of the American consensus that seems most in doubt today. In an age of abortion, AIDS, crack, insider trading, scandalous televangelists, and constant political corruption, it seems rather fanciful to call ourselves a virtuous people. Murray was aware that a deterioration in public moral standards was possible and, perhaps, already underway (pp. 39-43). And yet, if anything, these developments seem to prove Murray's point: true freedom is ordered freedom, and without order, a free society will experience social problems that may ultimately undermine its freedom.

5. Murray's fifth tenet is a defense of human and historical rights. He says that the American Bill of Rights was a "tributary to the tradition of natural law, to the idea that man has certain original responsibilities precisely as man, antecedent to his status as citizen" (p. 37). The Declaration of Independence states that God is the author of these rights. Our constitutional Bill of Rights is not a "top of the brain concoction" sanctioning radical individualism and license; it is deeply rooted in natural law, history, and tradition.

The historical components of our scheme of rights derive from the long history of English law. Even in medieval thought, the notion of *homo liber et legalis,* "the man whose freedom rests on law," was recognized. The Bill of Rights embodied many of the historical rights of Englishmen (p. 38).

Let us remember, however, that Murray did not claim that history is the only source of rights, as historicists, positivists, neo-Kantians, and Hegelians would. Murray used the historical argument to show that rights were not a rationalist invention. He would certainly grant that any right that our human nature requires would be a natural right even if it did not have an historical basis in a given society.[29]

28. See Cuervo, "Public Philosophy in a Democracy," pp. 209-26; and Kristol, *On the Democratic Idea in America,* pp. 4, 13.

29. I have not gone into Murray's extensive treatment of American church-state relations here because it is a rather substantial topic in its own right. But some aspects of Murray's analysis of this subject could probably be considered as additional tenets of his public philosophy.

The Origins, Growth, and Authority
of the Public Philosophy

Murray suggested that at this point we should ask where the public philosophy comes from and why it is binding upon our society. He begins his analysis of this question by noting that "the public consensus of the West, and of the United States as an historic participant in the Western style of civilization, would remain the public consensus, even if it were held, as perhaps it is held, only by a minority within the West. The validity of the consensus is radically independent of its possible status as majority or minority opinion" (p. 98).

This statement answers the first question Murray raises about the public philosophy. "Do we hold these truths because they are true, or are these truths true because we hold them?" Murray clearly favors the former alternative. "The second question follows. If the warrant for the validity of the propositions of the consensus is not the sheer fact of their general acceptance, what is this warrant?" (p. 98). To answer this question, Murray first investigates the origins of the public philosophy and then examines what he considers to be the only real basis for its authority — the doctrine of natural law.

Murray looks for the origins of the public philosophy by summarizing a portion of a series of lectures given by the economist Adolf A. Berle gathered under the title *Power without Property* (1959). Murray explains that Berle draws on Lippmann's *Public Philosophy* for an explanation of why American corporate capitalism seems to refrain from "excesses which often make concentrated power odious" and why business is often willing to accept government regulation (p. 101).

We should remember that Murray and Berle were writing during the 1950s, at a time when industry and corporations were considered a "power system" managed by a few men, a large-scale machine that had to be supervised in the public interest. This description seems partially outdated in our current era of entrepreneurialism, deregulation, and new technologies. But the general idea — that business must serve a general interest rather than simply a narrow, selfish interest — still applies. Berle's general thesis is that potential (and actual) excesses by big business are checked by a set of widely accepted "value judgments" resembling the public consensus theory that had recently been explained by Walter Lippmann.

Murray summarizes Berle's arguments about the place of the public philosophy in the business-government relationship. Berle seems to regard the public philosophy as a *given* in any healthy society, though he grants that it often exists at a general level and is seldom spelled out in any detail. The loose nature of the public philosophy allows it to have a "growing end" that gives it the capacity to analyze and deal with new, unanticipated issues of economic morality.

Let us now review Murray's summary of Berle.

1. The public consensus is "a set of ideas, widely held by the community" which holds that certain uses of power are wrong and contrary to the "interest and value system of the community." This body of doctrine contains standards of judgment to be applied to individual cases or situations (p. 101).

2. The consensus originates as a "product of thought and experience," not as a "spontaneous fact in the minds of many individuals." It is a product not of rational calculation but of the effort of many generations of society to deal with practical moral problems (pp. 101-2).

3. The consensus exists as a "hard core fact," but it is not explicitly spelled out and is almost completely unorganized. "The principles of the public consensus, some of which are well enough defined as to be inchoate law, have never been stated. Yet men in each industry are fairly well aware of them." This fluid nature of the public philosophy makes possible its "growing end" (p. 102).

4. The public consensus is not a finished but a growing and developing body of doctrine. It is "subject to constant examination, criticism, and evolution" (p. 102). There is a point of contact between the consensus and the "ongoing economic life of society," replete with new issues and new challenges.

5. The public philosophy is not identical to public opinion, although it is related to it. In a well-ordered society, public philosophy forms the basis of public opinion. The "specific conclusions" that a large portion of the community reaches "in some particular situation" derive from "some unstated but very real premises" — which is to say, the public philosophy (pp. 102-3).

6. Which people are the "depositaries of the consensus and the agents of its development and application?" At one level, anyone who works on the "margin" between economic theory and practice will discover the moral implications of new questions. In a more fundamental sense, "the conclusions of careful university professors, the reasoned opinions of specialists, the statements of responsible journalists, and at times the solid pronouncements of respected politicians" are sufficiently "principled, free, disinterested, and informed" to make this

group the "real tribunal" and developers of the public consensus (p. 103).

7. The public consensus serves as the " 'final arbiter' of the legitimacy of economic power and of the rightfulness of its uses." It validates sanctions imposed by the public on uses of economic power deemed to be wrongful (pp. 103-4). "This is the supreme function of the consensus — to determine the nature of the economy, to specify its style, and thus to insure that the style of the economy accords with the whole larger style of life that the American people has adopted as its own — the 'democratic style' that identifies the American people as a people and characterizes its action" (p. 104).

8. Finally the consensus furnishes the basis for criticizing existing law and for demanding changes in it. Like any true political theory, the public philosophy provides a paradigm or standard for judging political (or in this case, politico-economic) practice (p. 104).

In commenting on Berle's arguments, Murray points out that the consensus is doctrine, not just a set of converging public opinions or a least common denominator. The consensus finds its validity not in who accepts it but in its own inherent justice. It commands public agreement on the merits of the arguments that can be made for it (p. 105). But while it is a doctrine, the public philosophy is not an ideology that imposes itself upon reality "in violation of reality's own dynamisms and structures" in the interest of some utopian scheme. The inexplicit, growing nature of the public philosophy leaves what Berle calls the "non-dogmatic quality of American political economic action" intact (p. 106).

According to Murray, "The consensus is not simply 'the facts.' It is a set of principles or standards in terms of which to pass judgment on the facts" (p. 107). We have seen that the public philosophy originates as a product of thought and experience, that it reflects on the morality of new economic situations, and that it allows us to raise criticisms and demand changes in existing arrangements. However, we have still not answered the question of the "non-contingent element" that makes the public philosophy valid and obligatory upon society.

Murray does point out that decisions about the basic direction of society are not spontaneous. "The economy itself does not decide that it shall be a 'democratic' economy" (p. 108). The direction that the economy shall take is a matter of moral decision. Thus, the public consensus is a moral conception, and its validity and intelligibility rest on a moral theory. Murray at this point offers the proposition that only the theory of natural law "is able to give an account of the public moral experience that is the public consensus" (p. 109).

Murray argues that natural law is not an exclusively Catholic doctrine: its basic process and teachings are available to virtually all human beings (p. 109). He states this in two sets of premises, the first of which deals with human intelligence:

1. "Man is intelligent."
2. "Reality is intelligible."
3. "Reality, as grasped by intelligence, imposes on the will the ob-ligation that it be obeyed in its demands for action or abstention" (p. 109).

Murray's second set of premises is based on the belief that moral reality is especially permeable to human intelligence, even though intelligence admittedly has its limits:

1. "Intelligence can grasp the ethical a priori . . . that what is good is to be done and what is evil avoided" (pp. 109-10).
2. "After some elementary experience of the basic situations of human life, and upon some simple reflection on the meaning of terms, intelligence can grasp the meaning of 'good' and 'evil' in these situations" (p. 110).
3. "Intelligence, with the aid of simple reasoning, can know, and know to be obligatory, a set of [primary] natural-law principles that are derivative" (p. 110). These primary principles of natural law are accessible to the reason of virtually all human beings. Agreeing with Aquinas, Murray adds the qualification that in a few particular instances, such as mental defect, excessive passion, or lack of critical detachment, moral reason may fail in these primary areas, but these are exceptional cases (p. 110).
4. The last area open to human reason is reserved for the *wise*. This is the ability to understand complex moral situations. This field of natural law is restricted due to the need for more expert knowledge, greater disinterestedness, and prior understanding of these more complicated relationships and institutions. People who can grasp (and teach) about these matters are those whom George Washington called the "wise and honest." In time, this group came to include both philosophers and jurists (pp. 110-11).

It is in this secondary area that the "wise and honest" confront new problems and build up the growing end of the public philosophy.[30]

Murray holds a twofold theory of human nature and history, and we must understand this theory if we are to avoid confusing his arguments with those made by historical determinists or moral relativists. We must remember that Murray considered some aspects of human nature to be permanent, while at the same time granting that history presents us with new moral and social situations that "change" human nature's secondary details in the sense of growth and self-improvement.

First, Murray argues that "the fundamental structure of man's nature is, of course, permanent and unchanging; correlatively constant are the elementary human experiences." This is a stumbling block for ethical relativists, despite the fact that in their personal lives they generally observe the natural laws related to these basic human experiences (e.g., fulfilling contracts, loving their wives and children, fleeing ignorance). These structures of human nature are so basic that even relativists behave as though they believe in natural law in these areas (p. 112).

But second, Murray writes that

history, as any history book shows, does change what I have called the human reality. It evokes situations that never happened before. It calls into being relationships that had not existed. It involves human life in an increasing multitude of institutions of all kinds, which proliferate in response to new human needs and desires, as well as in consequence of the creative possibilities that are inexhaustibly resident in human freedom. (Pp. 112-13)

Over the course of history, the human race has spread across the globe and encountered a considerable variety of circumstances. Murray agrees with Aquinas, who states that "the nature of man is susceptible of change." "As all this happens, continually new problems are being put to the wise; at the same time, the same old problems are being put to every man, wise or not" (p. 113).

30. Public philosophy became a subject for secondary analysis by scholars beginning in the late 1970s. Examples would include Richard J. Bishirjian's *A Public Philosophy Reader* (1978) and my own *Public Philosophy in a Democracy* (1980).

Murray and Aquinas are not, in these remarks, embracing Montesquieu's cultural relativism or the idea that human nature is malleable in its essentials. For Murray and St. Thomas, there are two aspects of human nature: the formal, which may not change, and the material, which may vary in some respects. "In this sense the same things are not always and everywhere good and just. They have to be determined by the law" in the sense of custom or the declaration of the wise (p. 114). Of course, human nature is also open to individual moral self-improvement through compliance with the dictates of natural law or religion.[31]

In view of these arguments, Murray concludes that he has demonstrated that natural law, in its Thomistic version, is the "noncontingent element" that makes the public philosophy legitimate and binding. He states this conclusion as follows:

1. The principles of the consensus are secondary or "remote" principles of natural law. They are responses to historical (new) situations encountered in economic, social, or political life (pp. 117-18). For instance, the relationship between stockholders and corporate management was once such a new moral question. Even though these principles are not always legal enactments per se, they do constitute a sort of law.

2. The elaboration of the public philosophy "is the task of the wise and honest." Their expertise and detachment is needed in these matters, since these skills are "beyond the competence of the generality." The wise develop the consensus and "give 'instruction' to the generality" on remote principles of natural law (p. 118).

3. The inherent authority of the consensus, which makes its principles matters of *necessary observance*, lies in the fact that it is found, after careful inquiry by the wise, to be in accord with *reason*, which is the distinguishing characteristic of the human soul. This makes the consensus a matter of necessary observance, and the principles of the consensus often take on the character of public law (pp. 119-20).

Murray adds that even powerful persons are inclined to act according to reason and to desire that their actions be recognized as legitimate. Even when their moral inclination fails, "these men of power are at least 'natural' enough to submit to the just interventions of the public power in support of the public consensus" (pp. 120-21).

31. Hallowell, *The Moral Foundation of Democracy,* pp. 100-101.

How Open Can Society Be?

There is one last issue raised by Murray in his chapter on the origins and authority of the public consensus, a theme that is actually found throughout *We Hold These Truths* — namely, the question of how open society can be.

While still focused on the economic context of the origins and authority of the public consensus, Murray points out that both Aristotle and Aquinas would view modern commercial society with "foreboding," since commerce introduces both materialism and "alien customs and mores" into a society. In a larger context, Murray observes that

> the "open society" today faces the question, how open can it afford to be, and still remain a society; how many barbarians can it tolerate, and still remain civil; how many "idiots" can it include (in the classical Greek sense of the "private person" who does not share in the public thought of the City), and still have a public life; how many idioms, alien to one another, can it admit, and still allow the possibility of civil conversation? (P. 117)

Murray's question is especially relevant for contemporary American society. Some persons demand the opening of our society to an extent that was virtually unthinkable in the past. Three versions of this demand are particularly noteworthy:

1. Government must be "neutral" to all questions of morality, especially personal morality.
2. The essence of freedom is the ability to "choose," even when the object of choice, such as abortion or deviant sexual behavior, is condemned by traditional morality, public philosophy, or even public opinion.
3. Neither individuals nor groups nor governments may "impose their values" on people who wish to make and act on such choices.

As the above examples indicate, the moral code of the West is now up for grabs in the political arena. In the past few centuries, modern philosophers have questioned the basis of the moral code, but they have had a clear understanding of what the code comprised, and they have not challenged the code itself. For instance, John Locke, in his *Essay concerning Human Understanding*, argues (virtually to the point of relativism) that people are not created with innate practical (moral) principles in their minds. But he then proceeds to argue that the tenets of morality — including prohibitions against murder, theft, and the procurement of abortion — are not in question.[32]

Today, with the demand for choice and governmental neutrality, no person's reading of morality or public philosophy seems authoritative. Murray refers to this tendency as solipsism and points to its disastrous consequences: "the view that my insight is mine alone and cannot be shared by another, much less by a community . . . is, of course, the destruction of the classical and Christian concept of reason" (p. 129). Early in *We Hold These Truths,* Murray speaks of the "barbarian," the perennial task of whom is to "undermine rational standards of judgment, to corrupt the inherited intuitive wisdom by which the people have always lived, and to do this not by spreading new beliefs but by creating a climate of doubt and bewilderment in which clarity about the larger aims of life is dimmed and the self-confidence of the people is destroyed" (p. 12). Ultimately, this leads to a solipsist vocabulary and the breakdown of society's dialogue, and "civility dies with the death of the dialogue" (p. 14).

If the public philosophy is to be revived in this age of solipsism, we must turn to the insights of John Courtney Murray, Walter Lippmann, John Hallowell, and their successors. We must refute the neutralist point of view, which says that we are constitutionally committed to becoming a nation of idiots, as Murray used that term. We must reassert ourselves as a virtuous people carrying on a civil conversation.

32. Locke, *An Essay concerning Human Understanding* (Oxford: Clarendon Press, 1975), 1.3. Cf. Alasdair MacIntyre, *After Virtue: A Study in Moral Theory,* 2d ed. (Notre Dame, Ind.: Notre Dame University Press, 1984), pp. 12-15, 39-45.

We Held These Truths:
The Transformation of American Pluralism
and the Future of American Democracy

Kenneth L. Grasso

If we do not deny our malaises or seek to drown them, the experience of them can be turned to rational account.

JOHN COURTNEY MURRAY, S.J.

I N RECENT YEARS, a host of commentators occupying disparate positions on our political spectrum have concluded that all is not well with the American body politic. The signs that something is seriously amiss are numerous. In the political arena, for example, we have experienced a decline in public-spiritedness and a loss of any overarching sense of community or conception of a common good to which private interests must be subordinated. Ironically, as our public life has increasingly come to approximate the model of politics put forward by the interest-group school of democratic theory, the product has not been the "equilibrium" anticipated by that school but rather something approaching political paralysis and a dramatic decline of public confidence in our institutions. Simultaneously, the American polity has become increasingly polarized. Today's ongoing debate regarding abortion provides a good indication of the fundamental nature of the division besetting the American body politic, its explosive character, and its resistance to resolution through compromise. There is, furthermore, every reason to expect this polarization to continue and intensify. Our politics seems to have become, in Alasdair MacIntyre's apt phrase, "civil war carried on by other means."[1]

During recent decades a dramatic change has taken place in the character of American pluralism. In earlier periods of our history, as Francis Canavan, S.J., has observed, America was "a pluralist society composed of a multitude of religious branches that sprang from a common stem." Thus, "lush as the variety of creeds in America" may have been, "by far the greater part of them held the Bible in common and in most respects taught substantially the same moral code."[2] Today, however, our pluralism has been transformed from a religious to a moral pluralism. As a people we no longer agree about what a human being is, about what is good and bad for human beings, or about the basic moral principles and structure of social relations that should govern human life. The obvious question that suggests itself is whether there might be a connection between the emergence of this new form of pluralism and the malaise that afflicts us today. Might this new pluralism be the cause of many of the difficulties besetting our public life?

The notion that "pluralism" can be other than a salutary thing is a difficult one to communicate in America today. Traditionally we have extolled America's pluralism as a source of strength, as one of the secrets of our success: *e pluribus unum*. Indeed, we have become accustomed to think of pluralism as an unqualified good. Yet the fact remains that pluralism can mean many things, and can indeed be problematic. There is, after all, a limit to how pluralistic a society can be while still remaining a society at all.

Several decades ago, John Courtney Murray, S.J., pointed out that the changing character of our pluralism posed a whole series of urgent questions, questions with profound implications for the future of the American experiment in self-government: "How much pluralism," for example, "and what kinds of pluralism can a pluralist society stand? And conversely, how much unity and what kind of unity does a pluralist society need in order to be a society at all, effectively organized for action in history?"[3] Likewise,

---

1. MacIntyre, *After Virtue* (Notre Dame, Ind.: University of Notre Dame Press, 1981), p. 236. For a good overview of the broader cultural crisis of which this political crisis is a part, see William A. Donahue, *The New Freedom* (New Brunswick, N.J.: Transaction, 1990).

2. Canavan, "The Pluralist Game," *Law and Contemporary Problems* 44 (Spring 1981): 24-25.

3. Murray, *We Hold These Truths: Catholic Reflections on the American Proposition*

how open can . . . [our "open society"] afford to be, and still remain
a society; how many barbarians can it tolerate, and still remain civil;
how many "idiots" can it include (in the classical Greek sense of the
"private person" who does not share in the public thought of the
City), and still have a public life; how many idioms, alien to one
another, can it admit, and still allow the possibility of civil conversation? (P. 120)[4]

In this essay I will use Murray's concept of the "public philosophy"
to explore the transformation of American pluralism and its implications
for the future of American democracy. Indeed, I will suggest that the
change that has taken place in the character of American pluralism is
responsible, in large part, for the difficulties that beset our public life
today. Before turning our attention to these matters, however, we would
do well to turn our attention to the work that offers what is perhaps the
most important treatment of American pluralism in order better to
understand the original structure of American pluralism.

Pluralism and the American Experiment in Self-Government

The work in question is, of course, *The Federalist*, the classic exposition
of the Constitution and its political theory written by Hamilton, Madison, and Jay under the pseudonym Publius. "There is," Publius argues,
considerable "diversity in the state of property, in the genius, manners,
and habits of the people of different parts of the union." And, he
continues, "there are causes as well physical as moral, which may in a
greater or less degree permanently nourish different propensities and
inclinations" (#60).

(New York: Image Books, 1964), p. 132. Subsequent references to this volume will
be made parenthically in the text.
    4. Raising questions such as these is a dangerous business in our intellectual
climate. To raise them, as Murray points out, is to run the real risk of being
anathematized in many circles as a proponent of the imposition of a public orthodoxy and thus as an enemy of democracy, for although "we will tolerate all kinds
of ideas, however pernicious, . . . we will not tolerate the idea of an orthodoxy"
(p. 91). This, in turn, raises the question of whether some influential conceptions
of pluralism do not themselves mask a hidden orthodoxy. "Pluralism," writes
Richard John Neuhaus, "is a jealous god. When pluralism is established as dogma,
there is no room for other dogmas" (*The Naked Public Square* [Grand Rapids:
William B. Eerdmans, 1984], p. 148). Cf. Canavan, "The Pluralist Game."

This pluralism, a fact of life in a large heterogeneous country such as the United States, was an essential element in Publius's solution to the central theoretical problem addressed by *The Federalist* — namely, the problem of self-government with justice. Historically, however, popular governments have not fared well. The source of the difficulties that have beset them, Publius contends, is factionalism. A faction may be defined as "a number of citizens, whether amounting to a majority or minority of the whole, who are united and actuated by some common impulse of passion, or of interest, adverse to the rights of other citizens or to the permanent and aggregate interests of the community" (#10).

How can the effects of factionalism be controlled? As a result of the diversity inherent in our extended republic, our "society itself will be broken into . . . many parts, interests and classes of citizens." Since in a pluralistic society no single interest will command a majority, the making of laws will require the formation of a coalition consisting of a variety of groups, and this will require considerable compromise. This need to construct a coalition consisting of a number of diverse groups will "render an unjust combination of a majority of the whole, very improbable, if not impractical" (#51). "In the extended republic of the United States, and among the great variety of interests, parties and sects which it embraces," concludes Publius, "a coalition of a majority of the whole society could seldom take place on any other principles than those of justice and the general good" (#51).

There is more to Publius's solution to the problem of self-government with justice than pluralism, however. Statesmanship and deliberation, for example, both play a prominent role in Publius's "republican remedy," as does the idea of a virtuous people.[5] Publius's solution presupposes a citizenry capable of producing a wise and public-spirited political elite capable of "refining and enlarging public views" and choosing to be represented by leaders of this character rather than demagogues who pander to popular passions and parochial interests. It presupposes, in the final analysis, a citizenry both capable of recognizing and committed to rejecting the "wicked and improper" projects of factions. "As there exists," writes Publius, "a certain degree of de-

---

5. For a discussion of the dimensions of Publius's solution to the problem of self-government with justice that transcend a reliance on pluralism alone, see Kenneth L. Grasso, "Pluralism, the Public Good and the Problem of Self-Government in *The Federalist,*" *Interpretation* 15 (May-June 1987): 324-45.

pravity in mankind which requires a certain degree of circumspection and distrust: So there are other qualities in human nature, which justify a certain portion of esteem and confidence. Republican government presupposes the existence of these qualities in a higher degree than any other form." Do the American people possess the "qualities" presupposed by republican government? "I must own," answers Publius,

> that I could not give a negative answer to this question, without first obliterating every impression that I have received with regard to the present genius of the people of America, the spirit, which actuates the state legislatures, and the principles which are incorporated with the political character of every class of citizens. I am unable to conceive that the people of America in their present temper, or under any circumstances which can speedily happen, will choose . . . men who would be disposed to . . . pursue a scheme of tyranny or treachery. (#55)

Given his emphasis on America's pluralism, how can Publius so confidently generalize about the American people's moral character? Indeed, in light of the far-ranging diversity to which he calls attention, in what sense can the inhabitants of America be said to be a "people" at all, much less a virtuous people? If Publius's discussion emphasizes America's pluralism, it simultaneously calls attention to the larger context within which this pluralism exists. The political order established by the Constitution will not be inhabited by a mere aggregation of groups and individuals bound together only by geographical proximity and a common set of legal and political forms. Rather, it will be inhabited by a "people," by "a band of brethren united to each other by the strongest ties." "Providence," he writes, "has been pleased to give this one connected country, to one united people, a people descended from the same ancestors, speaking the same language, professing the same religion, attached to the same principles of government, [and] very similar in their manners and customs" (#2). The American people can be said to be a people because they are united by a common culture, a common way of life, a community of beliefs and values. Publius recognizes that the pluralism of which he speaks exists within the horizon of a "people" constituting a "community."

The existence of this cultural capital is auspicious, because the political unity to be established by the Constitution will build upon this pre-existing cultural unity and the substantive moral consensus it reflects. At the same time, the American people's status as a virtuous people — and consequently their ability to govern themselves with justice — stems from the profound influence that this culture and the ethic it embodies has exercised on their characters. Thus, it is the formative influence of this culture, combined with the republic's diversity and certain "inventions of prudence" (e.g., the separation of powers), that Publius believes will enable America to reconcile democratic government with the demands of justice, freedom, order, and the common good.

It is not altogether surprising, however, that some commentators have overlooked this aspect of Publius's thought. Despite its importance, the idea of the virtuous people is mentioned only briefly in *The Federalist,* and its implications are never really explored. Yet the question of the nature and function of this capital is central to any understanding of the American polity and the difficulties besetting it today. It is here that Murray can be of assistance to us.

Murray and the American Public Philosophy

At the time of the founding of America, Murray observes, there existed a "public philosophy," a "public consensus," which embodied "a whole body of concepts, principles and precepts bearing upon the political life of man; together with a certain general style of thinking about all the problems of politics and law." This public philosophy "furnished the premise of our newly fashioned institutions; and it permeated them as their inner principle of life." From this philosophy

> we drew the moral concept of freedom under law, both divine and human, and the concept of justice, and the concept of human equality. From it too, we derived the political ideas of representation and consent. This philosophy fashioned for us the conception of the legal order of society as subject to a higher law whence it derives its binding force upon the conscience. This philosophy, therefore, taught us that human law is neither simple fact nor sheer force, but a special form of moral direction brought to bear, coercively, upon the action of society in the interests of freedom and order. In this philosophy the state is part of the moral universe, subject — as the individual man is — to the objective canons of justice. Therefore the state is not omnipotent; it is limited in its power and action by rights that are

inherent in the human person, and it is dedicated by its very nature to the service of the human person and to the furtherance of his innate destinies, both temporal and eternal.[6]

"Only partially," Murray continues, "was this public philosophy committed to paper, in the form of law." The public philosophy was not a mere collection of political and legal principles; it embodied a whole tradition of moral thought, of which the American people were "the living repository" (p. 279). This is not to suggest that they could fully articulate this philosophy if called upon to do so, or defend it in the manner of professional philosophers. Rather, they held it "almost intuitively, in the form of a simple faith rather than an articulate philosophy." It was an "inheritance," a "patrimony" (p. 91). This public philosophy, this intuitive "wisdom," constituted the cultural capital the existence of which Publius took for granted, and upon which his solution to the problem of self-government with justice trades.

What is the source of this patrimony, of this public philosophy? Its source is found in what Murray terms the tradition of reason or tradition of civility — that is to say, in "the ancient tradition whose central assertion was the existence of a rational order of truth and justice, which man does not create, since it is the reflection of the Eternal Reason of God, but which man can discover, since he is himself made in the image of God."[7] While readily admitting that the formal "expression" of the principles underlying the American Republic experiment in self-government (e.g., the Declaration of Independence) may indeed have been "colored to some extent by eighteenth century ideology,"[8] Murray insisted that it was rooted in a more ancient and far richer tradition. Whether consciously or not, in the founding era, Americans "did their thinking within the tradition of freedom that was their heritage from England" (p. 49), a heritage with roots deep in the Middle Ages and that had found expression in the common law.

At the heart of this heritage were, on the one hand, the Christian concepts of dyarchy, limited government, and the sacredness of the human person; and, on the other hand, the tradition of natural law,

6. Murray, "Freedom, Responsibility and the Law," *Catholic Lawyer* 2 (July 1956): 215-16.

7. Murray, "Freedom, Responsibility and the Law," p. 215.

8. Murray, "Leo XIII: Separation of Church and State," *Theological Studies* 14 (June 1953): 160.

the origins of which "go back to Heraclitus and to the greatest of Greek philosophers and Roman jurists" and which received its "developed expression" in the Middle Ages through the work of "St. Thomas Aquinas and the later scholastics" (p. 285).[9]

From the moral framework supplied by the tradition of civility, a whole constellation of political principles emerged and found expression in the institutions and structures of American government, such as constitutionalism, limited government, and the like. This public philosophy not only informed America's political structures but also provided the moral framework within which these institutions were meant to operate. The political equipment created by the Constitution was designed to be operated by a people who had internalized the tradition of civility. The "great act of faith in the capacity of the people to govern themselves" underlying the American Experiment was rooted "in the belief . . . that the people are the living repository of a moral tradition . . . that enables them to know what is reasonable in the action of the state" (p. 279).

The decisive effect of the tradition of civility on the character of the American experiment can be seen clearly in the moral dimensions of the American idea of a free society. Rooted in a dualism derived from the Christian tradition, the American constitutional system, at the same time that it denies the government the power to regulate the community's religious life, acknowledges "the sovereignty of God as . . . the first principle of its political organization." The American system

> neither supposes nor effects an exile of God from society. . . . The state itself, in its distinction from society, rests on no pretence that even political life can be organized "without any regard for God or for the order established by Him." On the contrary, the constitution of the U.S. has to be read in light of the Declaration of Independence, in which there is an explicit recognition of God and of an order established by Him — the order of human rights, which is part of

9. For Murray's analysis of the political implications of Christianity, see *We Hold These Truths*, pp. 193-210, and "On the Structure of the Church-State Problem," in *The Catholic Church in World Affairs*, ed. Waldemar Gurian and M. A. Fitzsimmons (Notre Dame, Ind.: University of Notre Dame Press, 1954), pp. 11-32. The tradition of natural-law theory reflected in Aquinas's thought is not, Murray stresses, to be confused with the individualistic and rationalistic law-of-nature theories spawned by the Enlightenment. See *We Hold These Truths*, pp. 48-50, 280-317.

the universal moral order to whose imperatives the political order must be obedient.[10]

Thus, America's commitment to individual freedom was grounded not in religious indifferentism or skepticism or moral subjectivism but in the objective moral order. The American idea of freedom "had an inner moral structure. Freedom was not conceived in terms of the sheer subjective autonomy of the will. Man's freedom, like man himself, stood within the moral universe. It meant the objective right to act; it meant what Acton defined as 'the right to do what one ought,' a right, therefore, that is rooted in reason and sanctioned by inviolable divine law."[11]

This moral framework decisively separated the American experiment's understanding of freedom from understandings rooted in a thoroughgoing subjectivism:

America has passionately pursued the ideal of freedom, expressed in a whole system of political and civil rights, to new lengths; but it has not pursued this ideal so madly as to rush over the edge of the abyss, into sheer libertarianism, into the chaos created by the nineteenth-century theory of the "outlaw conscience," *conscientia exlex,* the conscience that knows no law higher than its own subjective imperatives. Part of the inner architecture of the American ideal of freedom has been the profound conviction that only a virtuous people can be free. It is . . . an American belief that free government . . . is possible . . . only when the people as a whole are inwardly governed by the recognized imperatives of the universal moral law. (P. 47)

Just as the tradition of civility gave the American idea of freedom a moral dimension lacking in theories that ground freedom in sheer subjectivism, so it also gave it a social dimension that the latter lacked: "freedom was also conceived in terms of social relations. It was a responsibility no less than a right — a right to claim what is due to oneself, and a responsibility to respect what is due to others. This responsibility is accepted when freedom in society is claimed."[12]

10. Murray, "Leo XIII: Separation of Church and State," pp. 159-60.
11. Murray, "Freedom, Responsibility and the Law," p. 216.
12. Murray, "Freedom, Responsibility and the Law," p. 216.

The State of the Union and the Status of the Consensus

Does the consensus, the public philosophy, that launched the American experiment still endure? As the 1950s progressed, Murray reluctantly concluded that this question must be answered in the negative. The question of the endurance of the American consensus can, he observes, be asked at "two levels." The first is the level of "the people at large," who would be expected to possess the public philosophy "almost intuitively, in the form of a simple faith rather than an articulate philosophy." The second "is the level of the 'clerks,' the intellectuals," who would be expected "to be in conscious possession of the public philosophy as a philosophy; for them it would be a personal acquisition and not simply a patrimony." "On both these levels," Murray concludes, "I am inclined to think the Noes have it." "By one cause or another," the American consensus "has been eroded" (pp. 91-92) — in fact, it "has been eroded, eclipsed, discarded."[13] "Today," he reluctantly concluded,

> no such moral tradition lives among the American people. . . . Those who seek the ironies of history should find one here, in the fact that the ethic which launched Western constitutionalism and endured long enough as a popular heritage to give essential form to the American system of government has now ceased to sustain the structure and direct the action of this constitutional commonwealth. (P. 279)

"Another idiom" foreign to the consensus that launched the American experiment "now prevails" (p. 52).

The eclipse of the public philosophy, Murray was convinced, did not bode well for America's future. "Granted," he wrote,

> that the unity of the commonwealth can be achieved in the absence of a consensus with regard to the theological truths that govern the total life and destiny of man, it does not follow that this necessary civic unity can endure in the absence of a consensus more narrow in its scope, operative on the level of political life, with regard to the rational truths and moral precepts that govern the structure of the

13. Murray, "Catholics in America — A Creative Minority — Yes or No?" *Catholic Mind* 53 (October 1955): 593.

constitutional state, specify the substance of the common weal, and determine the ends of public policy. (P. 80)

"No society in history," he concluded, "has ever achieved and maintained an identity and a vigor in action unless it has had some substance, unless it has been sustained and directed by some body of substantive beliefs" (p. 90). Thus, "the consensual will to an organization of political authority" must be informed by, and cannot be divorced from, "the will to a common life in a body politic" — which is to say, "the will to form a state, an order of peace and justice, whose contents are not purely formal or procedural but substantive and material."[14]

Indeed, inasmuch as the "material moral homogeneity" supplied by the public philosophy constituted "the dynamic of our free society,"[15] the erosion of the public philosophy and the vacuum it created at the heart of our public life endanger the very viability of the American experiment in self-government. Murray quoted Walter Lippmann's observation that "if we go back to the beginning of modern democratic movements in the 18th century, we can distinguish two diverging lines of development. The one is a way of progress in liberal constitutional democracy. The other is a morbid course of development into totalitarian conditions." America, Murray continues, "started out on a good line, inspired by the public philosophy. We seem to have shifted to the bad line, in consequence of the decay of the public philosophy."[16] The United States, he lamented, has become "a mass democracy rapidly slipping its moorings in reason."[17]

The severity of the crisis engendered by the loss of the public philosophy was not to be underestimated. It jeopardized not only the vitality of our democracy but its very survival. "The great experiment of the American constitutional commonwealth," Murray warned, "is not intelligible and cannot be made to work except by men who possess the public philosophy within whose context it was conceived."[18]

14. Murray, "Free Speech in Its Relation to Self-Government," *Georgetown Law Journal*, vol. 37, p. 658.
15. Murray, "Free Speech in Its Relation to Self-Government," p. 661.
16. Murray, "Catholics in America," p. 594.
17. Murray, "The Bad Arguments Intelligent People Make," *America*, 3 November 1956, p. 123.
18. Murray, "Catholics in America," pp. 593-94.

Consensus and Political Order

The loss of the public philosophy entailed a fundamental change in the nature of our pluralism. Specifically, it resulted in a transition from a religious to a moral pluralism, a transition from a community consisting of a plurality of churches and faiths divided by religious questions but united in their adherence to a common set of substantive moral principles to a community united only by geographical proximity and the acceptance of a common set of political and legal procedures.

In the disintegration of the public philosophy and the transformation in the character of our pluralism it entailed, we have identified the cause of the myriad difficulties besetting our public life today. "If our public affairs are going badly," as Murray has observed, "it is because we lack a public philosophy" (p. 93). Why should the transition from a religious pluralism to a moral pluralism have such disconcerting consequences? Why is a purely procedural consensus — a consensus limited to the methods to be employed in settling disputes, in contradistinction to a substantive consensus of the type we have been describing — an insufficient basis for a political order? Why, in Murray's terminology, does a political community depend for its "stability" and "progress," its "identity" and "vigor in actions," on such a substantive consensus?

An answer to these questions, Murray insists, requires an appreciation of "the three-fold function of the ensemble of truths that make up the public consensus or philosophy." To begin with, it is through the public consensus that "the people acquires its identity as a people and the society is endowed with its vital form, its entelechy, its sense of purpose as a collectivity organized for action in history." It is thus this consensus that "furnishes the premises of the people's action in history and defines the larger aims which that action seeks in internal affairs and in external relations" (p. 21). This determination of goals is necessarily "a moral act," necessarily involves substantive moral judgments. Secondly, this substantive consensus furnishes "the standards according to which judgment is to be passed on the means that the nation adopts to further its purposes. These means, in general, are what is called policy." Finally, this consensus "furnishes the basis of communication between government and the people and among the people themselves. It furnishes a common universe of discourse in which public issues can be intelligibly stated and intelligently argued" (p. 87).

The lack of a public philosophy that reflects a stable and enduring consensus regarding the community's purposes will manifest itself initially in confusion, drift, and paralysis in the policy arena. To illustrate this principle Murray cited the difficulties that beset American foreign policy in the post–World War II period. These difficulties, he maintains, were the result of the fact that although a negative consensus did exist (i.e., anticommunism), we lacked a positive consensus specifying the ultimate objectives of our foreign policy. Confronted with "the massive fact of world disorder," America faced a series of questions: "What kind of order in the world do you want? What are its premises and principles? What is to be the form of its institutions — political, legal, economic? How do you propose to help organize this disorganized world? Or do you propose not to help?" (p. 94). The lack of "any convinced or convincing answers to these questions and others of such tenor," the lack of a substantive agreement regarding our "political and moral ends" was, Murray insisted, the cause of the "confusions" and "ineffectivenesses" that plagued our foreign policy then (and that continue to plague it today).

The question of our ends or goals as a community is an inescapably moral question. What is the model of the good society the community seeks to advance via its public policies? What are its principles? What conception of human nature, of what is good and bad for human beings, of the structure of social relations proper to human life, does it reflect? Even a cursory survey of the history of political thought and practice will reveal that these questions admit a wide array of answers; and, absent a consensus regarding the proper answers, a community will be hard pressed to reach agreement regarding laws and policies. If we disagree fundamentally about the moral principles and ends that should govern our public life, arriving at policies capable of generating widespread support and successfully sustaining these policies over a long period of time will be, at a minimum, extremely difficult.

The stalemate and confusion resulting from the erosion of the public consensus are not restricted to the policy arena. At the heart of civil society, as Murray observes, is a public argument, an ongoing dialogue. He quotes the remark of Thomas Gilby, O.P. (who in turn was echoing Aquinas) that "civilization is formed by men locked together in argument." The "specifying note" of civil society — in contrast to "a mass or a herd or a huddle" — "is its rational deliberative quality." "The distinctive bond of the civil multitude," Murray writes, "is reason, or more exactly, that exercise of reason that is argument" (pp. 18-19). "Civility" — and, with it, civil society — "dies," therefore, "with the death" of this dialogue (p. 26).

The creation and maintenance of this civil conversation, however, is a demanding task. There are "laws of argument, the observance of which is imperative if discourse is to be civilized," and the civil conversation consequently presupposes "a special kind of moral virtue" that must be "laboriously cultivated by the discipline of passion, prejudice, and narrow self-interest" (p. 19). "The whole premise of the public argument," furthermore,

> if it is to be civilized and civilizing, is that the consensus is real, that among the people everything is not in doubt, but that there is a core of agreement, accord, concurrence, acquiescence. We hold certain truths; therefore we can argue about them. It seems to have been one of the corruptions of intelligence by positivism to assume that argument ends when agreement is reached. In a basic sense the reverse is true. There can be no argument except on the premise, and within a context, of agreement. *Mutatis mutandis,* this is true of scientific, philosophical, and theological argument. It is no less true of political argument. (Pp. 21-22)

Without a public consensus, the public argument will not even "carry us into disagreement" — disagreement not being "an easy thing to reach" — but rather into "confusion." Lacking the common moral understandings, the common frame of reference, and, as it were, the grammar supplied by the public philosophy, a community will "have no common universe of discourse." More specifically, different meanings will attach to the very terms to be utilized in the public argument, such as "truth, freedom, justice, prudence, order, law, authority, power, knowledge, certainty, unity, peace, virtue, morality, religion, God, and perhaps even man." The result will not be civilized argument, but "sheer confusion, in which soliloquy succeeds to argument," and public discourse will become "merely quarrelsome or querulous" (pp. 26-27). When the public consensus disintegrates, people can no longer be locked together in rational argument which is succeeded by appeals to passion, prejudice, and self-interest; public issues cease to be intelligibly stated or intelligently argued; and the body politic is thereby progressively devitalized.

The disintegration of the public consensus does more than merely

sap the community's vitality. Over time it undermines the community's
very stability and ability to cohere. In a healthy political community,
Murray observes, politics "should be simply a controversy over means
to ends already agreed on with sufficient unanimity." A society lacking
a public consensus about its purposes and ends is "a disintegrating
society" (p. 81). Murray never systematically elaborates on this point,
at least to the best of my knowledge, but it is scarcely an obscure or
idiosyncratic issue. The idea that the basis of human community is
found in *homonoia,* like-mindedness, is an old one, the roots of which
are deep in the classical and Christian traditions.[19]

An essential precondition of a viable political community is the
ability to generate unified action toward common goals. In the long
run, force and fear alone are incapable of generating such action.
To sustain a regime that lacks legitimacy by coercion and terror alone
involves a tremendous expenditure of energy and resources, an
expenditure that cannot be sustained indefinitely, and that, in any
case, does not generate a united and active pursuit of common
objectives but a mere passive acquiescence. The recent history of
Eastern Europe and the former Soviet Union provides an object
lesson in this regard.

This active cooperation and support on the part of the citizenry
characteristic of a healthy polity — what Daniel Bell calls *civitas*[20] —
manifests itself in a variety of ways. It manifests itself, to begin with,
in law-abidingness, in a willingness to obey the laws even when such
obedience runs contrary to the immediate dictates of self-interest and
when detection or punishment is unlikely. It manifests itself in a willingness to utilize freedom in a responsible manner and hence a willingness
to abstain from actions that, although legal, would be damaging to the
well-being of others or the community as a whole. It manifests itself in
a willingness to subordinate self-interest to the demands of the common

19. On the concept of *homonoia* in classical and Christian political thought,
see Gerhart Niemeyer, *Between Nothingness and Paradise* (Baton Rouge: Louisiana
State University Press, 1971), pp. 193-200. The idea that a viable society is rooted
in a "like-mindedness" has received ample support in modern social science. As
Robert N. Bellah, one of contemporary America's preeminent sociologists, observes, "it is one of the oldest of sociological generalizations that any coherent and
viable society rests on a common set of moral understandings about good and bad,
right and wrong, in the realm of individual and social action" (*The Broken Covenant*
[New York: Harper & Row, 1975], p. ix).

20. Bell, *The Cultural Contradictions of Capitalism* (New York: Basic Books,
1978), p. 245.

good — in a willingness, in other words, to make sacrifices and bear burdens for the good of others. It manifests itself in a sense of community, in a sense of civic amity, of partnership in a common enterprise — and hence in a sense of openness, trust, and goodwill (as opposed to suspicion, hostility, or fear) among the various individuals and groups that constitute the community. The presence of all of these things is vital to the health of the body politic.

This *civitas* cannot be created by governmental fiat or by a mere agreement about legal and political procedures. "No mere legal document," as Canavan has pointed out,

> can create or maintain unity . . . if the necessary social conditions for it are lacking. Cyprus, divided between Greek Christians and Moslem Turks; Lebanon, rent by multisided strife among Christians and Moslems and their subdivisions; and Northern Ireland, where the legitimacy of the state itself is a political issue, prove the point. . . . The constitution of a country can be a potent force in unifying it, but there is an antecedent unity upon which it must depend.[21]

What is the source of the "antecedent unity" that is a *sine qua non* of a viable political order? A clue is provided by Tocqueville's observation that "no society can prosper" or even "manage" without "common" beliefs. "Without ideas in common, no common action would be possible, and without common action, men might exist, but there could be no body social. So for society to exist and, even more, for society to prosper, it is essential that all the minds of the citizens should always be rallied and held together by some leading ideas."[22]

The ability of a society to engage in united action for a common end is dependent upon the presence of what Murray calls a "common thought." When the members of a community "think alike," when they are in agreement about the goods that constitute the goals of public life, then they will be able to "join together in some manner of common action to make their common thought or purpose prevail" (p. 33). At the heart of a vigorous and vital political community, therefore, will be found a consensus about the goods that constitute the goal of public life, an ensemble of substantive truths. These truths are the "entelechy,"

21. Canavan, "Unity in Diversity," *The World & I*, September 1987, pp. 49-50.
22. Alexis de Tocqueville, *Democracy in America* (Garden City, N.Y.: Doubleday, 1969), pp. 433-34.

the "vital form" (p. 21) that transforms different and potentially diverse individuals and groups into a people, a society, organized for action in history. These truths confer upon the people their identity and provide the basis for common action rooted in agreed-upon principles and goals.[23]

What happens when, over time, the consensus, the public philosophy, erodes? The answer is that the community whose life it ordered, whose entelechy it constituted, whose principle of unity it supplied, disintegrates. The most dramatic example of this occurs when a community becomes polarized into two bitterly opposed ideological, religious, or ethnic camps that are unable or unwilling to coexist in peace and that consequently erupts into civil war. One immediately thinks of contemporary Lebanon in this context.

There is, however, a slower and more subtle version of this process of disintegration. According to Bell, the loss of the public philosophy issues in "the loss of *civitas,* that spontaneous willingness to obey the law, to respect the rights of others, to forgo the temptations of private enrichment at the expense of the public weal — in short, to honor the 'city' of which one is a member. Instead, each man goes his own way, pursuing his private vices, which can be indulged in only at the expense of public benefits."[24] As a society slowly loses the entelechy that united and structured it, that integrated individuals and groups into a community, a body politic, it will gradually splinter into a multitude of disparate individuals and groups, which, far from viewing each other as partners in a common enterprise and exhibiting an attitude of friendship and trust toward each other, will instead view each other with hostility, fear, suspicion, and resentment. Simultaneously, as civic amity and a community of purposes and values gradually disappear, these groups will be both increasingly unable to reach agreement about policies and increasingly unwilling to sacrifice

23. "In the maintenance and formation of a true community," writes Lippmann, "the . . . [public] philosophy is . . . like the thread which holds the pieces of the fabric together. Not everyone can have mastered the philosophy. . . . But if among the people of light and leading the public philosophy has, as the Chinese say, the Mandate of Heaven, the beliefs and habits which cause men to collaborate will remain whole" (*The Public Philosophy* [New Brunswick, N.J.: Transaction, 1989], p. 135). For an incisive discussion of the function of the "shared perception of truth" as the "form" of society, see Stanley Parry, "The Restoration of Tradition," *Modern Age* 5 (1961): 125-38. Cf. Niemeyer, *Between Nothingness and Paradise,* especially pp. 189-90.

24. Bell, *The Cultural Contradictions of Capitalism,* p. 245.

their own interests for the good of others or the whole. Obviously, unified action on the part of such a community will become difficult if not impossible, and political paralysis will become a real possibility. Moreover, as the nation's laws and policies increasingly come to be viewed as representing not common purposes but merely the will of the stronger groups, government will increasingly lose its moral authority. The disintegration of the public consensus will thus issue in a progressive devitalization of the body politic, until all that is left is a multiplicity of disparate individuals and groups held together by inertia, fear, and coercion. "When the adherence of the whole body of people to the public philosophy is firm," concludes Lippmann, "a true community exists; where there is division and dissent over the main principles the result is a condition of latent war."[25]

The Eclipse of the Tradition of Civility
and the Decline of Democracy

Eschewing as it does the methods of coercion characteristic of authoritarian regimes, a democratic society must rely for its vitality on the willingness of the individuals and groups that compose it to cooperate freely to secure the common good. It must rely for its vitality, that is to say, on a consensus regarding the goods that will inform its public life and the civic amity that such a consensus engenders. But a democratic society requires not just any consensus: it requires a public philosophy embodying the precepts of the tradition of civility that constitute democracy's moral foundation. Only a people that has internalized the moral norms flowing from this tradition — only a virtuous people — can reconcile freedom and self-government with the imperatives of justice, order, and the common good. If democracy is a particularly fragile form of government, it is so in large measure because it demands so much of the citizenry, because it depends so heavily on their moral character and sound judgment for its vitality and stability. "In any phase," writes Murray,

> civil society demands order. In its highest phase of freedom it demands that order should not be imposed from the top down, as it were, but should spontaneously flower outward from the free

25. Lippmann, *The Public Philosophy*, p. 135.

obedience to the restraints and imperatives that stem from inwardly possessed moral principle. In this sense democracy is more than a political experiment; it is a spiritual and moral enterprise. And its success depends upon the virtue of the people who undertake it. Men who would be politically free must discipline themselves. Likewise institutions which would pretend to be free with a human freedom must in their workings be governed from within and made to serve the ends of virtue. *Political freedom is endangered in its foundations as soon as the universal moral values, upon whose shared possession the self-discipline of a free society depends, are no longer vigorous enough to restrain the passions and shatter the selfish inertia of men.* (P. 48; italics mine)

In a democratic society, a people governs itself. This means that the laws will reflect their convictions, their values, and, in the final analysis, their moral character. A debased people cannot govern with justice. Indeed, in a very real sense a debased people cannot govern at all. Among a people ignorant of, or in rebellion against, the imperatives of the universal moral order, freedom and self-government cannot long endure.[26]

Indeed, without the public philosophy and the moral framework it supplies, democracy ceases to be an intelligible system of government. "I take it," writes Murray,

> that the political substance of democracy consists in the admission of an order of rights antecedent to the state, the political form of society. These are the rights of the person, the family, the church, the associations men freely form for economic, cultural, social, and religious ends. In the admission of this prior order of rights — inviolable as well by democratic majorities as by absolute monarchs

26. The classic statement of this elementary political truth is found in the writings of Edmund Burke: "Men are qualified for civil liberty in exact proportion to their disposition to put moral chains on their own appetites; in proportion as their love of justice is above their rapacity; in proportion as their soundness and sobriety of understanding is above their vanity and presumption; in proportion as they are more disposed to listen to the councils of the wise and good, in preference to the flattery of knaves. Society cannot exist unless a controlling power upon the will and appetite be placed somewhere, and the less of it there is within, the more there must be without. It is ordained in the eternal constitution of things, that men of intemperate minds cannot be free. Their passions forge their fetters" (*The Works of Edmund Burke,* vol. 4 [Walham, Mass.: Little, Brown, 1866], pp. 51-52).

— consists the most distinctive assertion of the service-character of the democratic state. And this service-character is still further enforced by the affirmation, implicit in the admission of the order of human rights, of another order of right also antecedent to the state and regulative of its public action as a state; I mean the order of justice. (P. 308)

If "the political substance of democracy" is found in the admission of an order of human rights and an order of justice antecedent to the state, what is the basis, the foundation, of this affirmation? An answer to this question

must inevitably carry us to a metaphysical decision in regard of the nature of man. Just as we now know that the written letter of a Bill of Rights is of little value unless there exist the institutional means whereby these rights may have, and be guaranteed, their expression in social action, so also we know — or ought to know — that it is not enough for us to be able to concoct the written letter unless we are likewise able to justify, in terms of ultimates in our own thinking about the nature of man, our assertion that the rights we list are indeed rights and therefore inviolable. . . . Otherwise we are writing on sand in a time of hurricanes and floods. (P. 304)

The political substance of democracy has as its foundation a metaphysical decision regarding the existence of an objective and universally obligatory moral order discoverable by the human mind that includes the aforementioned orders of rights and justice, "an order of human ends that imposes itself on the human and political conscience as imperatively necessary, apart from any antecedent free consent to strive for these ends."[27] The affirmations of the public philosophy constitute the ultimate justification for democratic government.

To reject the moral absolutes of the tradition of civility is to deprive democratic government of its very foundation. If the orders of justice and rights that are at the heart of democracy have no objective foundation in reality, then these orders are necessarily reduced to the status of mere human conventions, and democracy is deprived of any foundation other than the subjective preferences of a particular community at a particular point in time. But if this is

27. Murray, "Free Speech in Its Relation to Self-Government," p. 657.

indeed the case, the logical conclusion, as Walter Berns has written, is that "the majority can do no wrong," because, absent an objective order of rights and justice, "there is no ground on which to rest an objection to the majority's rule."[28] If democratic institutions and practices have no foundation other than the subjective wills of the members of a community, why may the members not will the abolition of these institutions and practices? And, even within the context of democratic forms, why, if the orders of justice and rights are no more than human conventions, should individuals, groups, and majorities respect them?[29] Why should individuals not use their freedom in an irresponsible fashion? Why should liberty not be allowed to degenerate into license? Why should the majority not tyrannize over the minority? Given the realities of politics and the historical track record of democracy, these questions cannot be dismissed as unfair, nor the concerns they reflect as unwarranted. Sooner or later all societies must be prepared to face what Irving Kristol calls "the ultimate subversive question: 'Why not?'"[30]

The naked public square, the public square stripped of the transcendentally grounded moral norms provided by the tradition of civility, is, as Richard John Neuhaus has so forcefully argued, a very dangerous place. "Democratic government," he writes, "is premised upon the acknowledgement of transcendent truth to which the political order is held accountable." When this "transcendent point of refer-

28. Berns, *The First Amendment and the Future of American Democracy* (Chicago: Regnery Gateway, 1985), p. 210.
29. For a brilliant defense of the view that the moral foundation of democracy is found in the tradition of civility, see John H. Hallowell, *The Moral Foundation of Democracy* (Chicago: University of Chicago Press, 1954). Purely procedural restraints, he persuasively argues, "divorced from all other considerations, cannot logically . . . impose substantive restraints and . . . [are] no guaranty even of the continuation of the procedure itself," because "individuals will adhere to a particular procedure only so long as they recognize some good in it." This good, in turn, "must, of necessity, be derived from something beyond the procedure itself." Likewise, the mere establishment of democratic institutions and practices does not necessarily guarantee the "continued existence" of the institutions and practices or "the presevation and enlargement of human freedom." These institutions and practices "are the means to freedom, but they are not identical with it." "It is the way in which" these forms "are conceived and the way in which they are used that will ultimately determine their efficacy as instruments of freedom." See Hallowell, *The Moral Foundation of Democracy*, pp. 46-47, 65-67.
30. Kristol, *On the Democratic Idea in America* (New York: Harper & Row, 1972), p. 20.

ence" is lost, the result is the loss of any "agreed upon authority . . . higher than the community itself." In such a moral vacuum, "political action" becomes, "in every sense of the term, thoroughly demoralized," and concepts such as good government and just government become "meaningless, for there is no measure of goodness or justness apart from government." In such a demoralized political culture, freedom cannot long endure, because "without an understanding of transcendently grounded rights all rights are then subject to be overridden either by abstract principles or by raw majoritarianism."[31]

By rendering the political substance of democracy unintelligible, the eclipse of the tradition of civility simultaneously renders democracy unworkable. This tradition, Murray maintains, offered a philosophy of human rights that was rooted in and inextricably connected with a prior "philosophy of right, justice, law, juridical order, and social order" (p. 309). It thus held forth the possibility of what Murray (echoing Clinton Rossiter) describes as a regime of "ethical, ordered liberty" (p. 51). The rejection of the tradition of civility, however, detaches the idea of freedom "from its polar terms — responsibility, justice, order, law" (p. 194) and thereby precludes the establishment of such a regime. The public philosophy, the tradition of reason, placed politics solidly within a moral framework. Without this framework, all that is left is sheer subjective will, and the only political question becomes whose will is to be supreme. Thus, without the moral framework provided by the tradition of reason, a democracy will be forced to choose between an anarchic individualism and an untrammeled majoritarianism, between absolutizing the arbitrary will of the free individual armed with his subjective rights and absolutizing the arbitrary will of the majority.

Decades ago, Walter Lippmann illustrated this principle as it relates to a variety of basic democratic institutions and practices. His analysis of the right to private property is a case in point. From the standpoint of the tradition of civility, "an absolute right to private property or to anything else that affects other men, cannot be entertained."[32] The tradition understood the right to private property as a limited right, the justification of which is grounded not in "the acquisitive and possessive instincts of men" but in what Lippmann (echoing Blackstone) terms "the grand ends of civil society."[33] The tradition

31. Neuhaus, *The Naked Public Square,* pp. 120, 76, 221.
32. Lippmann, *The Public Philosophy,* p. 116.
33. Lippmann, *The Public Philosophy,* p. 120.

specified that the ends or goals that justify the institution of private property simultaneously set its limitations.

Under the impact of classical liberalism, however, the approach of the tradition of civility to private property was abandoned and replaced by the conception of private property as a purely individual and "absolute" right. The idea of an absolute right to private property, however, "inevitably produced intolerable evils" and at the same time precluded the establishment of legal remedies to these abuses. This development had profound consequences. To begin with, by ignoring the purposes private property is intended to serve, and thus failing to define and enforce the duties that constitute its "rational justification," this new approach to private property effectively deprived the institution of private property of its foundation. At the same time, it polarized the community into two hostile camps — "the minority who had so much absolute property" and "the propertyless" majority — between which there was "no connecting bond, no consensus, within the same realm of rational discourse." The community was thus confronted with "a dangerous and false dilemma": "the alternatives, it appeared, were to defend absolute property against the growing discontent of the propertyless, or to abolish private property."[34]

Through the loss of the public philosophy, property rights were divorced from correlative duties, justice, and order, and the community was trapped in an unreal dichotomy of absolute property rights on the one hand or none whatsoever on the other. In short, in a community that lacks the moral framework supplied by the tradition of civility, it becomes impossible to reconcile order and liberty, to steer a course between the Scylla of unbounded personal license and the Charybdis of majority tyranny. "Trapped in a false antithesis of unlimited freedom vs. unlimited power," such a society, Murray concludes, "will swing helplessly between the extremes of individualistic anarchy and totalitarian tyranny."[35]

The eclipse of the tradition of civility will not issue in the immediate collapse of democracy but in a slow process of devitalization the contours of which we have already considered. The dynamic of this decline will be exhibited perhaps most clearly in the decision-making process. Compromise is undeniably an essential feature of

34. Lippmann, *The Public Philosophy*, p. 122.
35. Murray, "Leo XIII: Government and the Order of Culture," *Theological Studies* 15 (March 1954): 5.

democratic politics, but it does not occur automatically. The ability of a democratic society to achieve "compromises on a consistent basis," as R. Bruce Douglass has pointed out, will "depend heavily on the attitudes with which citizens" approach public affairs. Will "they exercise self-discipline in making demands on government," or will "they instead try to grasp for themselves" as much as they can? Will "they be willing to bear burdens and accept sacrifices for the good of society," or will "they try whenever possible to pass the burdens and sacrifices off on others?" Will "they respect the rights of minorities," or will "they assume that all that matters is the might of numbers?"[36]

It is questionable, to say the least, whether the sense of community, the civic amity and trust upon which compromise depends, can be sustained in the absence of the common purposes and values, the like-mindedness supplied by the tradition of civility. Indeed, the loss of the tradition of civility makes it almost inevitable that groups will simultaneously intensify their demands and become inflexible in their pursuit of them.[37] It is equally questionable whether rational deliberation about the issues of the day can be sustained apart from the common premises and shared universe of discourse supplied by this tradition.

Beyond generating stalemate, polarization, and civic strife in the short term, however, the disintegration of the public consensus must ultimately result in a loss of faith in the democratic state itself. In the end a people accords legitimacy to a state on the basis of how well it serves common interests, purposes and values. Free elections alone are not enough to guarantee the legitimacy of the democratic state. Its

36. Douglass, "Liberalism as a Threat to Democracy," in *The Ethical Dimension of Political Life,* ed. Francis Canavan, S.J. (Durham, N.C.: Duke University Press, 1983), p. 33.

37. One thinks in this context of Burkhardt's comment that when established standards are overthrown, all that remains is the pursuit of power or pleasure — neither of which, it might be added, constitutes a promising foundation for democratic government. Cf. George Weigel: "this bloodiest of centuries has empirically validated the Founders' . . . belief in the necessity, for humane social life, of civic virtue grounded in transcendent moral norms. . . . We can agree with Nietzsche and Dostoevsky that a culture in which nothing is fundamentally true is a culture in which anything is permitted. Permissiveness can take many forms, of course. Relativism-leading-to-radical-permissiveness can result in 'a gentle . . . nihilism' in which the path of least resistance to the trend of the moment is the cultural path of choice. It can lead to a 'brutal nihilism' of the Nazi sort. But to nihilism, debonair or gruesome, it inexorably leads. And nihilism is incompatible with an experiment in democratic republicanism" (*Catholicism and the Renewal of American Democracy* [New York: Paulist Press, 1989], p. 194).

legitimacy will depend on the extent to which its laws and public policies are perceived to represent something more than the self-interest of the majority, something more than the will of the stronger party. If the decisions of the majority on a particular issue are to be seen as legitimate by the minority, they must be perceived as representing a good-faith judgment about what courses of action best advance shared interests, purposes, and values.

The loss of the shared purposes and values supplied by the public philosophy reduces politics to a mere calculus of power among self-seeking groups and reduces political decisions to nothing more than a register of the relative strengths of the contending parties. It thus lays the groundwork for the delegitimization of the democratic state. As Thomas A. Spragens, Jr., has written, the more

> the policies of [a democratic] system are . . . perceived as the product of purely self-interested logrolling, the more that system will be subjected to intensified demands and afflicted by loss of support. The system loses support because it loses its moral legitimacy, and intensified demands are placed on it as each group seeks to compensate for the real or imagined influence of its rivals. For both reasons, the system suffers from an erosion of its authority and, with it, a diminution of its capacity to govern effectively. The system thus becomes progressively less stable.[38]

The long-term viability of such a democratic state is, at a minimum, problematic.

Conclusion

Several decades ago T. S. Eliot noted modern man's propensity to fantasize about systems so perfect that no one will have to be good. The widely held view that a procedural consensus alone offers a secure foundation for a democratic society is clearly a case in point. A free society, like all societies, will necessarily be pluralistic, but for a society to cohere in the face of religious and ethnic diversity and a multiplicity of divergent economic interests and socioeconomic groups, it must be

38. Spragens, *The Irony of Liberal Reason* (Chicago: University of Chicago Press, 1981), p. 303.

united by an ensemble of substantive truths. Political unity, in short, presupposes, and must be informed by, an antecedent moral unity. The type of pluralism proper to a stable and vigorous free society is a diversity existing within the context of an overarching unity created by a common acceptance of the tradition of civility.

The transformation that has taken place in the character of American pluralism thus has disturbing implications for the future of the American experiment in self-government. This transformation has profoundly altered our character as a people, dissipating the moral capital on which Publius relied, and thereby eroding what George F. Will has aptly termed "the intangible prerequisites of free government."[39] The malaise besetting our public life today is a direct result of the change that has taken place in the structure of American pluralism. The effect of this change has been to undermine the moral and cultural preconditions of a viable democratic polity and to produce a phenomenon that Michael Crozier has characterized as "anomic democracy."

As to what the future may hold, perhaps Murray should be given the last word. The loss of the public philosophy, he maintained, has launched America on "an impossible experiment" that, in a very real sense, endangers the future of American democracy. If the American Republic is ever overthrown, he wrote,

> I would suggest that it will not be overthrown by communism. It will be overthrown because it will have made an impossible experiment. It will have undertaken to establish a technological order of most marvelous intricacy, which will have been constructed and will operate without relation to true political ends; and this technological order will hang, as it were, suspended over a moral confusion; and this moral confusion will itself be suspended over a spiritual vacuum.[40]

Confronted with this vacuum and the political and moral chaos it invited, America had, Murray believed, two basic alternatives. The first was to continue this impossible experiment and face the prospect of inevitable disintegration into either "the political chaos of formlessness" or the "moral chaos of tyranny" (p. 24). The second alternative

---

39. Will, *Statecraft as Soulcraft* (New York: Simon & Schuster, 1983), p. 22.
40. Murray, "The Return to Tribalism," *Catholic Mind* 60 (January 1962): 7.

was "a new moral act of purpose and a new act of intellectual affirmation, comparable to those which launched the American constitutional commonwealth, that will newly put us in possession of the public philosophy, the basic consensus we need" (p. 92). Much has changed in the more than two decades since Murray's death. Today, the crisis is graver, the peril is greater, and the hour is later. The basic alternatives, however, remain the same.

Murray's Natural-Law Articulation
of the American Proposition

Peter Augustine Lawler

JOHN COURTNEY MURRAY'S *We Hold These Truths* seems, at first, not to be a book in the proper sense at all but merely a collection of essays written for various occasions over a decade. But in terms of purpose, the book is a whole. It is also a whole in terms of argument. The same argument is made, time and again, in different ways. The book's thread of unity is its repeated exploration of "the American proposition," which Murray also calls "the public consensus or public philosophy of America."[1] Murray constantly defends his own "proposition . . . that only the theory of natural law can give an account of the public moral experience that is the public consensus" (p. 109).

Murray means to show what is required to make the American "moral experience" intelligible, what makes America a whole composed of free and rational beings, creatures made in the image of God. *We Hold These Truths* is a work of political philosophy, although it is not only that. It shows how one of those "whom St. Thomas calls 'the wise'" can provide illumination and direction to moral and political life (p. 111).

Through this demonstration, Murray says he fulfills his "duty" as a citizen, to know and show the worthiness of what holds together citizens as citizens (p. ix). But Murray writes not primarily as a citizen

---

1. Murray, *We Hold These Truths: Catholic Reflections on the American Proposition* (New York: Sheed & Ward, 1960), p. viii. Subsequent references to this volume will be made parenthetically in the text.

116

or even as a lover of philosophic reason but as a Catholic. He writes not only to show the compatibility between citizenship and the rational life but the compatibility between reason and revelation as well as between the political community (especially *his* political community) and revelation. He means to show how each of these human goods is part of the whole human person.

Although he was an American citizen, Murray noted that he viewed the American proposition primarily from the outside. The book's subtitle is *Catholic Reflections on the American Proposition,* not *A Catholic American's Reflections.* . . . His existence and duty as a citizen were subordinate to his "Catholic faith and morality." *The* question for him was the compatibility of American democracy with this faith and morality, in contrast to the average American citizen, who would reverse the order of the question (p. ix). For a Catholic, he asserted, *the* political question is "the right attitude to adopt toward the established polity" (p. 43). All Christians are called to judge their particular polity by a transpolitical, universal standard.

Murray criticized Catholic theorists whose acceptance of America is rooted, at least in principle, only in "expediency in the narrow sense — the need to accept what one is powerless to change." According to their view, it is permissible for a Catholic to be an American citizen not because America is good in itself but because the peace and security of any established polity is useful for the practice of one's faith. Catholic American citizens should do their civic duty, say these theorists, but they should do so without any principled devotion. From the perspective of a devoted citizen, the Catholic's relationship to his polity so understood seems parasitical and hence suspect.

Murray rejected the extreme Augustinianism or Platonism of this view even in theory as contrary to the harmonious or "integral" spirit of the doctrine of natural law (pp. 63, 182-85). He said that Catholics as Catholics can affirm the goodness of the American proposition or public philosophy with "conscience and conviction" (p. 43). America is worthy of their devotion, although not, of course, of their highest devotion. Catholics as Catholics can be good American citizens. In one respect, as we shall see, they can even be the best.

The reason for this affirmation is "the evident coincidence of the principles which inspired the American Republic with the principles which are structural to the Western Christian political tradition" (p. 43), the principles that receive their fullest articulation in the Catholic tradition of natural law. This "coincidence," like all salutary coincidences, is fortuitous, even "providential" (p. 30). Catholics did not, after all, found America, and the American founders undeniably exhibited hostility toward the Catholic Church as church. But Catholics, as Catholics, can still experience the American founding as good.

This coincidence is not some inexplicable accident. America is a good polity because "the Fathers of the Republic" received as an inheritance and worked within the political tradition established by "the Fathers of the Church," their intellectual Fathers (pp. 41-43). The Republic's Fathers viewed themselves as modern men rebelling against what their fathers had given them. But the tradition was nonetheless vigorous, because their rebellion was not radical (not even as radical as they thought). "The Fathers [were] building better than they knew," says Murray (pp. 30, 66), because they remained, more than they knew, within the Catholic Church's "own tradition of thought, which is wider and deeper than any that America has elaborated" (p. xi).

Catholic thought, more profound and more comprehensive than American thought, comprehends the Republic's Fathers better than the foundations of the American proposition did. Catholic reflections on this proposition cannot be sustained without some criticism and even some suspicion of the founding fathers (p. 20). Murray explicitly follows Lincoln in affirming their proposition with a sort of filial piety while attempting to deepen or transform its meaning (pp. viii-ix). Even the idea that America is devoted to a proposition was articulated not by the Fathers but by Lincoln.[2]

Many of the rhetorical features of Murray's extraordinarily carefully and elegantly written book are Lincolnian. He writes of our "ancient heritage" as Lincoln spoke of our "ancient faith." The phrase "Our Fathers" comes from Lincoln, which blurs, for the sake of piety and contrary to the Republic's Fathers' rationalistic spirit of innovation, the distinction between our political and religious beginnings.

This indistinctness, for Murray, is more than merely rhetorical. The heritage or faith of the Republic and the religion really do coincide in decisive respects — and without reducing American religion to "political religion," as Lincoln tends to do.[3] Murray implicitly criticizes

2. The interpretation of Lincoln here follows that of Harry Jaffa in *Crisis of the House Divided* (Chicago: University of Chicago Press, 1982). For supporting details and documentation of the argument, consult this volume.

3. The phrase "political religion" comes from Lincoln's Address to the Young Men's Lyceum (1838). For a criticism of Lincoln's reductionism, see John Gueguen, "Modernity in American Ideology," *Independent Journal of Philosophy* 4 (1980): 79-87.

Lincoln for his reductionism (p. xi). Lincoln's "abstract principle," which Thomas Jefferson asserted in the midst of a revolution, finds its most profound articulation in the thought of Thomas Aquinas. Murray's theme is that our "ancient faith" is also, truly, a "rational faith" (p. 10), as well as the Christian faith. Jefferson was more pious than he knew.

Lincoln's tendency was to particularize the proposition, to make it seem less abstract or universal, to make it the American nation's own. The crisis the nation faced in his time, above all, was of *devotion* to the project the Fathers had given to us. Murray's tendency is to generalize the proposition, to make it less America's own by locating it in a larger, more rational, and more universal tradition of thought.

In Murray's time, the crisis faced by the nation, and the West as a whole, is the contemporary denial, from almost all quarters, that human beings really can hold moral truths in common. He makes clear what the crisis is before he makes clear what the proposition is. He does say that he does not agree with Lincoln that it is only that all men are created equal. He contends that Lincoln "asserted" the proposition's "imperiled part" in the midst of a "national crisis" (pp. vii-viii). Lincoln, it seems, self-consciously reduced the whole to a part because the crisis the proposition faced was only partial. It was only a *national* crisis, and it involved only *part* of the proposition. The idea that moral truth might be held in common was not questioned.

But today, Murray says, "civil war" is "the basic fact of *world* society" (p. viii; italics mine). This conflict is essentially a series of "religious wars" over the "spiritual substance" of human existence and institutions — wars that lurk not far beneath the apparent "civic amity" of American religious pluralism (pp. 19, 24, 128). Murray asserts that "there is no element of the [American] theorem that is not menaced by active negation, and no thrust of the project that does not meet powerful opposition" (p. viii). The proposition, conceived as Murray conceives it — as both natural-law theory and as practice or historical project in that theory's light — is now threatened, in its entirety, throughout the world.

The crisis is primarily theoretical. Devotion to the project is imperiled by the fact that the very foundations of the theory are no longer considered credible. There has been "a loss of confidence in the power of reason to fix the purposes of political life" (p. 130). The defense of the American proposition today must be persuasive not only to Murray's fellow citizens, as *their* project, but to all human beings, as a truth that they can experience as true independently of their willing it. Murray, much more than Lincoln and the Republic's Fathers, is compelled, for political reasons, to bring the transpolitical, "metaphysical" foundation of the proposition to light. His beginning cannot be a defense of this or that part of the proposition. It must be a defense of the idea that there can be such a proposition. He argues for the existence of "a certain body of objective truth . . . accessible to the reason of man" (p. ix).

That such truths exist is the "traditional conviction" or "assertion" that has sustained the American proposition. If this faith in a "realist epistemology" is denied, Murray asserts, then "the American proposition is eviscerated . . . in one stroke" (pp. viii-ix). This denial is found almost everywhere today, perhaps especially in American universities. The "traditional conviction" is defended in the American intellectual world only in the Catholic community (pp. 40-41).

Murray does not deny that the contemporary repudiation of the Republic's Fathers' way of defending their proposition is reasonable. Their propensity was to accept without much thought "the serene, and often naive, certainties of the eighteenth century" (p. viii). These certainties "have crumbled" in the face of what is "genuine and true" in the thought of "Darwin, Freud, and Marx" (pp. viii, 310). The Fathers' superficial version of natural-law and natural-rights thinking depended to a great extent on the Lockean abstraction of the prepolitical and presocial state of nature, an unempirical, even misanthropic beginning that, by itself, generates "individualistic, rationalistic nonsense." The idea of the state of nature is no longer credible anywhere. The Fathers' certainties are our nonsense (pp. 310-16).

Insofar as the American proposition is understood to have originated in the thought of the Republic's Fathers, we can legitimately question its axiomatic character, says Murray (p. viii). The Fathers focused on reason, not piety or uncritical traditionalism, as the moral and political standard. They were convinced that their proposition must pass the test of reason to constitute the public philosophy.[4] They themselves would recommend that the proposition now be aban-

4. For interpretations of the American founding that stress its rationalism, see Harry Jaffa, *How to Think about the American Revolution* (Durham, N.C.: Carolina Academic Press, 1978); Walter Berns, *The First Amendment and the Future of American Democracy* (New York: Basic Books, 1976); and Thomas Pangle, *The Spirit of Modern Republicanism* (Chicago: University of Chicago Press, 1987).

doned unless a better argument than the one they gave for it could be found. Murray's contention is that there is indeed a better argument than they knew to defend the goodness of the polity they constructed. Only the Catholic tradition or community of thought, or the wise within it, can give American citizens what they most urgently need to perpetuate their proposition legitimately. It is in this sense that Murray asserts that Catholics are the best American citizens (p. 43).

Today's defense of the American proposition cannot be as serene or superficial, nor as unconsciously traditional, as that of the Fathers. Our reflection must be more profound, says Murray, because the depths of the problem of human freedom "stand revealed to us" as they were not to the Fathers (p. 321). They neither perceived nor affirmed the "naked essence" of the modern experiment, whereas we have no choice but to confront it (p. 308).

According to Murray, the experiment is disintegrating even as it succeeds. It is constituted by the attempt to realize "the Cartesian dream." The "dream today is largely reality; man is the master and possessor of nature." But the owner of nature has achieved his conquest at the cost of "his own identity" (p. 200). The dynamic of conquest has been an increasingly radical dissatisfaction with all traditional or "given" answers to the question "What is man?" as dogmatic limitations to human freedom (pp. 126-28). We no longer understand ourselves to be limited or defined by our nature or God. Freedom is primarily freedom from nature and God for self-creation. The modern faith centers on the belief that self-creation is possible, that the conquest of nature will somehow solve the problem of human freedom.

But the modern view of freedom is, at its core, only destructive or negative. It has been undeniably successful in its efforts to "destroy an order of political privilege and inaugurate an era of political equality." It has not been able, however, "to erect an order of social justice or inaugurate an order of freedom" (p. 319). It is still freedom *from* this or that limitation for nothing in particular. Its tendency, contrary to its intention, has been to obliterate everything that is distinctively human. Its effect has not been to raise man up to divinity but, as Eric Voegelin has explained, to reduce him in theory to an indistinguishable part of some deterministic system and in practice to an indistinguishable part of some "monistic" social whole (pp. 130-31). "Communism," Murray concludes, "is . . . political modernity carried to its logical conclusion," by which he means that "all that is implicit or unintentional in modernity . . . has become explicit or deliberate in the Communist system" (p. 211). The modern experiment ends up revealing to itself that it cannot solve the problem of human liberty except by denying, quite unreasonably and hence violently, that such liberty exists at all.

Murray asserts that communism marks the end of modern history and thought, though not the end of history itself. Its logical solution to the problem of human liberty is not empirical. The problem, in truth, remains unsolved. The end of history to which the communist system points is a "mirage" (p. 215). The real human experience at the end of the destructiveness of the modern era is "a spiritual vacuum . . . at the heart of human existence" (p. 216).[5]

The filling of this vacuum is a task that "postmodern" man must perform in one way or another. Our "anxious reflection" concerns "how . . . these hollow emptinesses [should] be filled."[6] Our search is no longer primarily for a way of achieving liberation from this or that constraint but for a "definition of freedom," for the "positive content" of liberty, for "ordered liberty" (p. 319). For us, there is, of necessity, "a new openness to the world of metaphysical and religious values" (p. 320). The modern experiment has demonstrated that there is no "purely secularistic" or superficial solution to the problem of human liberty. A reference to Nietzsche shows that Murray means, especially, to avoid the superficiality of Hegel and Marx (p. 216).

It is Murray's postmodern conviction that "the Basic Issues today can only be conceived in metaphysical and religious terms." Times are so untraditional that one must confront "the nature and structure of reality itself" (p. 199). As a result of this confrontation, postmoderns must make "a metaphysical decision in regard of the nature of man" (p. 321).

Murray's description of the postmodern task as a "decision" in response to "anxious reflection" is meant to be more unsettling than it has been. It means that it is no longer possible to be a conservative,

5. Our problem, then, is not communism at all: "I would here maintain that Communism is not the basic cause of our present confusions, uncertainties, insecurities, falterings and failures of purpose," says Murray. "I would go so far as to maintain that, if the Communist empire were to fall apart tomorrow, and if Communist ideology were to disintegrate with it, our problems would not be solved. In fact, they would be worse in many ways" (p. 88). The present disintegration of Soviet communism would seem to vindicate these sentiments.
6. Murray, "Reversing the Secularist Drift," *Thought* 24 (March 1949): 37.

that one must think and act radically. It also means that decisions other than the one for natural law are possible.

Murray's postmodern metaphysical decision is a radically untraditional affirmation of the truth embodied in the Western tradition. Another possibility, the one Murray associates with Nietzsche, is the radically untraditional rejection of the metaphysical decision, which would also be, in its way, a metaphysical decision. Murray understands that the result of the radically antimetaphysical decision, which modern thinkers prior to Nietzsche always fell short of making, would be a destruction of the West in theory and practice, the descent of the world into chaos and violence as a necessary precondition for the rebirth of human or spiritual life (pp. 216-17). The Nietzschean thesis is that the only way the "spiritual vacuum" can be filled is through this destruction, because the West lacks the resources to fill it itself (p. 290).

Murray agrees with Nietzsche, Heidegger, and existentialists of various varieties that a decision must be made in the face of the "impotent nihilism" (impotent because wholly secular) present at the end of modernity (p. 12). The existentialist understands a decision as a resolution to define the future through one's own self-assertion. This resolution comes in response to the nihilistic revelation, by the dynamic of Western thought, of the falsity of the West's defining assertion that "values" or morality have some metaphysical foundation. Values must be asserted against the emptiness of reality. A decision must be made because there is nothing but nothing, from a human or spiritual perspective, to be discovered.

Murray's use of "decision" calls to mind, in a word, existentialism's "decisionism," which, he recognizes, stands at the foundation of the relativism and tyrannical aspirations of contemporary social science (pp. 84, 322-24).[7] He denies that mere assertiveness or will can solve the problem of nihilism, which arises when the problem of human freedom seems insoluble (p. 12). He asks "whether the problem of freedom in the post-modern era can be satisfactorily dealt with in terms of philosophies (and theologies) which bear too heavily the stamp of modernity" (p. 198). Murray argues that existentialism's postmodern

7. For a discussion of the nihilistic extremes of relativism and decisionism, see my essay "Relativism, American Education, and Democracy," *Southeastern Political Review* 16 (1989): 1-16. My categories of relativism and decisionism are the equivalent of Ernest Fortin's categories of relativism and fanaticism; see "Natural Law and Social Justice," *American Journal of Jurisprudence* 30 (1986): 20.

124 Peter Augustine Lawler

solution does not constitute, at bottom, a rejection of modernity but rather an attempt to overcome modernity through the radicalization of its antimetaphysical bias. The problem of freedom is still approached through self-creativity. All postmodern projects, except for the recovery of natural law, are, in Murray's view, nihilistic attempts to cover up the nihilistic perception of the truth about reality (p. 217).

The emergence of the problem of nihilism signals the exhaustion of modernity. A decision must be made. To decide for natural law is, according to Murray, to "opt . . . for a metaphysics of right," for a standard that is not "subjective," a standard that exists independent of human decision. With this option, "objective law [or right] has the primacy over subjective rights" (p. 327). It is the decision, finally, that human beings are not free to decide, that the moral order is not a product of their ultimately arbitrary and, hence, free willing.

The metaphysical decision is not merely a decision. One cannot simply assert that "a metaphysics of right" exists. It depends on the discovery of the existence of "a metaphysic of nature, especially the idea that nature is a teleological concept" (p. 327) — a concept, in other words, that orders and directs human freedom. Murray asserts that natural-law doctrine is without "presuppositions," without elements that cannot be verified. The modern rejection of natural law was, most radically, an error (p. 109).

But to say that we can discover a natural teleology and even a "natural theology" is extremely controversial, especially in our time. It is an assertion that seems to oppose the foundation of modern natural science. Whatever its shortcomings in coming to terms with the problem of human freedom, this science seems to have authoritatively discredited the idea that human beings can find a grounding for their freedom in their spiritual existence in nature. Few postmodern thinkers are attracted to the metaphysical foundation of natural-law doctrine because few believe that the postmodern era can root itself in discredited premodern presuppositions.[8] Even most contemporary Thomists, including such very orthodox Catholics as Germain Grisez and John Finnis, accept the modern disjunction between nature and human freedom, and they transform Thomas's teaching accordingly. Others interested in recovering the morality of the tradition in view of modernity's culmination in moral nihilism,

8. See Leo Strauss, *Natural Right and History* (Chicago: University of Chicago Press, 1953), pp. 7-8.

such as Alasdair MacIntyre, do not view the "speculative" or meta-physical component of the tradition as recoverable.[9]

But the most telling example of this perceived tension between nature or metaphysical theory and morality is provided by Ernest Fortin. He calls for the full revitalization of the natural-law tradition's theory against "the bland and emasculated versions that are now being offered of it."[10] Natural-law theory, says Fortin, has "kept alive an ideal of human wholeness . . . because its understanding of the moral life was not guided by the abstractions of modern science."[11] Natural law apparently does fuller justice to the concrete reality of the human person than modern theory, which, in its various forms, always abstracts from phenomena that are distinctively human.

Fortin adds, however, that there are problems with natural-law theory, "particularly as regards its natural knowability." But he recommends that we ignore such "shortcomings," given the paucity of alternative theories and natural law's "particular suitability to a religious and cultural tradition such as ours."[12] But we cannot ignore his agreement with the modern critics of natural-law theory that at least much of its perception of moral order is not known to human beings by their natures. "The matter finally comes down to a choice between a truth that is good for the intellect alone and a salutary and beatifying truth that represents the good of the whole person."[13] He maintains that philosophers as philosophers do not believe that human beings can know the latter truth by nature.[14]

Fortin also holds that there is no "synthesis" that unites these two perceptions of truth. The "Great Tradition" is rooted not in a unity but in a "fundamental tension."[15] The candid and aware partisan of revelation

9. See John Finnis, *Natural Law and Natural Rights* (New York: Oxford University Press, 1980); and Alasdair MacIntyre, *After Virtue* (Notre Dame, Ind.: University of Notre Dame Press, 1982). For a critique of the failure of these authors to deal with natural or metaphysical issues, see Russell Hittinger, "After MacIntyre: Natural Law Theory, Virtue Ethics, and Eudaimonia," *International Philosophical Quarterly* 29 (1989): 449-61.

10. Fortin, "Natural Law and Social Justice," p. 1.

11. Fortin, "Natural Law and Social Justice," p. 20.

12. Fortin, "Natural Law and Social Justice," p. 19.

13. Fortin, "Rational Theologians and Irrational Philosophers: A Straussian Perspective," *Interpretation* 12 (1984): 356.

14. Fortin says that, even for Thomas Aquinas, "the status of the natural law as a philosophical concept was at best problematic" ("The New Rights Theory and Natural Law," *Review of Politics* 44 [1982]: 609).

15. Fortin, "Rational Theologians and Irrational Philosophers," p. 356.

must concede that he cannot know "the good of the whole person" according to nature. Unlike Murray, Fortin says that in the end the decision for revelation is against the philosophers' rational account of nature. The decision for natural law is in the end a decision for revelation.

Even some thoughtful contemporary partisans of natural law question Murray's view that natural-law doctrine concerning the natural or metaphysical foundation of moral order depends not at all on prerational and preempirical presuppositions. Murray does not, I think, adhere to that position consistently, much less demonstrate its truth.[16] As a whole, his book offers a more nuanced and more convincing defense of natural law.

The "metaphysical decision" is really a decision in the sense of being a choice from among plausible alternatives, none of which is wholly satisfactory to human reason. The choice for natural law, which according to Murray originates in part in human anger (pp. 316-18) or in the consciousness of a man protesting against injustice, may offend the intellect's desire for consistency or uniformity, which includes its desire to deny significance to human particularity or individuality. But it is still not a decision in the existentialist's sense, a willful imposition of value without or against reason. Murray contends that of all the alternatives available, natural law best comes to terms with the problem of human freedom. He also argues that it is the only theory that makes sense out of the American proposition. Natural law really does deserve to prevail over rival doctrines on empirical grounds alone.

Murray's affirmation of this conclusion is at the foundation of his critical defense of the American founding. He maintains that whatever theoretical pretensions the Republic's Fathers might have had, the American revolution "was less a revolution than a conservation" (p. 31). He "radically distinguishes the conservative Christian tradition of America from the Jacobin laicist tradition of Continental Europe." American liberalism defines liberty in terms of nature and God, whereas Continental liberalism knows of no standard but "autonomous reason" (p. 28).

Murray seems to say that natural law is part of a distinctively Christian tradition that the Fathers perpetuated more than rejected. The evidence he presents is the Declaration of Independence, as interpreted by Lincoln. That "landmark of Western political theory" placed, in Lincoln's words, "this nation under God" (pp. 28-30). This acknowl-

---

16. On this, see Robert W. McElroy, *The Search for an American Public Theology: The Contribution of John Courtney Murray* (New York: Paulist Press, 1989), pp. 156-57.

edgment of "the sovereignty of God over nations as well as individual men" is what "imparts to politics a fundamental human meaning." Politics, in America, is constituted and delimited by a "truth beyond politics," whereas for nations constituted by the Jacobin or secular liberal tradition, "religion is at best a purely private concern" (p. 28). The foundation of the natural-law tradition is the apprehension that human freedom defines itself under God's sovereignty. Hence political freedom "knows itself to be bound by the imperatives of the moral law" (p. 164).

The obvious objection to this interpretation of the American proposition is that the Constitution itself does not acknowledge the sovereignty of God but only the sovereignty of the people. Yet it is the document, as Murray himself says, that is the "object of reverence even to the point of worship among the American people."[17] Murray follows Lincoln most fundamentally in "constitutionalizing" the Declaration to save the Constitution from the moral superficiality of secularism. He says that "the Constitution of the United States *has* to be read in light of the Declaration of Independence." The necessity here is less historical or empirical than moral. Only with such a reading can Murray say that "the famous American phrase 'We the people. . . .' is the very negation of Jacobinism."[18] Other readings of the Constitution would reveal less continuity with the tradition.[19]

Murray again follows Lincoln in neglecting interpretations of the Declaration that could point to the Fathers' pretentious rationalism, to their at least partial kinship with the Jacobins. The Declaration refers to "Nature's God" and the Creator, and nowhere distinguishes between the two. The only appropriate or consistent conclusion, Murray suggests, is that Thomas Jefferson was a Thomist. But "Nature's God," interpreted in light of Jefferson's thought as a whole, is actually the

17. Murray, quoted by McElroy in *The Search for an American Public Theology*, p. 101.

18. Murray, "Leo XIII: Separation of Church and State," *Theological Studies* 14 (1953): 160.

19. See Gueguen, "Modernity in American Ideology"; and my essay "The Limits of the 'Secular Humanist' Interpretation of the Constitution," *The Journal of Political Science* 9 (1988): 49-58. And, for a critique of the pretentious, even tyrannical rationalism of the unamended Constitution's understanding of nature, see Aristocrotis, " 'The Government of Nature' Delineated," in vol. 3 of *The Complete Anti-Federalist*, ed. Herbert J. Storing and Murray Dry (Chicago: University of Chicago Press, 1981), pp. 196-213. Also worthy of note is E. A. Goerner's *Caesar and Peter* (New York: Herder & Herder, 1962); Goerner describes Murray's history as a "noble, Platonic tale" (p. 182).

God of the secular philosophers. The phrase has an antirevelationist and even anticreationist connotation.[20]

The references to the biblical God in the Declaration were meant to humor those of the revolutionary generation less "enlightened" than the leading fathers. The terms "Nature's God" and "the Creator" reflect very different theologies. For the political purpose of promoting revolutionary unity, the Declaration is, quite deliberately, theologically incoherent.[21] The synthesis Murray effects through his Thomistic natural-law interpretation is imposed from without, even if it is the only possible synthesis.

For Murray, the incoherence of the Declaration, which he plays down but does not deny, is the incoherence of the modern political experiment as such. Even the Republic's Fathers were modern enough to have rejected to some extent "the Christian revelation that man is a sacredness, and that his primatial *res sacra,* his freedom, is sought and found ultimately within the freedom of the Church" (p. 215). They rejected the credibility of divine revelation, and they tried to free natural law from its influence. Madison and Jefferson, the most "enlightened" of the Fathers, also opposed, in their "anti-ecclesiasticism" (p. 65), the church as an institution. But even they did not reject "the whole system of moral values, both individual and social, which had been elaborated under the influence of the Christian revelation" (p. 214). Their "values" were, more than they knew, a Christian inheritance. "Men of the eighteenth century," Murray observes, had "intelligences [that] were very superficially Christian" (p. 317), but they were Christian nonetheless.

The attempt of Jefferson and of the other leading fathers to dissociate the moral order of natural law and "Nature's God" from illumination by revelation was a pretentious impossibility. Jefferson's "moral values" depended, more than he knew, on the truth of the Christian idea of personal sacredness. Murray finally says that the whole American consensus, its proposition or public philosophy, "has its ultimate root" in this idea (p. 81). Murray insists that the proposition is eviscerated if this idea is denied. It turns out that "the spiritual substance of a free society" is always rooted in this "central Christian concept" (p. 198), whether or not the proponents of freedom realize it.

20. For an interpretation of the place of the God of the philosophers in the founding of America, see Paul H. Rahe, "Church and State," *The American Spectator,* January 1986, pp. 18-21.

21. See Michael Zuckert, "Self-Evident Truth and the Declaration of Independence," *Review of Politics* 49 (1987): 319-39.

It was a Christian discovery that "the whole of human life is not absorbed in the polis" (p. 333) and that human dignity is not primarily a "civil dignity" (p. 52). The Christian knows, as the Fathers asserted, that the state "has only a relative value" in service to the person's transpolitical dignity (p. 326). The Bill of Rights, in this light, was "a tributary to the tradition of natural law" (p. 37), "a product of Christian history" and, hence, Christian presuppositions (p. 39). Its idea is that "man has certain original responsibilities primarily as man, antecedent to his status as citizen" (p. 37). These responsibilities, as Madison said in his *Memorial and Remonstrance*, are the creature's duty, which he knows by his nature, to his Creator.

Murray claims to find in the religion clauses of the First Amendment the understanding of "the dignity of the person" he believes he ought to have found in Vatican II's "Declaration on Religious Freedom."[22] This dignity comes from the fact that the person is a "moral subject," capable of free and responsible choice. His freedom and responsibility, in turn, "are rooted in the given reality of man as man." He is aware that he should act freely "in accordance with his nature." He is free from political coercion to obey "imperatives" given to him by "the transcendent order of truth." He is required, by his nature, to establish his proper, dutiful relationship with his Creator.[23]

The religion clauses of the First Amendment, Murray suggests, actually correct the impression given by the unamended Constitution's apparent indifference to the existence of God.[24] They establish the point that American freedom is primarily freedom for religion (p. 151). They link the Constitution less ambiguously with the Declaration. Perhaps they even make the Constitution's theological interpretation of the Declaration less ambiguous. Madison's theology in the *Memorial and Remonstrance*, even if presented only for a political or rhetorical purpose, is more clearly or coherently part of the natural-law tradition than is the theology of the Declaration.

Murray does say that the First Amendment implies no theology,

22. For Murray's criticism of Vatican II's Declaration, see Francis Canavan, "Murray on Vatican II's *Declaration of Religious Freedom*," *Communio* 9 (1982): 404-5.

23. Murray, "The Declaration on Religious Freedom," in *Religious Liberty: An End and a Beginning*, ed. John Courtney Murray (New York: Macmillan, 1966), pp. 37-42.

24. For historical confirmation of this point, see Gary Glenn, "Forgotten Purposes of the First Amendment Religion Clauses," *Review of Politics* 49 (Summer 1987): 340-67.

that its substance is "simply political" (p. 69), but that disarming assertion is negated by his argument as a whole. He also says that politics, for Americans, points beyond itself, that it gets "its human meaning" from the truth about human sacredness or dignity that lies beyond it. Americans can agree about religious freedom "in the absence of a consensus with regard to the theological concepts that govern the total life and destiny of man" (p. 72), but if their proposition or political consensus is to be intelligible, they must agree that for some reason or other human life and dignity transcend political life. In other words, they must affirm a metaphysical assertion that is distinctively Christian. It would appear that in order to defend their proposition, Americans must acknowledge a limit to their theological pluralism. Religious pluralism, Murray says, is "inherently disintegrative of *all* consensus and community" (p. 73; italics mine). Any community, if it is to be a community, must acknowledge its limitations. The First Amendment, as well as the Declaration, are parts of the "conservative Christian tradition" because they are not merely political, because they imply a metaphysical decision about the nature of man. That their authors were not fully aware of that fact simply means that they built better than they knew.

All that has been said about the Republic's Fathers' "moral values" can be granted without addressing the problem that Fortin (but not Murray) says we should overlook: Is the understanding of natural law in the Catholic or Christian tradition theoretically correct or even plausible? The modern attempt to free natural law from revelation is based on the premise that the human being does not, in fact, know himself to be a creature by nature. To experience the world as created and oneself as a creature requires knowledge that reason itself does not provide. For the originators of the modern project, the "creationist" metaphysics of Thomistic natural law is actually a combination of elements from reason and revelation. What is called natural law does not depend solely upon what we know by nature, and hence it must be rejected in the name of nature.[25]

Murray seems to acknowledge the validity of this criticism on some occasions. He says that all non-Christian thought tends to be "monistic." For Aristotle, *the* pre-Christian philosopher for the tradition of natural law, "man in the end was only citizen, whose final destiny was to be achieved within the City" (p. 15). He did not know of man's transpolitical dignity or sacredness. For the decisively post-Christian

25. Strauss, *Natural Right and History,* p. 164.

philosophers, Rousseau and his essentially secular successors, human distinctiveness or dignity is equated with being a citizen. Their concern, according to Murray, was the recovery, against the influence of Christianity, of "the integrity of the political order." For them, the unifying consensus is essentially a "civic faith" that subordinates church to state (p. 21). Murray even observes that "the chief phenomenon of modern times has been the development of secular civil religions."[26]

It appears at this point that man does not know his genuine freedom or sacredness by the testimony of his nature alone, inasmuch as it was not discovered by those philosophers whose thought was unillumined by revelation. Murray himself goes so far as to say that "Christianity freed man *from* nature by teaching him that he has an immortal soul," which he would have known by his nature. By so doing, "it taught him his own uniqueness, his own individual worth, the dignity of his own person, the equality of all men, the unity of the human race" (p. 192). Christianity freed human beings from what appears to unassisted reason to be the limits of their natures. Their genuine worth or dignity was not given to them by nature.

Because of the influence of Christianity, Murray says, human beings no longer experience themselves primarily as citizens. In our Christian consciousness, "every fatherland" is, to some extent, "a foreign land" (p. 15). We know we are not fully at home in or constrained definitively by our polity. Human beings know that, finally, they are free from the political community.

The integrity of the political order cannot be restored in post-Christian times except by "totalitarian" means, because it requires the forceful suppression of this consciousness of personal freedom. The truth of St. Augustine's criticism of civil theology and even pagan natural theology cannot easily be eradicated from the world, precisely because the criticism is true.[27] Post-Christian restoration, to the extent that it occurs, is never really a political restoration. Murray observes that the modern secularist must make "denials" that the pagan secularist did not. Hence, post-Christian "unification of social life" is not only more "forcible" but takes place on "a lower level than . . . Aristotle's" (p. 133).

---

26. Murray, "The Return to Tribalism," *Catholic Mind* 60 (January 1962): 8.
27. On the perennial relevance of the critical thrust of orthodox Christian theology, see my essay "Thoughts on America's 'Catholic Moment,'" *The Political Science Reviewer* 17 (1988): 206-8; and "Natural Law and the American Regime: Murray's *We Hold These Truths*." *Communio* 9 (1982): 370-71.

Totalitarian projects are revolts against the truth, especially the metaphysical truth about human existence. Perhaps Murray means to say that Christian revelation illuminated for human beings what they can know to be true independently of revelation about their sacredness or dignity. Genuinely self-conscious individuals cannot help but define themselves as more than parts of a political community, as not simply "absorbed" in some "monistic" whole. They know that a merely "civil theology" or even an impersonal "natural theology" do not address the most profound longings, implanted in them by nature. In a discussion of the "imperatives" of his own nature, Murray says that "my situation is that of a creature before God" (p. 329). He calls the modern denial of this situation "a basic betrayal of the existential structure of reality itself" (p. 215). He also contends that "instinctively and by natural inclination the common man knows that he cannot be free if his basic human things are not sacredly immune from profanation by the power of the state and by other secular powers" (p. 204).

Human beings know that they transcend the city as well as impersonal natural necessity. They know they are not God. They know they are not self-created. Do they know, by their natures as free and rational mortals, that they are free, as persons, under God? Is any other conclusion by a self-conscious mortal a rebellion against the truth, an antimetaphysical revolt? It is certainly true that post-Christian "monism," culminating in communism, has been at war with human self-consciousness. Murray understands this monism as being grounded in various scientific attempts to deny, in the name of reason's autonomy, the reality and sacredness of human transcendence or freedom (pp. 322-26).

For Murray, unlike Fortin, the fundamental human decision is not between reason and revelation, but for natural law. It is for the proposition that human reason, as it attempts to come to terms with the apparently rationally unsatisfactory problem of human freedom, can be illuminated by revelation. Only in the light of its influence does reason remain genuinely empirical, does it avoid the intellect's characteristic propensity toward reductionism or "monism." Murray contrasts natural law's "integrally human . . . outlook on man and society" with that of the educationism of "rationalism" (p. 320).

The fundamentally Christian insight of natural law is that although the human being is a citizen or political animal, he is most fundamentally much more. This dualistic doctrine appears deficient to those committed to socialist idealism and to those who would revive the perspective of classical political philosophy, the "integral" perspective of the polis. From the perspective of the political community, the question remains whether natural law gives sufficient dignity to political life. To say, as Murray does, that the end of the political order is different from and subordinate to the total end of the human person is to say that citizenship is a means to a higher, more comprehensive end, and this undermines the devotion that the political community requires of its members in order to perpetuate itself. A large part — perhaps too large a part — of Murray's defense of America is that it is good for the Church, and not simply good in itself. His key criticism of America is its failure to recognize sufficiently that the freedom it promotes and protects is ultimately the freedom of the Church (pp. 69-72). Whether American political freedom is good in itself Murray, the Christian, actually seems to leave open (p. 195).

Rousseau's assertion that one "cannot be a citizen and a Christian at the same time" seems to retain some force against natural-law theory. No dualistic account of human nature will be without tensions. Murray admits that any attempt at integration or "synthesis" will remain "ever precarious" (p. 196). That is one reason why the American proposition requires constant "development on penalty of decadence" (p. vii). The distinctiveness of natural law lies in its inclination toward integration or synthesis rather than reduction. It keeps alive, as Fortin says, "the ideal of human wholeness" without forgetting that it is to be actualized most fully in a personal and transpolitical sense.

Perhaps the most radical socialist and classical criticism of Christianity's denigration of politics is that it uproots human beings from communal devotion for the loneliness of the isolated individual. This deracination, as Heidegger says, produces an anxious "homesickness" in modern human beings that cries out for some sort of radical cure.[28] This line of thinking suggests that Christianity produces the negative freedom that leads to totalitarianism. Hence postmodern thought must, in part, entail overcoming the effects of Christianity.

Murray's response here is to agree that if human freedom is freedom *from* political community or citizenship but *for* nothing in particular, or if it amounts to nothing more than the lonely freedom of the isolated conscience (p. 206), then it is simply a source of misery and not worthy of human beings. Human self-consciousness or individuality might, as it grows, readily reach the nihilistic conclusion that it is itself no

28. For a good treatment of Heidegger's thought on this point, see Harry Neumann, "What Is Bigotry?" *Modern Age* 31 (1987): 45-51.

good. The "extreme individualism" of Lockean or "classical liberalism" (p. 129), which is reflected to some extent in Madison's antiecclesiastical interpretation of the creature's freedom of conscience, generates the extreme collectivism of totalitarianism (pp. 213-14, 322).

In the end, the understanding of freedom that Christianity brought into the world can be defended only as "freedom of the Church," freedom for membership in a "genuine intellectual community" (p. 21), "an order of culture" (p. 35) that transcends politics and resists politicization. Murray contends that the modern experiment in freedom has been an attempt to find a "secular substitute" for freedom of the church (p. 201). Its experience has shown that there is no such replacement. The very idea of natural law, as opposed to the idea of the state of nature, suggests that the human person cannot sustain his liberty outside a community of thought and belief (p. 331). Limited government or constitutionalism as a human good depends upon the possibility of such a community.

The truth of the matter is that people naturally long for liberation, and they know that true liberation cannot be political or historical. The American proposition is good primarily because, under its largely natural-law understanding of freedom, religion is guaranteed the full freedom to achieve its own proper task of the spiritual liberation of man. No account of the American proposition or "moral consensus" is adequate that does not acknowledge all that is implied by this truth.[29]

29. One issue not addressed here is the significance of the disintegration of the natural-law consensus in the Catholic intellectual community since Murray wrote. Consider that he sometimes worried that the tradition was, in truth, not even particularly alive in that community but was "merely being kept in custody" (Murray, "Catholics in America — A Creative Minority," *Catholic Mind* 53 [1955]: 594-95). The destruction of the consensus has, in fact, critically energized those who still defend natural law. According to Ronald Lawler, "these are good days to be Catholic scholars. . . . When I was a young student, almost all Catholic moralists taught what the Church authentically taught. But as I look over the moral texts I knew in those days, I am impressed by their poor quality. When the teachings of faith were assailed in the revolutions of our time, it became necessary for Catholic scholars to provide far better defenses for positions that were assailed on every side" ("The Catholic Vision of Higher Education," in *Catholic Higher Education*, ed. Paul Williams [Scranton: Northeast Books, 1989], p. 72).

According to Murray, crisis requires and hence brings forth radical thought. For evidence that these are good days to be natural-law thinkers, see Hittinger, "After MacIntyre"; and Fortin, "Natural Law and Social Justice" and "The New Rights Theory and Natural Law."

Animadversions on
John Courtney Murray's
Political Ontology

David T. Mason

". . . but we have the mind of Christ."

1 CORINTHIANS 2:16

A CAREFUL AND CRITICAL READING of John Courtney Murray's *We Hold These Truths,* while thought-provoking, is a discomforting experience. I have identified two reasons for my stimulated disquietude.

First, the essays collected under this title solicit from our intellectually neglectful time a most unseasonal and painfully exacting remembrance: theology is a preserve of profoundly good thought that has much to contribute to serious political thinking. I say this not as a theologian but as one who would dare do political philosophy within the environment of busy nescience many today denominate a *science* of the political.

Second, the essays are yet another disturbing expression of one of the enduring dilemmas defining the Western intellectual enterprise of moral-political inquiry: theologians invariably locate themselves in a universe of discourse on political being that never quite matches that of political philosophy. Numerous treatises on ethical comportment enucleate but rarely confront this perplexing incongruity. The sources of and reasons for this discontinuity are as varied and complicated as intellectual history itself, of course, and would require an impossibly

lengthy excavation of the Western mind to locate and identify in full
detail.

I would locate a part of the explanation for the incommensurate
dialogues of traditional moral theology and of normative political
philosophy in *ontology* — that is, in the varying historical modal constructions of our being in the world and of our thinking about this
political being. I prefer to call the political-philosophical activity that
addresses "political being" by the name of *political ontology*. I shall shed
some light on the meaning of this expression presently. Here I wish
to observe that since the Ionian pre-Socratics and the emergence of
Western philosophy out of mythopoeic categories of thought, moral-
political inquiry has flowed in two separate, albeit closely parallel,
riverbeds. Political philosophy and theology traditionally have talked
to and about human being in the world. The difficult and, for some,
the more controversial point is that the "human being" *of whom* both
traditions have spoken has not been the *same* human being. Aristotle's
paradigmatic *zoon politikon* is not the *homo divinum animal* of Christian
theology, predicated on the Judeo-Christian ontological *imago Dei*. (The
correct translation of Aristotle's expression is "political being.") It is
indeed true that the two traditions have often participated in a common *Seinsfrage*, or questioning of human being, characterized by abun-
dant cross-fertilization if not always by a cordial relationship, but it is
also true that we are here confronting not one but two modes of inquiry
and normative prescription. The fact of these two intellectual traditions, however, should in no way be construed as an argument *for* two
such traditions.

Between them, it seems to me, theology and traditional political
philosophy encompass the vital ontological questions of the human
condition. Theology has always had the more daunting task of explaining human being to human being — its essential origin, meaning, and
ultimate destiny. These are *the* important questions and issues; they
abide in sapience and cannot be postponed for very long, no matter
how hectic and cluttered we make our world. Political philosophy has
failed most miserably and most spectacularly in those moments when
it has neglected these basic problematics of our sapient being in its
noble quest for political order and ethical well-being.

These complex and interrelated issues of being, knowledge,
comportment, morality, and order constitute the premises and subject
of Murray's critical argumentation. They also appear, as one should
expect of reasoned inquiry and critique, in his conclusions. I am of

the opinion that the basic initiative of Murray's critical evaluation of the American moral-political condition is sound. My critical notice, necessarily generalized, will address the philosophical journey that links his premises to his critical and his normative conclusions. This is an urgent and stimulating journey, due in no small measure to the fact that it is an *agon*, a valiant struggle to repair the gaps between discrepant modes of moral-political thinking. And although Murray's journey is incomplete, as all such journeys must be, it remains as insistent for us as it was for him. The prospective loosening of our polity from its necessary ethical moorings, which he identifies, is daily impressed upon our social consciousness. The question begging an answer today is whether *we* possess John Courtney Murray's intellectual courage.

By way of concluding my preliminary remarks, I shall make three observations. First, the critical essay that follows is formulated in cognizance of the fact that *We Hold These Truths* is a collection of essays that Murray wrote over the course of several years. Second, I am aware that Father Murray was by vocation and training a Catholic theologian and that the greater part of his intellectual labors was devoted to theological matters, though a not-inconsiderable portion may be viewed as a prolegomenon to an American civil theology. Third, I have no intention of criticizing Murray for not writing the book that I would have written had I written his book of essays. But this is not to say that I have no serious objections to his arguments. I have. The following essay is a critical reaction to and elaboration of his penetrating analysis of the modern political ontology of American democracy, particularly its structuring theory of moral knowledge. I share Murray's conviction that contemporary political thinking must become critical of its ethically disengaged cognitive insularity. There is no gainsaying the plain urgency of interrogating a political epistemology that is ignorant of political being qua moral being.

The Structure and Contents of Murray's Basic Argument

I shall begin at the end, so to speak, and work my way back to Murray's several theses and arguments. In one significant respect, the essays composing *We Hold These Truths* are oddly organized. One must await the final essay to gain clarification and partial correction of three substantially incomplete impressions conveyed throughout the preced-

ing essays. The first incomplete impression that I sustained until reading the final thirty pages or so of Murray's presentation is that he is
asserting that the tradition of *ius naturale*, in its civic actualization, is
primarily a creation of the Catholic historical, intellectual experience.
The second impression I found bothersome is Murray's vague sug-
gestion that this old moral philosophy of *ius naturale* presented a formal
structure of natural-law political rights. And the third impression,
which the final essay does not remove, is Murray's adherence to ontological dualism in his political thinking.

These are more substantial than mere quibbles about textual
arrangement. The absence of a substantive consideration of the
powerful intellectual antecedents of Roman and medieval natural-law
philosophy and the vagueness suffered as to the time of the philosophical extraction of democratic political-ethical rights within natural-law theory, until partially redressed in the final essay, tend to
isolate Murray's discussions within the philosophical tradition of the
Church. A mere editorial tinkering will not remedy the problems, for
the fundament of the difficulty here is to be found in the ubiety of
the two traditions of moral-political inquiry noted above. A deeper
probing reveals the simultaneous presence of these two structures of
inquiry in the essays. The very presence of both traditions and Murray's attempts to decoct, in effect, the critical and normative acumen
of each and train this wisdom on an ethically vacuous modern rationalism impart to the essays much of their vigor, complexity, and
richness. Thematically and substantively, though, the prevailing categories of his basic argument are drawn from the tradition of theological moral inquiry — which is to say, from orthodox Thomistic philosophy. And his normative vision of the morally constituted political
order has at its heart the problematic ontological bifurcation that
remains, at work's end, unreconciled.

Ontological bifurcation, the descriptive or prescriptive presentation of a particular or comprehensive arrangement of the human
condition as two orders or dimensions of being, is not peculiar to the
moral-political thought of Christian theology. It is the defining
character of the ethical ideal-realism of Plato's influential political
philosophy. And, though differently formulated, it also structures the
subjectivist realism of contemporary empiricist political theory.

There is nothing surreptitious, moreover, about Murray's presentation of his normative vision. Early on, he explicitly states that, for
him, "the principles of Catholic faith and morality stand superior to,

and in control of, the whole order of civil life."[1] Does this claim disqualify him from political inquiry? I do not think so. Theologians dwell politically, too, and it is an empty intellectual conceit that would confine discussion of civic morality exclusively to "political" discourse. I do think, however, that his religious convictions place extraordinary demands on him in the context of his traditional and chosen universe of inquiry to be diligently open and faithful to the formulation and development of the nontheological tradition of political philosophy and to be sensitive to the fruits and intellectual influences of this inquiry. Murray's essays do not always meet these formidable and largely self-imposed demands.

Murray's interrogatory is profoundly ontological. It queries the American public credo regarding the conception, status, and definition of the ethical human being that it "holds" to be politically *true*. In this critical examination I ask Murray's text or basic argument to clarify and elaborate its *under*standing of the larger sapient political ontology of ethical human being in the world, of which the American polity and attendant intellectual experience is one *Seinsmodus* in a historical con-catenation of sapient modes of political being. This critical questioning is also prompted by, among other considerations, the inescapable fact of wandering valorizations in philosophical inquiry that inevitably re-quire the coloring of all thinkings in specific shadings, which is one source of systemic thinking.

What, then, is Murray's thesis? As the preceding remarks imply, Murray is engaging some of the fundamental and most important questions about human beingness. And he accomplishes this with a deceptively simple presentation of profoundly complicated ideas. The basic argument of his essays involves an interplay or weave of three distinct components: intellectual history, philosophical critique, and normative prescription. However, the warp and weft of these com-ponents constitute a single piece of moral-political argumentation that seeks to recover a natural-law ethic of political comportment that is *not* "political" in the modern sense of this term.

I believe it is fair to say that the informing thesis of his essays is presented in several formulations that correspond to the threefold architecture of his basic argument. Establishing the framework for his

---

1. Murray, *We Hold These Truths: Catholic Reflections on the American Proposition* (New York: Sheed & Ward, 1960), p. ix. Subsequent references to this volume will be made parenthetically in the text.

intellectual-history presentation, as well as for his critique, Murray makes a significant claim about the intellectual foundation and democratic content of the American Bill of Rights: "The 'man' whose rights are guaranteed in the face of law and government is, whether he knows it or not, the Christian man, who had learned to know his own personal dignity in the school of Christian faith" (p. 39). The Bill of Rights, especially the First Amendment's ordering distinction between church and state, is a historical product of the Christian intellectual legacy, Murray holds, albeit endowed at the founding with "a special embodiment adapted to the peculiar genius" of the American experience (p. 66).

The development of his intellectual-history thesis is primarily concerned with establishing, in natural-law philosophy, the saliency of Thomistic-Scholastic conceptions and, in political reality, with the ontological imperative of affirming the intrinsic sanctity or sacredness of human beings. As for the former, Murray submits the traditional claim that the natural law is a moral law that is rationally intelligible and thus ethically compelling for a sapient being possessing moral consciousness. Ultimately, Murray urges, the natural-law "dictates of common human reason are the dictates of God, who is Eternal Reason, the Logos" (p. 116). As for political reality, Murray advances the argument that the modern democratic idea of political freedom found its original articulation in the Church's early formulation of spiritual-sacerdotal freedom. In contrast to the classical world, Murray writes, the Christian world introduced "a Great Idea" — namely, "a radical distinction between the order of the sacred and the order of the secular" — an idea that was appropriated, although in altered form, by the modern political world (p. 202). The original formulation, Murray notes, was advanced by Gelasius I in A.D. 494 as "the freedom of the Church to be a participant in the freedom of the Incarnate Son of God, the God-Man, Christ Jesus." This freedom, Murray elaborates, possesses two dimensions: the immunity of the Church's "spiritual authority" in its several aspects from any secular restriction and the "intrapolitical" freedom of Christian people to participate in the "integral supernatural life" of their being within the earthly Church, *res sacra in temporalibus*. The foundation of this thesis, from which Murray derives the structuring ontological theory or "general theorem" of his critique and his normative argument, is the ontological concept of the human being as sacred, *res sacra homo*. The powerful import of the Gelasian doctrine, Murray postulates, is that there is more to politics than politics in the political ontology: the Church must be free to attend to, and to nourish, the essential spiritual beingness, freedom, and supernatural needs of human being in the world. Thus, the Gelasian thesis (which is Murray's basic thesis) of supra-intrapolitical sacredness, *res sacra*, articulated "the limiting principle of the power of government." That is to say, the Idea *qua* institution of the spiritual freedom of the visible Church "asserted an astounding new freedom on a title not of this world." And in its original formulation, Murray emphasizes, people "found their freedom where they found their faith — within the Church" (pp. 198, 202-5 *et passim*). An important corollary of this basic thesis, which assumes significance in Murray's critique, is his assertion that "the type of humanism called 'classical' has had little influence on American culture" (p. 177).

The thesis of Murray's critical discussion is similarly founded, addressing the disjunction that he perceives between the intellectual "patrimony" of the Church and the modern, secularized American political mind. His critical thesis, generally stated, is "that the political experiment of modernity has essentially consisted in an effort to find and install in the world a secular substitute for all that the Christian tradition has meant by the pregnant phrase, the 'freedom of the Church'" (p. 201). The primary target of his critique is the modern or positivistic epistemology, which he says "has declared the Gelasian doctrine to be heretical and has outlawed it, in the name of modern orthodoxy, which is a naturalist rationalism" (p. 210). The political self-understanding of the modern democratic world, he avers, is "monistic," conflating in a single notion of indivisible sovereignty the elements of secular democratic power, technical reason, and soulless morality. This "democratic monism," Murray declares, reduces complex political life to "a political technique" — namely, the device of majority vote naively founded in the presumed moral conscience of "the people." Part mystical political sentimentalism and part modern rationalism, this ethically untutored monistic reduction is resulting in a perverse spiritualization of the secular order that is clearly antithetical to the Christian concept of the political state "as a limited order" subordinate to "the organized moral conscience of society [that is] formed and mobilized by the Church" (pp. 208-9).

Within the context of American political culture, these dynamics of secularism and rationalism have created havoc in the public mind. But they have been assisted in this, Murray argues, by an internecine battle of minds, the clash between Protestant and Catholic conceptions of moral-political principles of comportment. It is a battle that has been won and lost. Protestantism traditionally has distrusted human reason. It has nourished, in the practice of self-interpretation of Scripture, a religious-moral subjectivism that is political-epistemological kin to modern scientific rationalism.

In Murray's view, the Protestant mind once prevailed. It articulated what he calls the "old morality" of the American polity, individualistic and mystical in its belief that personal moral goodness would somehow translate into a political morality of collective goodness. Today, however, this "old morality" reposes in effective ruin, its lack of philosophical and political sophistication all too evident (pp. 276ff.).

But the "new morality" pushing through the ruins and shadows of the old is even more frightening. It is narrowly rationalistic, subjective, pragmatic, and immanentist in its ersatz ethical orientation. It, too, he claims, rejects "the whole style and structure of natural-law morality" (p. 279). The political-epistemological reciprocal of Murray's thesis here is that the American public mind is *losing* its civic mind to the extent that it continues to neglect the inherited, authentically founded ethical truths and political vocabulary of traditional natural law that are still vital in the Catholic legacy.

Moving to his normative argument, Murray claims that "the growing conviction as to the ultimate impotence of the old attempts to solve the problem of human liberty and social order in purely secularistic, positivist terms [has] created a new openness to the world of metaphysical and religious values" (p. 320). The premodern formulations of reason, order, freedom, and truth once again appear attractive in their recovered wisdom. There is, Murray stipulates, promise of a "return" to the enduring ethical-ontological substance of the historical traditions of moral-political inquiry.

Murray's normative argument is an ambitious, prescriptive restatement and synthesis of his presentation of the intellectual history of natural-law philosophy and his critical discussion of modernity. The heart of his normative presentation is the metaphysics of natural law. It is an ontological-epistemological thesis, he stipulates, that harbors "vital resources" for the modern political condition. The epistemology of natural-law knowledge is realist; it "asserts the real to be the measure of knowledge" and is grounded in the nature of man. This epistemology presumes an ontology whereby and wherein "nature is a teleological concept, [meaning] that the 'form' of a thing is its 'final cause,' the goal of its becoming [and] that there is a natural inclination in man to become what in nature and destination he is — to achieve the fullness of his own being" (pp. 327-28). Further, the ontology and epistemology of natural law presuppose a natural theology, "asserting that there is a God, Who is eternal Reason, *Nous,* at the summit of the order of being, Who is the author of all nature, and Who wills that the order of nature be fulfilled in all its purposes, as these are inherent in the natures found in the order" (p. 328). Finally, Murray stipulates that because the human being is a rational and teleological being, the natural law presupposes a morality in the order of nature that "is an order of reason and therefore freedom. The order of being that confronts his intelligence is an order of 'oughtness' for his will; the moral order is a prolongation of the metaphysical order into the dimensions of human freedom" (p. 328). Pulling his stipulations together, Murray presents his basic normative thesis: natural law is "immanent in the nature of man, but transcendent in its reference" (p. 329).

This normative thesis is the least developed and the least compelling component of Murray's basic argument. The logic and the substance of the theological predicates of his presentation overpower the moral-political contents of the ancient *Wiederkehr* that he tardily and parsimoniously introduces. This normative formulation is a nebulously eloquent, though unmistakably bifurcated, political ontology of *res sacra–res publica.*

To be sure, I have presented only the skeleton of his argument's initiatives; these must be elaborated. I turn, then, to the primary tasks — namely, the critique of Murray's basic argument and the exploration of possibilities for expanding his project of refounding the moral consciousness of contemporary American political culture. I will begin by critically examining the philosophical presuppositions of his presentation.

A Critical Thinking about Murray's Thinking about Political Being

Each and every act of philosophical thinking is an expression of presuppositions. Although trivially obvious, we frequently lose sight of this fact in the cool excitement of marshaling *our* individual clarity of thought against another's fuzzy thinking. Yet, in the activity of self-conscious cognition, the most one can ever hope to achieve is that one's thinking is also a reflexivity. For *reflexivity* — the critical thinking about our thinking about our being in the world — binds thought to the inclusive ontology of sapient being in the world.[2] This reflexivity is nothing more than the ancient motor-power of traditional philosophy, science, *and* common sense. We execute it, more or less profoundly, every day when, to give an illustration from epistemology, we quite simply *know* that the fact-value distinction of empiricism is sheer suppositional and methodological delusion (i.e., formally embraced illusion). Moreover, reflexivity, which founds grand philosophy in mundane common sense, is the bond of our *common* sapience. Some philosophers, I realize, abhor any formulation that suggests their profundities are somehow "common." This is a pity. Even philosophers — indeed, especially philosophers — are in need, to paraphrase Ernest Hemingway, of a built-in, shock-proof nonsense detector. And reflexivity does not demand the sort of gratuitous obscurantism found in the opaque philosophical Eurospeak of, for example, deconstructionism and sundry linguistic analytics that incessantly talk about the *talk* of thinking but never get around to thinking about the ontological substance of thought.

Now, Murray is sensitive to the relation between presuppositions and thinking. His essays appear to initiate an exercise in critical thinking. In his introduction he states that public discourse is necessary to "preserve" the heritage of the learned, extracted truths of civility that abide in the "depository of the public mind." This locus of truth, however, is vulnerable to the preying vicissitudes of sophistry, skeptical delights, "forgetfulness," and the eventual destruction of the public consensus on civil truth. "High argument alone will keep it alive, in the vital state of being 'held,'" he writes. Life-informing truths are fragile entities that live *in* the becoming order of human being. And though wrested from "the structure of reality" in the activity we call philosophy, and held to be true "because they are true," they must yet be subjected to the "constant scrutiny of political experience" and the "life of man in society" (p. 11). But he then makes a statement that appears to delimit reflexivity. Following a caveat that this scrutiny must constantly recur "to first principles," he observes in a runic, parenthetical remark that "one is, I take it, on the brink of impotence and nihilism when one begins to be aware of one's own awareness of what one is doing, saying, thinking. This is the paralysis of all serious thought; it

2. I discuss this issue of reflexivity and the matter and details of political ontology in my forthcoming book *Greek Political Ontology*.

is likewise the destruction of all the spontaneities of love" (p. 12). In fact, he is clearly rejecting commitment to critical reflexivity, advocating in its stead "reflections" informed by a priori, unchanging truth principles.

The notion of "reflection" as a critical activity of philosophical sapience is slippery. Some thinkers argue that it is, in its modern or current usage, an empiricist doctrine that allows us to view ideas as examinable, internal "things." Often identified as *introspection,* this is an epistemological fable introduced to the modern world by Descartes and elevated to the level of philosophical nonsense by Locke and his Enlightenment disciples. Others, including Murray, view it in a Platonic sense; philosophical reflection is the *bios theoretikos,* the thinking of transcendent, eternal absolutes that no thinking, then, now, or ever, will deabsolutize. Reflexivity asks: What is the relationship of presuppositions to this Platonic reflection? How does this reflection distinguish between those truths we hold true "because they *are* true" and those truths we hold true because we *say* they are true or because we *want* them to be true?

Murray has an answer to these questions. They are the questions of "the barbarian at the gates of the city," who comes clad as businessperson, liberal scholar, pragmatist, technician, utilitarian, and ethical relativist. Murray's rejection of reflexivity reveals, I think, an epistemological relationship that structures and colors his political thinking. First, his introductory remarks exhibit a profound intellectual conservatism, a combination of diffidence at the prospect of what Camus called metaphysical rebellion, particularly in the public mind, and an adherence to a fixed, received wisdom, what he describes as "the inherited intuitive wisdom by which the people have always lived," which a critical "awareness" presumably threatens (p. 12). At times he seems to speak in a voice that combines Burke, Carlyle, and St. Paul: "society is rescued from chaos only by a few men, not by the many. *Paucis humanum vivit genus.* It is only the few who understand the disciplines of civility and are able to sustain them in being and thus hold in check the forces of barbarism that are always threatening to force the gates of the City" (p. 13). Second, his remarks intimate the dualistic configuration of his forthcoming ontological and epistemological formulations.

Thus, my first major criticism of Murray's basic argument pertains to his conception of the nature or ontology of thought. I am not persuaded that reflexive consciousness (i.e., being "aware of what one is doing, saying, thinking") necessarily portends the arrival of nihilism. When allowing for the American cultural shadows within which he pens these sentences — the ugly and destructive witch-hunts of the fifties, their now-comical sleuths skulking about in the irrational ambience of "The Red Scare," mixed with the strange, new phenomena of the "Beat Generation" and rock music and, for many, the worrisome incipience of mass secularism and consumerism — Murray's condemnations are understandable, yet philosophically excessive. Indeed, at moments they bespeak a structuring intellectual orthodoxy that *in principle* is not unlike that of the "modernity" he critiques. Murray knows that authentic philosophy is not a ritualistic activity and that it cannot, as a life-informing corpus, consist in finished-fact truth. If such were the case, *political* philosophy would become institutionalized and the political philosopher and the public intellectual would be reduced to systemic housekeepers. Murray says as much. But his conception of philosophy, his view of truth, and his scope of inquiry and critique are too limited by theological presuppositions. Here we confront the politics of knowledge.

Murray's ontology of thought is an aristocracy. Mine is a democracy. In my understanding of sapience, reflexivity queries *all* truths, no matter how great, ancient, or pedigreed, asking them *why* they are true and worthy of being held. A cognitive-philosophical agent of checks and balances, this critical awareness does not come to the examination of truth *with* truth; it comes with the enduring ontological questions that most "systems" of thought prefer not to think, much less ask. *Of course* there is danger in this reflexive conception of philosophy! Many will see in it the specter, even the reality, of anarchy or ethical relativism. The fear of prudentially unfettered and untutored critical thinking is wise. But the fear of an authentic philosophical consciousness, I am prepared to argue, is almost always a fear or caution engendered from the desire to preserve some reigning orthodoxy. It is also an expression of comprehensive distrust of critical reason.

Every epistemological aristocracy raises the intellectual barbarian's visage and warns of his imminent visitation. Such is the character of the politics of knowledge. But these aristocrats also know that the politics of knowledge invariably involve the social-cognitive sanctification or elevation of "truth." When truth, of any kind, is not subject to reflexive critique — whether bred of fear of nihilism or the worship of "held" truth or outlawed by decree — the result is cognitive immurement. And the consequent awareness is the intellectual consciousness

one finds expressed, say, in *Exsurge Domine* (the 1520 papal bull ordering the burning of Martin Luther's writings; Luther later retaliated in
kind, publicly burning scores of books on canon law and Church
philosophy). Or it is the "consciousness" found in the popular media
today, wherein amorphous banality, strident self-interest, moral vacuity,
and every imaginable commodity fetish become "concept"-for-a-day
on the American merry-go-round of intellectual "excellence." Sadly,
the unreflexive consumers of this consciousness are the constituents of
a republic of intellectual turnips in which "philosophy" is debased to
the scribbling of lists.

The philosophical awareness of reflexivity is this: it is a critical
consciousness of reigning, learned consciousness, a critical thinking
about serious thinking that is sapience aware of what it is doing, saying,
thinking in the world. In the absence of reflexivity, "nihilism" is *ontologically* meaningless; so is "truth." Moreover, in political reality the
politics of knowledge is as real as the civil politics of power, positive
law, resource allocation, and other activities of maintaining a *commonwealth*, for the latter proceed upon the constructions of the former.
Where there is no critical spark of reflexivity, there is no authentically
illuminating thinking. There is only the ritualistic incantation of cognitive recipes and the liturgical reading of the obscure tables of "truths"
crowding the hallowed library of the public mind.

This Murray says, but incompletely. He protects certain truths
(those he brings to his criticism) from critical scrutiny — which is to
say, from the fray of the ineradicable politics of knowledge. But if
knowledge is not coextensive with the purview of critical sapience,
then there exists a very good possibility, as both intellectual history
"and" political history demonstrate, that an institutionalized bifurcation between thought and being will define the political ontology.
Worlds of sapience-debilitating ontological distinctions obtain in the
separation of *Ecce Veritas!* from *Ecce Homo Sapiens!* In such thought-
being bifurcation, sapient being encounters its sapience as ontological
"other." A part of sapient being in the world is thus not *of* the world
and thus not accessible to critical thought. In effect, this is precisely
what Murray endorses when he claims that only "a few men" (and,
by extension, a few great ideas) can stave off chaos. He is not advocating intellectual tyranny; neither is he advocating a democracy of
critical sapience. I have no illusions in this matter. I believe the matter,
the problems, and the politics of truth are more complicated than
Murray lets on, or realizes. For example, his failure to elaborate the

spiritual-religious consciousness to which he alludes, shortly after his "few men" assertion, is telling. It presumes the Augustinian two-cities doctrine and renders the citizen an explicitly bifurcated being — a *political* being (from classical antiquity) and a sapience-transcendent *spiritual* being (from Christianity). Such may be sound fideist theology, but it makes reflexive political thinking profoundly problematic, if not impossible.

Murray's Intellectual History

Murray's representation of the intellectual history of Western political philosophy is incomplete. Therein, the diverse voices of Hellenic, Hellenistic, and Roman political thinkers and texts tell not their own respective histories but that of the early and medieval church's intellectual experience. This is my second major criticism of Murray's essays. I do not believe this foreshortened and mildly tendentious presentation of the antecedent or pre-Christian expression of political philosophy is a fatal defect. I do believe that the philosophical content of Murray's argument, as regards this antecedent political thinking, is insufficiently crystallized. His argument will be meaningfully augmented by briefly exploring and elaborating the wealth of classical formulations dwelling silently in his essays.

Consider, first, Murray's claim that it is the formal sapience of "the Christian man" that informs the ethical-political contents of the founding American consensus. This claim is at once overstatement and understatement. It simultaneously exaggerates the saliency of religion's influence and diminishes the presence of secular and orthodoxy-neutral thinking in the founding American intellect. This assertion by Murray is also problematic. First, it is structured by negation. That is, it is first and foremost an argument against Enlightenment rationalism through which Murray uncritically produces a piece of intellectual history *de novo*, paying inadequate attention to the fact that classical philosophy is architectonic for both medieval and modern political philosophy. Second, the substance of the classical contribution to the uniquely American synthesis of democratic and constitutional theorizing is sheared off in his unexplored claim that the humanism of classical republicanism "has had little influence on American [political] culture" (p. 177). Our modern understanding of the term *republic* has come to us through the Aristotle-Polybius-Cicero-

Machiavelli tradition, reinvigorated in the English and American republican thinkers. And though I am reluctant to enter the Hartz-Hallowell-Pocock-Diggins debate regarding the seminal intellectual influences on the founding, the following observations are in order.

Thomas Jefferson, a deist, did not participate in the theism of "the Christian man." He was an Enlightenment rationalist. And he was a philosopher of republicanism who, I am told, kept a copy of Cicero's *De Republica* at bedside. His view of traditional, institutionalized religion vis-à-vis the political life can be gathered from his Virginia Bill for Establishing Religious Freedom and in his famous "wall of separation" letter to Nehemiah Dodge. Jefferson, like his fellow deist Tom Paine, took nothing on its face — which is to say, unreflexively — and this included "Lockean" liberalism, the claims of the Christian tradition, neoclassical republican thought, the rationalistic optimism of the French *philosophes,* and a host of native schools of political thought. Madison's thinking was equally eclectic and equally impossible to reduce to and capture within Christian orthodoxy. And it is to be noted that the Bill of Rights was urged on Madison by Jefferson for prudential reasons — specifically, to thwart the antifederalist drive for a second Constitutional Convention, which they agreed would be a disaster for the new republican experiment and its charter. Thus, a *republican* ethos did obtain. The framers were critically alive to the touch of vital intellectual history *beyond Christian categories.*

One is able to discern standing beside Murray's Christian man at the American founding the presence of the ancient Greek philosopher, Moses and the Decalogue, the Hellenistic neo-Platonist, the Roman Stoic, and a virtual army of Jewish, Arab, and critical Christian thinkers, including John of Paris, Marsilio of Padua, and William of Occam, as well as antisectarian, "modern" political philosophers from Machiavelli to Hobbes to Jefferson. It is quite simply inaccurate, as Murray claims, that " 'the West' [is] a concept that has no meaning apart from Christianity" (p. 198). Or if it is accurate, as an isolated, constitutive historical truth, then it is banal; equivalent statements may be uttered, respectively, of the ancient Hebrews, the Greek pre-Socratics, the classical *polis,* the Roman *res publica,* the Enlightenment, the Industrial Revolution, and any additional, intellect- and polity-defining moments that might come to mind. Conceptually, "the West" is incomprehensible as anything other than an organic historical-intellectual matrix, a matrix in which the Catholic Church and,

later, sectarian Christianity played very important but not conceptually monolithic roles.[3]

As suggested, natural-law philosophy long antedates Scholasti-
cism, beginning with the articulation of Western philosophy in Ionia,
when the early mythopoeic vessels of religious categories were redefined as the cosmological-ontological vessels of reflexively self-
conscious thinking. This transformation was started by a group of
sixth-century B.C. thinkers known as the *Physikoi*. They looked to nature
(physis) for ethical principles of order *(kosmos)*. One such principle or
natural law was the *Logos* of Heraclitus. He argued that all human
beings are potentially capable of knowing the ethical instruction of
nature's *Logos,* in that the human soul *(nous),* or informing individual
logos, naturally harmonizes Nature's Law. The *Physikoi* are accorded
the status of "the first philosophers," acknowledged even by Plato,
because they transfigured the act and contents of thinking about our
sapient being. In the place of self-exculpatory polytheism and animism,
they installed the rationally liberating principles and forms of critical
and ethical thinking requisite for integrating ontological theories of
political order and moral obligation.

Following the classical period of Greek philosophy, Hellenistic
Stoicism elaborated the naturalistic ethical ontology of the *Physikoi*.
In the developmental and varying formulations of Zeno of Citium,
Chrysippus, Panaetius, and Seneca, the conception of an integrated
rational-ethical cosmos was taken well beyond what is presented in
the surviving fragments of the *Physikoi*. Greco-Roman Stoicism contains a theological dimension not common to earlier Greek philosophy, a dimension that anticipates, together with neo-Platonism, the

---

3. Much of the Hartz-Pocock et al. debate is reductionist in nature. It is true
that several of the informing principles of modern democratic political philosophy
are secular restatements of Judeo-Christian precepts of human dignity and the
universal preciousness of every human being. But it is questionable that the political
content of these principles exclusively originates in this religious tradition, as *The
Federalist Papers* numbers 18 and 63 and John Adams's critique of ecclesiastical law
indicate.

The American founders were intellectually eclectic. It simply will not do to
make them captive to any single tradition of thought. Certainly Jefferson, Madison,
Adams, Paine, and the others were familiar with the Christian tradition. For very
few, however, did individual political educations end there. On intellectual-political
"concessions" to religion in America at the time of the revolution, see Gordon S.
Wood, *The Creation of the American Republic, 1776-1787* (Chapel Hill, N.C.: University
of North Carolina Press, 1969), pp. 118-99.

monotheistic Christian ontology of a universal divine-natural law and a universal humanity.

With Panaetius (ca. 185-110 B.C.) Stoicism is brought to Rome. The Roman conception of *humanitas* is based, in part, on Panaetius's tutoring of critical thinkers such as Cicero in Greek political thought, as synthesized in the ethical philosophy of Stoicism. *Humanitas* thus expresses, in addition to Stoic universalism, echoes of Plato's transcendent ethical *Agathon* and Aristotle's ontological *spoudaios*. More to the point, the political philosophy of *humanitas* sustains the classical world's *integrated meaning* of political-ethical being. *Arete* and *virtus* are incomprehensible apart from the classical ontology of political thought, particularly that of Plato and Aristotle, for whom *episteme* (science) was ethical in content. This is most vividly expressed in Aristotle's definition of political science *(politike)* as "the architectonic science" of ethical human being, which he erected on recovered *Physikoi* premises. It is this ancient-classical ethical naturalism, among other significant influences that we cannot here explore, that suffuses the moral sapience of universalistic Stoic natural law and the republican political theory of Polybius, Cicero, and, later, Marsilio.

Stoicism, then, with considerable philosophical cargo, constituted the intellectual environment of the Roman jurists' articulation of *ius naturale*. Of course, the changing political context was the proximate pressing stimulus.

Begun in the first century B.C., the juristic elaboration (i.e., codification) of natural law assumed great urgency in the second and third centuries A.D. Severe and complex problems had been generated by the enduring confrontation between *ius civile* (the older law governing Roman citizens) and *ius gentium* (the various legal systems and principles of the peoples who had been absorbed into the empire). In the hands of the jurists, the eventual *ius civile–ius gentium* synthesis, in time and usage, became equivalent to *ius naturale*, though not identical in content. The legal or juristic law *(lex)* was compatible with the older Stoic conception of the general moral law *(ius)*; the jurists did not view as necessarily corrupt positive law that contradicted the philosophical corpus of *ius naturale*. These two terms, important in later canonical and modern natural law, were used interchangeably by the Roman jurists, with *ius* possessing the more expansive denotations of both juridical rule and abstract, ethical principles of right conduct. But, as noted above, no structure of democratic "political rights" was articulated in the Roman natural-civil law (or in its medieval redefinition).

Though Murray is aware of the origin of natural-law philosophy in antiquity, and though he mentions the contributions of the classical periods, he does not explain these crucial intellectual linkages as they bear on his *theological* understanding of traditional natural-law thinking. In fact, Murray claims that the traditional natural law received its "developed expression . . . in St. Thomas Aquinas and the later Scholastics" (p. 301). This raw assertion is untenable. By omission, he allows a rather charitable reading of the political project of the medieval canonists, which is perplexing in that he is an acknowledged authority on this period.

The *jus canonicum,* canon law, at length reformulated the Greek-Hellenistic-Roman natural law within the unsettled context of the intellectual and doctrinal desiderata of the medieval church at odds with its political environment. The avowed purpose of canon law was to articulate the independent institutional legitimacy of ecclesiastical authority in matters of Church governance, faith, doctrine, and morals. The prevailing practice of canon law, as Otto Gierke amply demonstrates, was a politics of knowledge (i.e., elaboration of the justification for the dominance of the secular political order by the Church), a project that extended from the eleventh to the sixteenth century.

The theological theory of canonical political thought was that the community is a single corporate body with two authoritative realms, spiritual and temporal.[4] But the intellectual, political reality of the day consisted in a prolonged battle to surmount this *sacerdotium et regnum* dualism by absorbing the secular order into the ecclesiastical. The authoritative, though ambiguous, basis for this assimilation had been posited by Pope Gelasius I in what Murray identifies as the confrontation of old and new ideas. In response to Emperor Zeno's *Henotikon,* declaring the secular ruler's power to do theology and participate in the governance of the Church, Gelasius enunciated his doctrine of the interdistinct spheres of ecclesiastical and secular authority. Gelasius's statement became the focus of the politics of knowledge that occupied the High Middle Ages, during which period several popes and many canonists moved to place all power in the *sacerdotium.* Gelasian dualism became, ironically, a project in political monism!

The working premise of these canonists' argument was derived,

---

4. The political part of canon law was predicated on some notable fictions, including the fraudulent "Decretals" attributed to St. Isidore of Seville and the "Donation" of Constantine.

inter alia, from Scripture and Augustine. Secular authority is a consequence of the fall; it is divine in origin but ancillary and therefore subordinate to the ecclesia's authority, which comes directly from God. According to Otto Gierke, "this absorption of the state is . . . clearly proclaimed by Gregory VII. . . . Then Innocent III gave the doctrine the juristic shape in which it passed into the Canon Law. . . . When Boniface VIII has given to this doctrine a final form [in *Unam Sanctam*] it is widely spread abroad by the canonists."[5] The canonists politically viewed the *ecclesia* as the *civitas*. Thus, Gierke argues that "it is a mistake to represent the great Popes as proclaiming, and the common opinion of the Middle Ages as accepting, only . . . 'indirect power in temporalities' " (i.e., in secular affairs).[6]

The canonists' labors in this project were only incidentally supported by the philosopher-theologians. St. Thomas Aquinas creatively reworked the old natural-law philosophy into the *Lex Aeterna,* now viewed as the source of all other law, principally *lex naturalis.* Now, too, positive law *(lex humana, lex positiva)* may not contradict natural law, as a general rule. The fundamental point, though, is that in St. Thomas the architectonic vessels of classical moral-political philosophy *and* the categories of patristic theology were reflexively reconfigured and synthesized into an expanded theology. But canon law, when viewed as a project in the politics of knowledge, is seen to have been less interested in a theological philosophy of natural law and more interested in legitimating the *ecclesia* as the sole interpretive voice of the theologian's divinely ordained natural law heard throughout the temporal political ontology of sapient being in the world. *Political* epistemology thus walks with Murray's Christian man.

On this expanded reading, the *jus canonicum* emerges as an instrument of disputation, potentially casting into doubt Murray's thesis of the unclouded origin of *political* freedom. As the legalist opposition was quick to point out to the canonists, "freedom" had no univocal social signification in this dispute. The canonists were arguing for *libertas ecclesiastica* as superordinate abstraction and as power. The political reality of freedom was altogether different, as a brief examination of feudal law illustrates (e.g., *Homo Ecclesiasticus,* a church vassal, an agricultural worker). The *Feodarum Consuetudines,* a twelfth-century publication that became the

5. Gierke, *Political Theories of the Middle Ages* (1900; rpt., Boston: Beacon Press, 1958), pp. 105-6.
6. Gierke, *Political Theories of the Middle Ages,* p. 108.

basis of subsequent digests of feudal law, defines *liber* as the condition of *exemption from* the service or jurisdiction of another. It is the grim political reality of unfreedom, together with the church's power politics, that prompted opponents such as Marsilio, Nicholas of Cusa, and, later, Machiavelli to invoke the older tradition of republican political theory to interdict the canonical politics of the new Christian freedom.[7] Murray is, of course, correct in his statement that traditional natural-law philosophy has no Roman Catholic presuppositions. But the statement is rather beside the point of a reading of the intellectual history of natural law, in which only Roman Catholic presuppositions matter.

Murray's Critique

In his critical argument, Murray focuses on the Enlightenment antecedents of America's philosophically naive and oxymoronic moral-secularism. He is profoundly disturbed by the secular basis and import of the modern rationalist epistemology and its political derivative, "democratic monism." He views the modal political ontology of modernity as an "indictment of Christianity" and thinkers such as Marsilio, Hobbes, and Rousseau as "prophets of modernity [who are] united in viewing the freedom of the Church . . . as a trespass upon, and a danger to" the modern political order (p. 207). Thus the political philosophy of John Locke, "that most decadent of all philosophical things, a nominalist" (p. 309), is nothing more than the uncritical "reflex of the socio-philosophical individualism of a superficial age" that apotheosized the morally untutored reason of the self-interested individual (p. 306).

7. The political conflict between *sacerdotium* and *imperium* is only part of the story of the Middle Ages. The perhaps more significant dynamic involved two modes of political philosophy. "Beneath this movement, however, there was an internal contest, which in the history of ideas was of more importance than all the external differences between partizans — namely, the contest between properly Medieval and 'Antique-Modern' Thought" (Gierke, *Political Theories of the Middle Ages*, p. 3). This contest, I have argued, is nearly invisible in Murray's presentation.

Elsewhere, however, Murray is critical of the political project in the medieval Church to absorb the secular order. In a 1948 paper, for example, he criticizes the medieval Church for at times ignoring the Gelasian intent and the legitimate autonomy of the political sphere. See Murray, "Governmental Repression of Heresy," in *Proceedings of the Catholic Theological Society of America* (Chicago: Catholic Theological Society of America, 1948), pp. 26-98.

As stated above, I agree with Murray's critical initiative. But, as with his intellectual history, his analysis of Enlightenment epistemology is somewhat narrow; and his critique of the modern American political mind is inadequate, due primarily to his unwillingness to admit historical humanistic influences of classical republicanism. This, in turn, permits him to argue for the special salutary value of the church's patrimony of natural-law philosophy as normative-epistemological corrective.

The ontological premise of Murray's critical argument is that the citizen's sacred beingness, *res sacra homo,* is a distinct and related order of spiritual freedom. This, of course, is the Gelasian thesis: it is the church, not the secular order, that recognizes and sustains sacredness and thus constitutes, "on a title not of this world," a necessary *spiritual order* and authority *qua ecclesia* in the temporal political ontology. Hence, a political thinking that does not recognize or heed this title is suspect or, as in the modern configuration of political thought, hostile. And this hostility, which today holds the Gelasian doctrine in outlawry, has its origins in the seventeenth- and eighteenth-century redefinition of moral-political philosophy. This brings us to Murray's Enlightenment critique, which focuses on the Locke-Rousseau nexus that he takes to be definitive for the structure and substance of modern political thought, mentioning Hobbes and Descartes peripherally.

In Locke's liberal individualism, natural law is reduced to "a collection of particular empowerments considered desirable for the preservation of 'property'" and "the free functioning of self-interest" (p. 309). Yet Locke was hardly original, Murray notes; he merely restates in a vulgarized form "the central medieval tradition of the supremacy of law over government, and of government by law which is reason, not will" (p. 313). Murray's critical assessment of Lockean individualism and natural law must be connected to the medieval corpus that they displace. This requires a brief look at the thought of Hobbes and Descartes, two central figures in the formulation of the rationalism of modernity. Hobbes's political philosophy constitutes the crucial link between medieval and modern natural-law theory. Descartes's philosophy shapes modernity's theory of knowledge, including its ignorance of being. Both thinkers are on the cusp of the Enlightenment and initiate much that occupies Locke, Rousseau, and the mind of modernity.

In his *Leviathan,* Hobbes extracts a presocial and inalienable "right of nature" from the old *ius naturale.* A law of nature *(lex),* he posits, is a negative dictate discovered by reason; a right *(jus)* is a liberty, even if brutishly executed. With this formulation begins the modern political philosophy of contractarian, natural-law theory. Hobbes redefines what he takes to be the traditional confounding of *jus* and *lex* in heretofore linguistic-conceptual misconstructions of the order and operation of natural law. Locke "liberalizes" Hobbes's severe, mechanistic political scheme, but in the matter of natural law he essentially follows Hobbes's individualistic initiative and elaborates its bourgeois accommodation and empiricist ethical nescience. The neoclassical humanistic formulation of Grotius's natural law is eclipsed in the Enlightenment rush to elaborate the Lockean contents of the Cartesian ontology of sapience.

What Hobbes is to modern political philosophy, Descartes is to the structure of modern epistemology. Murray's critique of this epistemology misses its salient feature. Descartes's *Cogito,* with its bifurcating *res cogitans–res extensa* construct, is ontological delusion. It expresses a subjectivistic theory of knowledge that does not know the knowing being and thus renders the *ego cogitans* worldless in epistemological illusion. This is the source of the malevolent "Cartesian dream" that Murray describes, in which the deluded, individualistic, worldless *ego* today appropriates nature, and its *self,* in a practiced political ontology of "rational" and ethical negation.

The great irony of Enlightenment rationalism in the American founding, however, is that the American rationalists did not uncritically endorse untutored individual reason, and not primarily out of religious convictions. Simply stated, the American political-intellectual order is *not* wholly identical to the ontology of modern positivistic thought. Murray mistakes dominance for complete "evacuation." This mirrors his neglect of the substantial influence of classical moral-political philosophy in the American republic, which yet holds "political" equivalent to a *pluralistic community* of sapient human dignities.

Murray simplifies the pluralism of the American political order. It is a pluralism that goes beyond theology, naturalist rationalism, secularism, and the plethora of technological-commercial illusions of well-being. We have a Constitution *because* the founders did not naively and mystically believe "the people" would be constant, politically rational republicans, *always* upholding the rule of law, respecting others' humanity, and exercising political power with the indifference of a Cincinnatus. Enlightenment optimism, in other words, was — and is — balanced by the historical skepticism of classical-modern republicanism and constitutionalism. This is the American elaboration of classical humanism Murray fails to detect. It prevents, or has prevented, Murray's "democratic monism" from becoming the *exclusive* self-understanding of the American political mind. Still, Murray is accurate in his perception of the reductionist tendencies of positivism and individualism, which obtain unique nourishment in a democratic context. I submit, however, that the principal defect of Murray's critique is its insensitivity to the role of reflexivity in *political* thinking. There is more locution than substance in Murray's claim that the American political community "is not the repository of the tradition of reason on any moral issue you would like to name" (p. 291). His indictment bespeaks not only exclusion but also a restricted view of the preserve of moral-political sapience.

The key to understanding Murray's political ontology, both as *Seinsfrage* and as a normative *Seinsmodus* of particular institutions, values, and practices, is realizing that he is making several arguments simultaneously: theological, historical, philosophical, political, epistemological, and ontological. Nowhere in the essays is this more evident than in his critique, where he contends that the epistemology of modern rationalism and the ontology of modern political thought are coeval and homologous. This uniform political sapience of modernity, he claims, has made the transcendent structure of Christian revealed values *immanent* in the historical political ontology.

Despite its eloquence, Murray's Great-Idea argument is not, at bottom, an argument *about the political ontology*. It is an argument for the authority of transcendent wisdom and judgment *in*, but not *of*, the political condition. His claim that Christianity "altered the structure of [classical] politics" when it introduced a competing center of spiritual and legal authority but that it "did not change the nature of politics, law, and government, which still remain rational processes" is confused (p. 289). *Of course* the theocentric Christian religion and its elaborate theology of the immortal created soul, redemption, the Church, faith, salvation, and the metaphysic of the eschaton altered both the contents and configuration of the classical self-understanding of *kosmos* and sapient political being. On the other hand, what Murray takes to be modernity's politics in the "image of political man" (i.e., the immanentization of the transcendent) is in fact the very ontological content of classical moral-political philosophy. It is the classical "nature of politics" and is eloquently expressed in Pericles's funeral oration and given political vitality in Aristotle's teleological conception of the *polis*.

The influence of Eric Voegelin is unmistakable here. Murray
is employing Voegelin's favored critical thesis of modernity's "immanentization of the eschaton." This is significant and yet unfor-
tunate, for Voegelin errs majestically in his interpretation of Platonic
political symbolism. Socrates was no doubt an exemplary philosopher; it is doubtful that he was the older political-theologian brother
of Christ whom Voegelin finds in his canonical reading of Plato's
dialogues. It is a common, though unwarranted, intellectual prejudice that views Plato as typical — indeed, as the source — of Greek
political philosophy.

Murray's Normative Political Philosophy

Murray recovers, after a fashion, the ancient tradition of moral-political
philosophy in his normative argument. This argument is a synthesis
of the Thomistic metaphysics of natural-law philosophy, natural theology, natural morality, and certain aspects of the classical tradition.
His argument is that the natural moral order, of which the political
ontology ought to be an expression, "is a prolongation of the metaphysical order into the dimensions of human freedom," by which is
rightly organized the political order (p. 328). The term *natural* means
rational and designates the sapient being. In sapience is freedom (i.e.,
transcendence of mere deterministic nature); in beingness is rational,
teleological nature. Finally, natural law, though "immanent in the [ra-
tional-sacred] nature of man, [is] transcendent in its reference" —
namely, the divine Creator of natural being.

These are the essential predicates of Murray's normative argument. The objective of his argument is to offer the traditional contents
of natural-law philosophy as an alternative normative philosophy to
that of the ethically nugatory moral-political thinking articulated within
the context of modern rationalism and secularism. I have no quarrel
with this goal. I do, however, have a problem with the formulation and
presentation of his traditional natural-law philosophy *as moral-political
theory*. My final critical remarks will focus on the ontologically bifurcated
character of his interpretation of natural law.

In his brief discussion of natural theology, Murray uncritically
conflates classical and Christian notions of theology, nature, and reason. Long before theology and natural law were Christian, they were
"immanent" — that is, political. This is to say that in its original formu-

lation, natural-law philosophy was anthropocentric in the sense of initiating the critical sapience that served to displace the political authority of religious mythopoeticism. Not even Plato's reworking of ancient soul eschatologies yielded a religious theocentricism, contrary misinterpretations notwithstanding.

Murray's thesis of the moral order of being as a "prolongation" of the metaphysical into the natural is remarkably opaque on the traditional conception of "nature." He asserts that the "situation" of the human being in the natural world "is that of a creature before God," from which point he goes on to stipulate the ultimate authority of natural law (p. 329). What he in fact does here is to transform a philosophical premise of earlier natural law into the very theological foundation of Christian natural law. In other words, Murray is not using the term *natural* in the sense in which it was employed in the older tradition. Classical thought (and here I mean the architectonic Greek *naturalistic* thinking) was very clear in its moral-political philosophy on the distinction between *physis* (nature) on the one side and *nomos* (convention, law) and *techne* (fabrication, creation) on the other side. Ancient-classical natural law was not "made by God." Murray's natural law is God-created law, derivatively "given," where earlier it constituted the ambient integrated order of natural being, *law as is,* the *is* of being-in-becoming *(genesis).* Murray's natural law significantly alters the logical and ontological status of nature and natural law prior to Christianity.

But it is Murray's description of the "reason" of human sapience that most vividly expresses the confusion of his appeal to the classical tradition. His description starkly exhibits the contrast between secular and theological moral-political philosophy. "Reason does not create its own laws," he writes, "any more than man creates himself. Man has the laws of his nature given to him, as nature itself is given. By nature he is the image of God, eternal Reason; and so his reason reflects a higher reason; therein consists its rightness. . . . Above the natural law immanent in man stands the eternal law in God transcendent," which is the ordering reason of all being (p. 330). This, I am prepared to argue, is *not* traditional natural-law philosophy; it is orthodox theology employing a selected natural-law vocabulary. More to the point, it is the Platonic ontological bifurcation between worldly being and Intelligible Being decked out in the Scholastic appropriation and reworking of Aristotle's naturalistic correction of Plato's idealism. And herein resides Murray's problem in formulating a moral-*political* natural law, with roots in secular philosophy, that is consonant with the Christian ontology: the traditional epistemological-ontological structure of the Christian order of all things, particularly epistemology, is Platonic, but the contents of its natural-law philosophy *qua* moral-political theory *would be* that of the *Physikoi*-Aristotle-Aquinas tradition, if it worked. The former counfounds the latter. This brings us to Murray's bifurcated political ontology.

He writes that "in the rational creature the immanent law is knowable and known; it is a moral law that authoritatively solicits the consent of freedom. St. Thomas, then, defines the natural law as the 'rational creature's participation in the eternal law.' The participation consists in man's possession of reason, the godlike faculty, whereby [the human being comports] himself freely . . . to the plenitude of self-realization of his rational and social being" (p. 330). The crucial term in this theological synthesis of Plato, Aristotle, and doctrinal presuppositions is *participation*. It is Plato's language and happens to be the reef upon which Plato's political philosophy ultimately founders in its vain attempt to reconnect the political world of *physis* and the *meta-physis* world of the ethical *Eide*. In Plato, "participation" *(methexis)* is a ghostly, magical principle that effects a cognitively illusory integration of the transcendent and the natural. It is illusory because the ontology of the "really real" entities, the Ideas or Forms, remains essentially distinct, different, and unrealizable, both in reflective thought and in mimetic-natural "reality." Murray's appeal to the Aristotelian "self-realization" cannot be squared with his unreflexive conception of human sapience and intractable sacred-secular and transcendent-immanent domains, in which dwell estranged vocabularies of being.

Murray's natural law, insofar as it would be a moral-political philosophy for our times, exists in an ontological limbo, caught somewhere between classical philosophy and modern, rationalistic natural law. Murray is not at home in either of these secular articulations of natural-law philosophy. And his natural law is not at home in the political condition. It does not speak to sapient political being in the world in an ontologically coherent language. It is ontologically incommensurate, which is to say that a moral-political law with its *posited* origin and substance in God's Ontological Library *is not necessarily political*. Attempts to make Murray's natural-law authority an ontological *real* would no doubt encounter his expressed skepticism toward "incarnational humanism," from which he retreats into theological paternalism: "true religion and profound humaneness . . . are not rivals but sisters. . . . [The Church] is less certain of man himself in his total being and less confident of his power to harmonize his whole human effort with his Christian faith, in that ever precarious synthesis known as Christian humanism" (pp. 195-96). Contrary claims notwithstanding, this is a theological expression of an ontological distrust of natural and free human sapience. Sapience *cannot* be manipulated, cannot be viewed as part of the "total being" of the human being for the philosophical purpose of common-ontological faculty identification and then be summarily subordinated to the privileged metaphysical wisdom of an institution whose title to epistemological authority and whose primary orientation are meta-ontological (i.e., "not of this world"). The gap between "metaphysics" and political "nature" cannot be bridged. Sapient *political* being has no standing in this metaphysical-theological sapience.

Ontologically — that is, in terms of sapient human being *in the world* — Murray's "participation" thesis holds that the political ontology, to be truly moral, must be made "part of the moral universe" of Eternal Law. And to accomplish this, the ontological structure of society must "be conceived in terms of a theorem with regard to the relation between the sacredness inherent in man and the manifold secularities" of the natural world (p. 199). Murray's natural-law argument, which mixes doctrinal thesis with ontological hypothesis, looks all too much like a reinvention of the moral-political wheel of natural-law philosophy found in ancient thought, but with a new second axle. It is his dualistic "Great Idea," I am prepared to argue, that makes Murray's "theorem" necessary within his theological universe of political discourse. But it cannot make his theorem a project in ontologically coherent *political* philosophy, any more than Hobbes's invocation of geometry makes his political philosophy coherent.

It would appear, then, that Murray is engaged in constructing a sacrosanct epistemology of political *theology*, distinct from a *political-theology* that is ontologically responsive to reflexive scrutiny.

It is important to remember that the intellectual life of Christianity was founded in its own unique metaphysical rebellion — which is to say, in reflexivity. An authentically free human sapience contains the ever-present possibility of ontological-epistemological reformulation, which *is* philosophy, science, *and* theology. The American separation of church and state is not hostile; it is a political-ontological recognition that in any belief system — sacred or secular — the sapient being is, *at best,* a fallible, uncertain, penultimate being. He or she may want to change a truth, or a great deal more. Surely theologians from time to time wonder whether their doctrines (or even their Great Ideas and Truths) might not be a misreading or a misconstruction of sapience in being. This is not to suggest that theology-based political thinking is without value. But is an institutionalized church's doctrinal thinking sufficient to accomplish transcendence, to effect *in our being in the world* a recognition of and response to ontological dimensions and possibilities beyond the most rudimentary? This is open to question — or should be. Murray writes early on in his essays that "religious pluralism is against the will of God. But it is the human condition; it is written into the script of history" (p. 23). How does Murray, or Gelasius, *know* "the will of God"? Here, again, is the theologian's aristocracy of orthodox knowledge (i.e., faith). Should religion and its attendant theology function as privileged authority over our critical sapience? This, too, is an open question — or should be — in the political ontology. The basic problems here are the authorship and locus of life-informing truth. Theological truths may be eternal, sacred truths, but what does this mean *in* the political ontology when such truths do not *belong to* all reflexive-sapient beings? In the ontology of sapience, "metaphysical truth" is sapience in search of its own authorship. Assigning this authorship to God is the ultimate political-ontological delusion. The brute fact is this: sacred theology is not civil theology. Thus far, the latter, yet mediated through the language of the former, has not arrived at an ontological understanding of political being.

There are alternative theological approaches. John Macquarrie, for example, dissents from Murray's conservative Thomism, arguing for an approach that includes "setting aside . . . the classic natural theology as employing an outmoded conceptuality and dubious metaphysical method" in its presentation of Christianity.[8] In his view, the traditional emphasis on "transcendence" in the transcendence-immanence bifurcation should be retired and replaced with an emphasis on the immanent ontology of sapient being in the world. I am reluctant to believe that St. Thomas would endorse Murray's tepid ontological immersion and fearful distancing from reflexivity. And though impossible to answer, one asks if St. Thomas would today accept the "straw" of his own ontological bifurcation? Hans Küng suggests that he would not.

8. Macquarrie, *New Directions in Theology Today: God and Secularity* (Philadelphia: Westminster Press, 1967), p. 87.

In his assertion that "theology should not simply be silent before God but should talk about him afresh, without the framework of a dualistic metaphysics," I take Küng to be saying that it is time to transcend a broken ontological-epistemological apparatus.[9] It is time for theology to scrutinize critically its traditional structures of the mind and confront what Küng, invoking Ernst Bloch, identifies as "transcendence without transcendence."[10] It would then confront *political being*.

Karl Barth's reflexive-theological alternative — the assertion that since God became human, humanity *is* the measure of all things — is a new-ancient idea that suggests that the actual Great Idea of Christianity is the liberating ontological integration of Being "and" being. Christ taught a healing *mode* of universal-ethical being, not an ontology/theology of rended being. Orthodox theology misread the ontological validation *in* the Incarnation. That this tradition resists reflexive scrutiny of its "mind-forg'd manacles" is to be questioned and *is* being questioned.

Human being is more than a crude dichotomy or a raw immanence. Our reflexive (i.e., spiritual) sapience validates this. No unifying, moral-political genius incarnate will emanate from a theology that cleaves to the *disjecta membra* of ontological dualism. Inevitably, a political *theology* is politics of knowledge. A transcendent reality will not settle this political competition in Truth. This is Mystery, not ontological understanding. Theology is in a unique position today to lead the way in a critical rethinking of our ontological self-understanding. God does not need theology, I suspect. The political ontology does. What is needed from theology is *ontological* discourse, clarification of the multivocal human condition, wherein tensions are not automatically dichotomies. Theology would *not* abandon God for transient conceits of sapience in this expanded *political-theological* project. Neither would it continue to sacrifice political being in a votary's fane of an institutionalized unreflexive metaphysic that is furtive, fugitive, and "other."

The political ontology of John Courtney Murray's *We Hold These Truths* is neither to be ignored nor accepted uncritically.

---

9. Küng, *Does God Exist? An Answer for Today* (1978; rpt., New York: Random House–Vintage Press, 1981), p. 501.
10. Küng, *Does God Exist?* p. 487.

III. MURRAY AND
THE CONTEMPORARY
PUBLIC ARGUMENT

Religious Freedom:
John Courtney Murray
and Vatican II

Francis Canavan, S.J.

RELIGIOUS FREEDOM IN THE UNITED STATES is popularly supposed to be guaranteed by the separation of church and state. The phrase "separation of church and state" in fact occurs nowhere in the Constitution of the United States, but it is useful for pointing to something prior to and deeper than itself: the distinction between church and state, a distinction as old as, but not older than, Christianity.

The ancient pagan world knew no such duality of church and state. For it, society was the *polis* or, later, the *imperium,* a compact and undifferentiated unity whose functions were not only those which we call political but also those which we call religious. The city or the Empire enforced laws and fought wars; it also worshiped the gods, and it saw no reason for regarding priests as being any less civic functionaries than magistrates or generals.

With the rise of Christianity there appeared for the first time a distinct social body that called itself the *ecclesia* or church. Unlike the people of Israel whom God had made peculiarly his own, the church was open to all who would accept the faith that it taught and would join it through baptism. Like Israel, it presented itself as having been founded directly by God and, while it acknowledged the authority of governments in temporal affairs, it claimed autonomy in all that pertained to man's relationship with God.

The editors of this volume would like to thank the editors of *Faith and Reason* for permitting the republication, with minor changes, of Father Canavan's essay.

167

Now there were two distinct authorities in society, the political and the religious, the temporal and the spiritual. The centuries since then have been filled with an unending debate, by no means yet concluded, on the proper relationship between them. Here we need only note that the question of that relationship, which in this country we call a separation of church and state, presupposes the distinction between them. If there were only the state, there would be no church to which to relate it or from which to separate it.

Given the reality of both church and state, however, drawing the line between their proper spheres leads ultimately to the idea of constitutional government — that is, government limited in its powers. Underlying this idea is a conception of society as organized in different ways for different purposes. Society is indeed composed of individuals, but not of individuals standing alone opposite the state. The family is a natural human grouping, and society is made up of families as much as of individuals. As society develops, it articulates itself into a multitude of economic, cultural, and other groups. Society overall is organized as the state, but only for certain purposes and for the performance of certain functions relative to those purposes. For the performance of other functions in relation to God, a Christian society organizes itself as the Church or the churches. The state and its organs of government thus come to have limited powers because they have limited goals and functions.

The late John Courtney Murray saw this constitutional conception of the state as basic to the American idea of religious liberty. Murray was certainly not the only American Catholic who wrote on church-state relations, nor was he the only or the principal person who influenced Vatican II's *Declaration on Religious Freedom*. But in the years before Vatican II, he was the most profound and articulate Catholic interpreter of the American understanding of religious liberty. If we are inquiring into the impact of the American Catholic experience on the document framed by Vatican II, we may well begin with his reflections on that experience.

Murray's writings on church-state relations and religious freedom were voluminous and, so far as I know, all of them appeared originally in periodicals. Some people write books, but Murray developed his thought in a series of articles that ended only with his death in 1967. Even his one published book, *We Hold These Truths*, was a reworking of previously published articles. His best statement of the institutionalization of religious liberty in the U.S. Constitution is found in chapter 2 of that book, under the title "Civil Liberty and Religious Integrity."

"The American thesis," he says in this chapter, "is that government is not juridically omnipotent. Its powers are limited, and one of the principles of limitation is the distinction between state and church, in their purposes, methods, and manner of organization."[1] The wording of the religion clauses of the First Amendment to the Constitution bears him out. On their face, these clauses state nothing but a limitation on the powers of government: "Congress shall make no law respecting an establishment of religion, or prohibiting the free exercise thereof." It is significant that the statement is made in the imperative rather than the indicative mood and in the language of law rather than of dogma. According to Murray, "these constitutional clauses have no religious content. They answer none of the eternal human questions with regard to the nature of truth and freedom or the manner in which the spiritual order of man's life is to be organized or not organized. Therefore they are not invested with the sanctity that attaches to dogma, but only with the rationality that attaches to law" (p. 49).

One may subscribe to these clauses for theological or philosophical reasons, and many have done so. But one may also accept them, as Murray proposes that we should, simply as good law, known to be good from experience rather than from theory. "If history makes one thing clear," he says, "it is that these clauses were the twin children of social necessity, the necessity of creating a social environment, protected by law, in which men of differing religious faiths might live together in peace" (p. 57). What the First Amendment gave us, Murray argues, was an adaptation "to the peculiar genius of American government and to the concrete conditions of American society" of "one of the central assertions" of "the genuine Western tradition of politics" — namely, "the distinction of church and state" (p. 66).

As Murray reads the First Amendment,

> it does not say that there is no distinction between true and false religion, good and bad morality. But it does say that in American circumstances the conscience of the community, aware of its moral obligations to the peace of the community, and speaking therefore

---

1. Murray, *We Hold These Truths: Catholic Reflections on the American Proposition* (New York: Sheed & Ward, 1960), p. 68. Subsequent references to this volume will be made parenthetically in the text.

as the voice of God, does not give government any mandate, does not impose on it any duty, and does not even communicate to it the right to repress religious opinions or practices, even though they are erroneous and false. (P. 63)

The religion clauses of the First Amendment are "not articles of faith but articles of peace . . . in a pluralist society" (pp. 56, 78). They are not, however, mere concessions to expediency. They are not only morally acceptable to the Catholic conscience but morally obligatory upon it because they arise out of the moral exigencies of the common good in our society. "The origins of our fundamental law," says Murray, "are in moral principle; the obligations it imposes are moral obligations, binding in conscience" (p. 63).

The American experience under the religion clauses, moreover, has validated their claim to serve the common good. "First, America has proved by experience that political unity and stability are possible without uniformity of religious belief and practice, without the necessity of any governmental restrictions on any religion." Murray is aware, however, that there is a limit to what this experience proves. He therefore adds a caveat: the nation depends for its existence and well-being on a moral consensus "with regard to the rational truths and moral precepts that govern the structure of the constitutional state, specify the substance of the common weal, and determine the ends of public policy," and experience has not shown us how, if at all, this consensus "can survive amid all the ruptures of religious division, whose tendency is inherently disintegrative of all consensus and community" (pp. 72-73).

"The second American experience," he continues, "was that stable political unity, which means perduring agreement on the common good of man at the level of performance, can be strengthened by the exclusion of religious differences from the area of concern allotted to government" (p. 73). That is to say, religious groups find it easier to differ without civil strife when political power is not open to them as an object for which they can strive.

"The third and most striking aspect of the American experience consists in the fact that religion itself, and not least the Catholic Church, has benefitted by our free institutions, by the maintenance, even in exaggerated form, of the distinction between church and state" (pp. 73-74). In this respect, says Murray, the experience of the church has been better in America than in Latin countries where the church's situation has alternated between privilege and persecution.

This last benefit of the American experience — namely, the freedom of the church — is of crucial importance to Murray. Under the American Constitution, he notes, religious freedom is guaranteed "not only to the individual Catholic but to the Church as an organized society with its own law and jurisdiction. . . . Within [American] society, as distinct from the state, there is room for the independent exercise of an authority which is not that of the state" (pp. 70-71). According to Murray, this independent spiritual authority has been the essential element of freedom in the political tradition of the Christian West.

He spells out this proposition in chapter 9 of *We Hold These Truths*, under the title "Are There Two or One?" The basic question is whether the government of the world is divided between two authorities, the temporal and the spiritual, each supreme in its own sphere, or whether there is ultimately only one supreme authority, that of the sovereign political state, within which religious bodies exist only as associations of private right. The Christian tradition insists that there are two, with the result that the freedom of the Church is the bulwark of the freedom of all else in a society in which the state is confined to its own limited sphere of jurisdiction and of action.

"Freedom of the church," says Murray, is a "pregnant phrase" (p. 201) that means more than it seems to at first glance. First of all, it naturally denotes the freedom of the Church as a spiritual authority to carry out its divine commission to teach, to rule, and to sanctify. But it also denotes the freedom of the Church as the Christian people "to live within her fold an integral supernatural life," a life with an "inherent superpolitical dignity" that transcends the goals and powers of the state and so founds a claim to immunity from subordination to the state and its temporal ends. Complementary to this are all those aspects of the temporal life of man that

> by reason of their Christian mode of existence, or by reason of their finality, . . . transcend the limited purposes of the political order and are thus invested with a certain sacredness. The chief example is the institution of the family — the marriage contract itself, and the relationships of husband and wife, parent and child. Included also are other human relationships in so far as they involve a moral element and require regulation in the interests of the personal dignity of man. Such, for instance, are the employer-employee relationship and the reciprocal relationships established by the political obligation. Sacred too is the intellectual patrimony of the human race, the

heritage of basic truths about the nature of man, amassed by secular experience and reflection, that form the essential content of the social consensus. (Pp. 203-4)

The protection of these aspects of life from the inherently expansive power of the state, Murray argues, has depended historically on the freedom of the church as an independent spiritual authority. A significant shift in the theoretical foundation of freedom came, however, with the rise of the modern liberal state. The "political experiment of modernity" (p. 206), to be sure, did not reject the

> whole system of moral values, both individual and social, which had been elaborated under the influence of the Christian revelation. . . . As a matter of fact, these values were adopted as the very basis for the modern political experiment. Modernity, however, has maintained that these values are now known to be simply immanent in man; that man has become conscious of them in the course of their emergence in historical experience; that, whatever may have been the influence of the Christian revelation on the earlier phases of this experience, these values are now simply a human possession, a conquest and an achievement of humanity by man himself. (P. 214)

While the moral values inherited from the Christian tradition were largely retained, the freedom of the church was rejected as "the mediating principle between society and state, between the people and the public power." Henceforth the people themselves, through free political institutions, would limit the power of government, and this program gave a new content to the idea of religious freedom.

> The key to the whole new political edifice was the freedom of the individual conscience. Here precisely lies the newness of the modern experiment. A great act of trust was made. The trust was that the free individual conscience would effectively mediate the moral imperatives of the transcendental order of justice (whose existence was not doubted in the earlier phases of the modern experiment). Then, through the workings of free political institutions these imperatives would be transmitted to the public power as binding norms upon its action. The only sovereign spiritual authority would be the conscience of the free man. The freedom of the individual conscience, constitutionally guaranteed, would supply the armature of immunity

to the sacred order, which now became, by modern definition, precisely the order of the private conscience. And through free political institutions, again constitutionally guaranteed, the moral consensus of the community would be mobilized in favor of justice and freedom in the secular order. (P. 206)[2]

The corollary of this way of conceiving religious freedom, as the development of European liberalism made clear, was the "thesis of the juridical omnipotence and omnicompetence of the state. . . . It was because freedom of religion and separation of church and state were predicated on this thesis that the Church refused to accept them as a thesis" (p. 68). Murray thought that the church was completely right in refusing.

On the other hand, he defended the American "separation of church and state," while conceding that it "exaggerates the distinction between church and state by its self-denying ordinances." But, he said, "it is one thing to exaggerate a traditional distinction along the lines of its inherent tendency; it is quite another to abolish the distinction. In the latter case the result is a vicious monistic society; in the former, a faultily dualistic one." The monistic society was the "lay state" of European liberalism, in which separation of church and state amounted to a subordination of the church to the state. But the American separation was a dualism whose fault was "some exaggeration of the restrictions placed on government." In American circumstances, this exaggeration was "necessary in order to insure freedom" (p. 69).

Murray therefore did not found his theory of religious freedom or his interpretation of the American experience of religious liberty on the freedom of the individual conscience. This appears clearly in a paper which he read at an Institute on Religious Freedom held at the Bellarmine School of Theology in North Aurora, Illinois, shortly after the conclusion of Vatican II.[3] He described the evolution of the argument for religious freedom in Vatican II as a movement away from freedom of conscience as its foundation toward what he regarded as a sounder political and juridical basis.

2. For a fuller exposition of this thesis, see chaps. 1 and 2 of John Hallowell's *The Decline of Liberalism as an Ideology* (New York: Horward Fertig, 1971).

3. The paper, entitled "The Declaration on Religious Freedom: A Moment in Its Legislative History," was later published (together with the other papers presented at the Institute) in *Religious Liberty: An End and a Beginning*, ed. John Courtney Murray, S.J. (New York: Macmillan, 1966), pp. 15-42.

The Declaration on Religious Freedom, Murray explains, went through three schemata; the third, with three revisions, became the final document. He says that it is fair to characterize the first schema "as a declaration of a theory of freedom of conscience." In it, "religious freedom is freedom of conscience, and freedom of conscience is to be positively defined as 'the right of the person to the free exercise of religion according to the dictates of conscience.' The object or content of this right is not simply negative — an immunity, a 'freedom from' coercion; it is also positive — a 'freedom for' action according to conscience."[4]

According to Murray, it was this second, or positive, aspect of freedom of conscience that "encountered an unresolved dispute within the Church with regard to the 'rights of conscience.' "[5] Both sides in the dispute agreed that, in the matters of faith, no one should be forced to act against his conscience. They disagreed on the extent to which the sincerity of one's conscience founds an obligation in other people to give one full scope to act in accordance with one's conscience.

The second schema, while an improvement on the first,

> asserted that the man of sincere conscience, even though he be in error, has the right to religious freedom, meaning the public profession, practice, and observance of his religion, and to its public teaching, according to the dictates of his own conscience. The foundation of his right is his own conscience and its sincerity. . . . This position was opposed by another, which asserted that the man who is in error, even though he be sincere, has no right to religious freedom, no right to the public manifestation of his error, whether in action or, more particularly, in public teaching. The reason for this counter assertion was that rights must be founded on the objective order of truth, not on the subjective dictates of conscience.[6]

Murray regarded both of these positions as "simplistic" and inadequate. In any case, since there was an unresolved dispute and no clear tradition in the Church on the "rights of conscience," the liberal line taken by the first and second schemata "could not be made the basis of a conciliar statement."[7]

4. Murray, "The Declaration on Religious Freedom," pp. 17-18.
5. Murray, "The Declaration on Religious Freedom," p. 26.
6. Murray, "The Declaration on Religious Freedom," p. 22.
7. Murray, "The Declaration on Religious Freedom," p. 26.

The third schema, however, began to move in the right direction and "took up the issue of religious freedom as formally juridical concept." In this concept,

> religious freedom is a freedom from coercion; it is an immunity; its content is negative. Historically, the First Amendment to the Constitution of the United States launched this conception. The freedoms of the First Amendment, including "the free exercise of religion," were understood to be certain specified immunities. . . . The political or civil freedoms of the First Amendment, unlike later freedoms or rights of the socio-economic order, were not claims on society and government for positive action, but assurances against coercive action by government and society.
>
> Hence the object of religious freedom as a juridical conception is not the actualization of positive values inherent in religious belief, profession, and practice. . . . The object of the right is simply the assured absence of constraints and restraints on individuals in their efforts to pursue freely the positive values of religion.[8]

But although the notion of religious freedom is negative in the sense that it consists in the absence of constraints and restraints, it does not connote hostility or even indifference to religion. In this notion,

> government denies to itself the competence to be a judge of religious belief and action. But this denial is not an assertion of indifference to the values of religion to man and society. . . . It is simply a recognition of the limited functions of the juridical order of society as the legal armature of human rights. Hence it is a recognition of the inviolability of the human person, individually and in association with others, in what concerns religious belief and action.[9]

Accordingly, Murray explains, the third schema changes the

---

8. Murray, "The Declaration on Religious Freedom," pp. 27-28. Here I must venture to correct Murray. The First Amendment does not protect persons from "coercive action by *government and society*," but only from government. What Justice Potter Stewart said of the freedom-of-speech clause applies equally to the religion clauses of the Amendment: "It is, of course, a commonplace that the constitutional guarantee of free speech is a guarantee only against abridgement by government, federal or state" (*Hudgens v. NLRB* 424 U.S. 507, 513 [1976]).

9. Murray, "The Declaration on Religious Freedom," p. 37.

foundation of religious freedom from the rights of conscience to "the dignity of the human person," on which papal teaching regarding the social, economic, and political order has put increasing emphasis in the twentieth century. He adds, however, that "it can hardly be said that the schema develops the idea satisfactorily; it does no more than suggest the line of development to be followed."[10]

The rest of Murray's paper is a sketch of what a properly developed argument for religious freedom based on "the dignity of the human person" would be. It concludes that

> an exigence for immunity from coercion is resident in the human person as such. It is an exigence of his dignity as a moral subject. This exigence is the source of the fundamental rights of the person — those politico-civil rights concerning the search for truth, artistic creation, scientific discovery, and the development of man's political views, moral convictions, and religious beliefs. In all these areas of human life, in which the values of the human spirit are directly at stake, the human person has the right to immunity from coercion. . . .
>
> This exigence is a thing of the objective order; it is rooted in the given reality of man as man. . . . It is identically the basic imperative requirement that man should act in accordance with his nature.[11]

Murray's doctrine on religious freedom is thus based not on the subjective rights of conscience but on the objective natural goals of civil society. From the latter, a theory of constitutional government can be inferred. He says that the Declaration on Religious Freedom moved, though not far enough, in the same direction. I have some reason, however, to doubt whether he was even as much satisfied with the final draft of the Declaration as he purported to be in this paper.

I presented a paper at the same Institute on Religious Freedom at which Murray spoke. In it I analyzed the Declaration as arguing "directly from the obligation to follow conscience to the right to do so" and concluded by saying that I was "not entirely convinced by the document's argument, which proceeds from the obligation to follow conscience to a rather elaborate series of rights that collectively constitute religious freedom." I then asked, "Does this argument really bear

10. Murray, "The Declaration on Religious Freedom," pp. 37-38.
11. Murray, "The Declaration on Religious Freedom," pp. 40-41.

the full weight that is put on it?"[12] It was not that I had any more quarrel than Murray did with the Declaration's conclusions, but I wondered if its argument fully sustained them.

Later that day I met Father Murray, and he said to me, in reference to the question I had raised, "You were much too kind."[13] I gathered from this remark and the explanation he gave of what he meant by it that he thought that the Declaration's argument, even in its final form, was still anchored to an analysis of conscience and its rights and obligations.

Everything I have said to this point has been a long windup for a very short pitch. If we take Murray as the leading American Catholic theoretician of religious freedom at the time of Vatican II (at which he was present as a *peritus*), it is not clear that he had a strong, still less a determinative, influence on its thinking. The experience of the American Church may have had a much greater influence, of course, simply as a historical experience rather than as a theory. This country had shown in practice that the Church could flourish in conditions where it was not established and where the free exercise of religion was guaranteed to all. That fact may well have impressed the Conciliar Fathers. But to estimate the impact of the American experience on Vatican II is a task for a historian and is far beyond my competence.

One thing, however, I do know about history: it does not stand still, and no historical experience is ever quite finished. John Courtney Murray died in 1967, just twenty years after the U.S. Supreme Court began to write our contemporary constitutional law on the meaning of the establishment-of-religion clause in *Everson v. Board of Education,* 330 U.S. 1, in 1947. He was thoroughly familiar with that case and its sequels up to the time of his death, and I know that he was not at all happy with the *Everson* opinion. I have sometimes wondered what his judgment on the American experience would be if it included all that the Supreme Court has done with the First Amendment, and with the establishment clause in particular, in the years since he died.

Murray, in his writings, and Vatican II, in the Declaration on Religious Freedom, located religious liberty not in the nonestablishment of religion but in its free exercise. The Declaration adverts to the

12. Canavan, "The Catholic Concept of Religious Freedom as a Human Right," in *Religious Liberty: An End and a Beginning,* pp. 78-79.

13. See also my comment on this incident in "Murray on Vatican II's Declaration on Religious Freedom," *Communio* 9 (1982): 404-5.

establishment of religion only in passing, where it says, "if, in view of peculiar circumstances obtaining among certain peoples, special legal recognition is given in the constitutional order of society to one religious body, it is at the same time imperative that the right of all citizens and religious bodies to religious freedom should be recognized and made effective in practice."[14] In the mind of the Council, an established religion is acceptable only if it does not impede the free exercise of religion. In Murray's mind, contemplating the American situation, the nonestablishment of religion was ancillary to its free exercise, a mere means to an end, not an end in itself.

The difficulty that our Supreme Court has had in reconciling the demands of the establishment and the free exercise clauses of the First Amendment with one another lies precisely in the Court's tendency to see the clauses as serving two equal and independent ends. The bar against an establishment of religion becomes an end in itself, with no clearly elaborated relationship to free exercise. There is, in addition, a well-organized and influential body of opinion in this country that urges the Court to make the nonestablishment of religion the supreme end, meaning that government may do nothing that has the effect of favoring religion, whatever inhibiting effect that policy may have on the free exercise thereof. Murray's reading of the First Amendment, therefore, cannot be said to hold the field.

It may also be that religious freedom as we have known it in America has depended on the particular kind of pluralism that resulted from a multiplicity of religious denominations that nonetheless shared a common biblical tradition. The common tradition made possible a consensus on the good of man at the level of performance, which is the level that counts in the government of a political community. As we have noted, Murray was well aware that our American experience had not shown us how the moral consensus on which the nation depends "can survive amid all the ruptures of religious division, whose tendency is inherently disintegrative of all consensus and community" (p. 73). The consensus has surely not become stronger in the years since he wrote. Rather, one has the impression that it is falling apart under the unrelenting pressure of claims to individual liberty as the highest good.

We also noted above that Murray held that our constitutional guarantee of religious liberty extends not only to the individual but

14. "The Declaration on Religious Liberty," in *The Documents of Vatican II*, ed. Walter M. Abbott and Joseph Gallagher (New York: Guild Press, 1966), p. 685.

also "to the Church as an organized society with its own law and jurisdiction" (p. 70). A substantial body of case law supports his statement; our constitutional law does protect the corporate freedom of churches.

But there is another way of looking at our constitutionalism that has its own validity and deserves consideration. A Methodist theologian, Stanley Hauerwas, agrees that "in America we have institutionalized the limited state." We protect the rights of institutions as well as of individuals. But in effect, he says, "the rights of the individual have become the secular equivalent to the church as the means to keep government in its proper sphere." That, too, is a not inaccurate description of the drift of a good deal of contemporary American law, and it leads us to ignore the

> fundamental tension between our commitments to the rights of the individual, preservation of intermediate associations, and the ability to retain a limited state. Indeed, the very language of "intermediate associations" already betrays liberal presuppositions which distort the moral reality of such institutions as the family. Whatever else the family is, it is not but another voluntary association. The very means used to insure that the democratic state be a limited state — namely, the rights of the individual — turn out to be no less destructive for intermediate institutions than the monistic state of Marxism. For it is the strategy of liberalism to insure the existence of the "autonomy of cultural and economic life" by insuring the freedom of the individual. Ironically, that strategy results in the undermining of intermediate associations because they are now understood only as those arbitrary institutions sustained by the private desires of individuals.[15]

Murray clearly would agree that a constitutionalism based solely or primarily on the rights of the individual is a weak one and leads eventually to a monistic society. He might also agree today that that is the direction in which our constitutionalism is moving.

All of this suggests that religious freedom is not simply a timeless principle but a moment in history. It does indeed depend on principles derived from the unchanging elements in the nature of man, and it

15. Hauerwas, "Christianity and Democracy: A Response," *Center Journal* 1 (Summer 1982): 44-45.

must so depend if we are to make an intelligible case for it. Otherwise our religious freedom rests upon an unstable voluntarism: we are free because we will to be free. But who can predict how long, in conditions of decaying consensus and increasing pluralism, freedom will be our strongest desire?

The underlying principles of religious liberty are necessary, but they are not enough. They depend for their realization in practice on sets of circumstances that come into being in history and may likewise pass out of being. Certain beliefs and convictions of a moral and religious nature must prevail among a people, certain balances of religious, social, and cultural forces must exist, and certain political and legal traditions must be strong in their society before that people can achieve religious freedom. We have had those sets of circumstances in America; they constitute our experience. It could turn out to have been a happy moment in history.

Beyond Murray's Articles
of Peace and Faith

Gerard V. Bradley

I N A DESERVEDLY RENOWNED CHAPTER of *We Hold These Truths,* John
Courtney Murray sketches two fundamentally different views of the
First Amendment religion clauses. He recommends and defends the
nonestablishment and free-exercise provisions as "Articles of Peace,"
allowing that many Americans incorrectly and unprofitably view them
instead as "Articles of Faith." I propose to examine our constitutional law
of church and state in light of Murray's compact typology. Two preliminary expositions are demanded by the task: What is the law? and
What is Murray's typology? The provisional conclusion: the law of the
clauses constitutes an Article of Faith. But Murray's typology is not
without its problems. The "faith/peace" distinction *may* have effectively
persuaded Roman Catholics of the moral legitimacy of America's pluralistic (and historically Protestant) regime, which seems to me one of its
intentions, but the distinction eventually subverted Murray's larger
stated aim to relate the *only* sensible account of the regime itself. Murray
unwisely hardened his distinction into a dichotomy — a dichotomy that
is inadequately expressed in his own thought. Finally, we will note how
the law partakes of *both* types in a way Murray contemplated but could
not articulate because of the limitations of his typology.

I

Any accounting of constitutional law to Murray's typology threatens to
derail at the station. Asking "What hath the Court wrought?" is not

simply a first step toward analysis; it is almost (but not quite) hopelessly contentious, an introduction to the Constitution after Babel. The problem is not that nobody knows what the law is but that everybody does: there are almost as many renditions of the corpus as there are renderers. *This* pluralism has many sources. One is relentless polemicizing. Religion-clause scholarship is commonly wedded to the scholar's own prescriptive vision, and the vision often colors the description of the corpus. Laurence Tribe is a classic example. In his work there is just no way to know where the law leaves off and Tribe begins.[1]

A second source of the pluralistic interpretation of the law lies in what one commentator called the law's "legendary inconsistencies."[2] The bill of particulars here includes puzzles like the constitutional permissibility of public bus rides for parochial school students to and from school but *not* for field trips. Also, the state may provide books but not maps — generating the infamous "atlas" problem: may the state provide books of maps? If there is sense to the law, it must be at some more penetrating level than this. But the specific cases are characterized by multiple opinions, all of them turgid. Judicial "analyses" are mainly vapid generalizations succeeded by proclamations of results. The law's instability is increased by judicial discontent, by the Courts' chronic hankering after a better way. By 1984 eight of the nine members of the Supreme Court had expressed deep regrets at the law's condition.[3] Since then the regrets have softened, but the analyses have grown more troubled. Some thought the Supreme Court hit bottom in that year, when the presence of plastic reindeer kept Baby Jesus from being removed from a Pawtucket nativity scene (*Lynch v. Donnelley*, 465 U.S. 668). But the Court confounded its critics by making such rescues an annual judicial ritual, and itself revisited the problem in 1989 in *County of Allegheny v. ACLU* (109 S.Ct. 3086). Since the crèche cases variously illustrate the contemporary predicament, a closer look at them is warranted.

The place to begin is the still-entrenched *Lemon* test (*Lemon v. Kurtzman* 403 U.S. 602 [1971]). This ruling held that in order for a governmental action to avoid violation of the establishment clause, it

1. See Tribe, *American Constitutional Law* (Mineola, N.Y.: Foundation, 1988).
2. W. Marshall, " 'We Know It When We See It': The Supreme Court and Establishment," *Southern California Law Review* 59 (1988): 495.
3. See G. Bradley, "Imagining the Past and Remembering the Future: The Supreme Court's History of the Establishment Clause," *Connecticut Law Review* 18 (1986): 827-43.

must possess a secular legislative purpose, its primary effect must neither advance nor inhibit religion, and it must avoid "excessive entanglements" with religion. But a sincere application of this test would clearly invalidate legislative chaplains, municipal crèches, and all other tokens of our religious sentiments. And, indeed, it was precisely to save such tokens that in *Marsh v. Chambers* (463 U.S. 783 [1983], a legislative chaplains case) and *Lynch v. Donnelley* (the 1984 crèche decision) the Court substituted an ad hoc historical test for the *Lemon* test. I call it the "roll call of ancient analogues." At first glance, this maneuver suggests analytical desperation — and it is that — but a closer look at the question to which it is the answer uncovers the central theme of our constitutional law.

In those two cases the majority asked whether the challenged practice had an eighteenth-century counterpart. The idea was that if it had such a counterpart, then the modern equivalent could be considered consistent with the First Amendment.[4] The *Lynch* Court found President Washington's Thanksgiving Day proclamation a persuasive counterpart. The dissenters instead sought the "intent" of the framers respecting nativity scenes — in other words, they wanted to know whether the framers erected crèches in their courthouses.

The minority analysis was more cogent. Although the first Christmas in America dates to 1492, the contemporary holiday took shape only in the nineteenth century. In the colonial period, New England Protestants, most of them Calvinist in theology, rejected any observance of the day, both as part of their rebellion against Anglicanism and on the grounds that Christmas was one of the "devices of men" and not grounded in Scripture. In 1659, the General Court of Massachusetts actually enacted a law to punish those who kept the day sacred. Dutch Reformed, Roman Catholic, Episcopalian, and Lutheran immigrants took a more positive view of the holiday and celebrated it according to their ancestral traditions. With the rise of immigration following the Revolution, and especially in the mid-nineteenth century, Christmas observances became common. Yet it was not until 1849 that New York and Virginia recognized Christmas as a legal holiday, and another forty-one years before the holiday gained legal recognition in all states.

---

4. This analysis can be distinguished from that which saved church tax exemptions in *Walz v. Tax Commission* (397 U.S. 664 [1970]). In that case, a long-standing continuous practice survived a close brush with the Establishment Clause.

This kind of historical polling *may* inform a search for the principles contained in the establishment clause in some small way, but it can do no more than that without ending in absurdity. Those who doubt that this is the case should linger over a few pertinent questions. As ludicrous as this may sound, Justice Scalia inquired in all earnestness of plaintiff's counsel in the 1989 crèche case whether they had poinsettias in Bethlehem.[5] To cite a comparable Easter symbolism, ought we be similarly concerned if a peacock appears in a "Season's Greetings" display? The peacock is, after all, a venerable symbol of eternal life, and some might hold that it adds to the religiosity of the scene. But would it not be more likely to suggest to a contemporary audience that the display was being brought to us by NBC?

The most recent appellate analysis to come across the transom presented for constitutional inspection the following material, the details of which are noteworthy:

> During the 1988 Christmas season, the Commonwealth of Kentucky erected a rustic stable on the grounds of the state capitol. The cost to the state was $2,400. The stable was furnished with a manger, two large pottery jugs, a ladder, carvings, and some straw, but not with figurines or statues commonly found in a crèche. The rest of the capitol grounds were decorated with Christmas trees, lights, and ornaments.[6]

When church groups reenacted the nativity using this creche, the ACLU sued. Lower federal courts rejected the challenge on condition that private funds defray state expense and that two "disclaimers" be posted. One said that the area was a "public forum" available to all religious groups. The other, in letters big enough to read from a passing car, warned that "the display was not constructed with public funds and does not constitute an endorsement by the Commonwealth of any religion or religious doctrine." As Russell Hittinger recently observed, one has the sinking feeling that the Court has lost a grip on the subject it is bound to adjudicate.

These contortions signal frantic attempts to prevent the complete secularization of public life. Put differently, *Lynch*'s sins may be forgiv-

---

5. That was because we needed to know whether poinsettias added to the religious symbolism or detracted from it (see 57 *U.S.L.W.* 3563).

6. *ACLU v. Wilinson*, 58 U.S.L.W. 2470 (U.S. 1990).

able, but our pardon should not obscure the secularist thrust this rear-guard action is meant to parry. That thrust itself stems from *Everson*'s determination that nonestablishment does not mean that government should treat all religions equally but rather that government may not aid, foster, promote, or encourage religion generally, or all religions.[7] Coupled with a fervid "prophylacticism" (the notion that it is better to overprotect rather than underprotect against even giving the impression of government encouragement), *Everson*'s effect was to encourage erasing all evidence of religion from government.

Whence the secularist principles? *Everson* grounded them in history, but its history was no better than *Lynch*'s. Indeed, *Everson* contented itself with little more than select quotations from Madison and Jefferson to support conclusions reached on other grounds. But what other grounds? Here begins the real detective work necessary to flesh out an account of the main thrust of the judicial project, which is our constitutional law.

Justice Robert Jackson asserted in 1948 that key establishment-clause issues are matters on which "we can find no law but our own prepossessions."[8] More recently, Justice Byron White, after previously admitting that history did not answer the vital questions, said that the Court has simply "carved out what [it] deemed to be the most desirable national policy governing various aspects of church-state relationships."[9] What is shaping the corpus? The justices' own conceptions of the rightly ordered polity. But since jurists usually get their models retail from cultural elites, you can bet some variant of liberal individualism determines the law.

Before investigating this issue in detail, let us pause to consider this vision's theater of operations. Is it limited to a discrete set of issues, a few lesser included aspects of "religion and public life" (e.g., school prayer, parochial school aid)?

To answer that, consider the doctrinal principle most influencing the corpus (and commentary), and ask whether it contains any intrinsic limitations on its applicability. "Endorsement" analysis has attained dominance in establishment-clause jurisprudence. The matter of its precise relationship to the still vigorous *Lemon* test, and the question

---

7. *Everson v. Board of Education*, 330 U.S. at 15-16.

8. *McCollum v. Board of Education*, 333 U.S. 203 (1948), 238. Murray entitled his critique of the *McCollum* decision "Law or Prepossessions."

9. *Committee for Public Education v. Nyquist*, 413 U.S. 820 (1973).

of whether it has been implicit in the corpus all along, are still disputed and need not detain us. But make no mistake: "endorsement" analysis is operative and central.[10] It is the analytical heart of the latest crèche case and commands a majority of the Supreme Court (evidenced by the 1989 crèche decision and also by the opinion in *Bullock v. Texas Monthly* [109 S.Ct. 890 (1989)], which struck down a Texas sales tax exemption for religious periodicals). Endorsement analysis is definitely *not* limited to token "displays" (as "ancient analogues" may be). It is in play regardless of context. Its academic supporters are legion. Laurence Tribe, to give but one notable example, has made it the centerpiece of his analysis of religious freedom.[11]

What is "endorsement" analysis? The kerygmatic preaching here is Justice Sandra O'Connor's and it is from *Lynch:* "Every government practice must be judged in its unique circumstances to determine whether it constitutes an endorsement or disapproval of religion" (694). In the view of those who approve of endorsement analysis, the vice in government "endorsement" of religion is that it conveys to holders of "nonendorsed" beliefs the idea that they are "outsiders," not full members of the political community. The controlling desideratum here is that every American can and should feel equally "at home" regardless of his or her religious belief. And endorsement analysis applies to all stripes of religious belief — in other words, government may not endorse religion as such, much less one brand of it.

This doctrine's breadth is commensurate with deeper justificatory principles. The Supreme Court regularly attributes the ambit of its efforts to the ubiquitously volatile sum of religion plus politics. They say no less than that

> ordinarily political debate and division, however vigorous or even partisan, are normal and healthy manifestations of our democratic system of government, but political division along religious lines was one of the principal evils against which the First Amendment was intended to protect. . . . The potential divisiveness of such conflict is a threat to the normal political process.[12]

10. See 109 S.Ct. 3086 (1989).

11. For a critical review of Tribe's church-state jurisprudence, including his use of "endorsement" analysis, see G. Bradley, "A Gracious Passage to Oakland: Tribe's Jurisprudence of the Religion Clauses," in *The Jurisprudence of Laurence Tribe,* ed. G. McDowell, forthcoming.

12. *Lemon v. Kurtzman,* 403 U.S. 622-23 (1971).

Religion and politics are everywhere a deadly mix. Judges stand ready to defuse these crises, which are beyond the calming capacities of politics. This "divisiveness" rationale for judicial superintendence of the field is as frequently cited as it is uncritically accepted. Scour the cases from beginning to end and you will find no basis for it besides assertions that, but for emergency rescues by courts, our society might go the way of Lebanon and Northern Ireland. (Of course, those tales are trimmed to fit the predetermined storyline. Each country is ravaged by "religious warfare," not — as in Lebanon — by a glorified gang war, or — as in Ireland — by political oppression.) The combined effect is no less than an almost universal agreement *not* on what the Court intends, but on the point that the Court — a nonpolitical institution — can and should superintend the whole of religion and public life.

What is the Court up to? I have argued elsewhere, on the basis of elaborate exegesis of the cases, that the only way to view the corpus is as one gigantic campaign to privatize religion.[13] The Court would limit religion's significance to "private" life, if not to individual psyches, and admit no *legitimate* influence upon our political life. "Divisiveness" rhetoric is nothing more nor less than a post hoc justification for privatization. It has no other intrinsic appeal, validity, or utility. It is the Court's rhetorical Munich or Vietnam — a historical memory so terrible that invoking it ends discussion even before the appropriateness of the analogy is explored. Of course no one wants the United States to become another Iran. But the real question is whether there is any warrant for suggesting that it might. In response, the Court rests upon unadorned ipse dixit or unsubstantial and inappropriate appeals to the framers.

Religion is the divisive factor, not political conflict generally or religio-political turmoil specifically. The Court does not, and could not realistically, expect to influence the actual content of religious belief, which is generated by and from nonpublic sources. Its focus, consequently, is upon the compelling quality of belief. So long as religious duty is taken as uniquely obligatory (i.e., what the one true God expects of all his children, believer and nonbeliever alike), religion threatens to irrupt and dominate the normative structure of the presently compartmentalized political sphere. This is so because faith's account of,

13. For an in-depth analysis of this topic, see Bradley, "Dogmatomachy — A Privatization Theory of the Religion Clause Cases," *St. Louis Law Journal* 30 (1986): 275-330.

for example, "equality" or "privacy" or "sexual orientation" or abortion or the origin of the species is, in the eyes of the believer, superior to the law's account. The Court's monopoly on such prescriptive thinking can be feasibly maintained only by relativizing belief, by inducing the believer to view the "social gospel" as just another "ideology" or "interest" that must be ordered within the public realm according to constitutionally derived norms of justice. To borrow an image from Lonergan, the Court intends control of the riverbed (i.e., the nature of belief) over which all streams (i.e., beliefs) must flow.

Anthropologist Mary Douglas cautions that "secularization," most commonly understood as a "naked public square" or evacuation of religion from political life, does not imply a diminution of private religious devotion.[14] The other definition of secularization — the politicization of belief itself — is inapposite to the judicial project, and for good reason. Except where it fits the contemporary political agenda, in which case its effects are redundant, politicized religion is the villain of the piece. I would insist that "privatization" similarly be given a particular definition. Under the influence of the great dogma of modernity — individual moral autonomy or "subjectivism" — the Court is trying not only to privatize but to "individualize" religion. Religious belief not only has no legitimate public aspirations but makes no well-founded intersubjective truth claims. The solitary heart is the locus of all religious experience. All extra-individual authority is suspect (as it is for the Quakers) if not indeed hostile to religious liberty.

II

As early as 1949 Murray saw the privatizing potential in the emerging corpus.[15] In *We Hold These Truths* he points to it as one example or kind of "faith" placed in the religion clauses. And there might be an end to it: by pursuing privatization the Supreme Court has "established," in effect, "articles of faith." But it is not that simple. In the remainder of this essay, I wish to render problematic Murray's distinction and recast his central insights into terms more consonant with his

14. Douglas, *How Institutions Think* (Syracuse: Syracuse University Press, 1986), p. 94.

15. See Murray, "Law or Prepossessions," *Law and Contemporary Problems* 23 (1949): 14-43.

thinking. His seminal expression of the distinction is compact enough to permit full quotation:

> On the one hand, there are those who read into [the religion clauses] certain ultimate beliefs, certain specifically sectarian tenets with regard to the nature of religion, religious truth, the church, faith, conscience, divine revelation, human freedom, etc. In this view these articles are invested with a genuine sanctity that derives from their supposed religious content. They are dogmas, norms of orthodoxy, to which one must conform on pain of some manner of excommunication. They are true articles of faith. Hence it is necessary to believe them, to give them a religiously motivated assent.
>
> On the other hand, there are those who see in these articles only a law, not a dogma. These constitutional clauses have no religious content. They answer none of the eternal human questions with regard to the nature of truth and freedom or the manner in which the spiritual order of man's life is to be organized or not organized. Therefore they are not invested with the sanctity that attaches to dogma, but only with the rationality that attaches to law. Rationality is the highest value of law. In further consequence, it is not necessary to give them a religious assent but only a rational civil obedience. In a word, they are not articles of faith but articles of peace, that is to say, you may not act against them, because they are law and good law. (Pp. 48-49)

Murray specifies his concerns in greater detail:

> Do these clauses assert or imply that the nature of the church is such that it inherently demands the most absolute separation from the state? Do they *assert* or *imply* that the institutional church is simply a voluntary association of like-minded men, that its origins are only in the will of men to associate freely for purposes of religion and worship?
>
> Further, does the free-exercise clause assert or imply that the individual conscience is the ultimate norm of religious belief in such wise that an external religious authority is inimical to Christian freedom? Does it hold that religion is a purely private matter in such wise that an ecclesiastical religion is inherently a corruption of the Christian Gospel?
>
> The questions could be multiplied, but they all reduce themselves

to two. Is the no-establishment clause a piece of ecclesiology, and is
the free-exercise clause a piece of religious philosophy? (Pp. 50-51)

My initial observation regards the intrinsic instability of Murray's
distinction. This instability can be seen by examining three conclusions
that might be drawn from Murray's premises. From a starting point
similar to Murray's concern that no particular religious view be intimate with our political institutions, "endorsement" analysis deduces
privatization. This is because, in present conditions of "pluralism," *any*
public religiosity may entail "outsider" status for some, or perhaps even
many, Americans. It may be that "endorsement" analysis is flawed (I
think so), but Murray's premises seem to entail it. Again, from premises
like Murray's, systematic liberal thinkers have construed "justice" to
privatize religion. One of the conditions of justice sounds very Mur-
rayan: we want principles of "justice" that do *not* implicate persons'
commitments on matters such as the meaning and purpose of life. To
do that effectively, we have to operate publicly without implicating
them. The only way to avoid implicating them is to leave them *out* of
public life. Since religion commonly carries answers to such questions,
religion ought be kept out of public life too. Finally, at least some
well-intentioned persons have synthesized Murray's disjunctive into
privatization. The *only* way to keep civil peace in our society is finally
to eliminate all public religion. With the most slippery-slope rhetoric
in all constitutional law, the argument is pressed that to defuse the
potentially deadly mix of religious belief and politics, we need a "wall
of separation" between religion and public life. The slightest breach
might detonate the load.

These observations counsel soft-peddling the distinction. But
Murray hardens it into a dichotomy: "from the stand point both of
history and of contemporary social reality the only tenable position is
that [they] . . . are not articles of faith but articles of peace" (p. 56).
The latter is the "*only* view that a citizen with both historical sense and
common sense" can hold (p. 56; italics mine).

Now, if Murray means that the dogmatic view of the First Amendment would force Catholics (and many other non-Protestants) into an
adversary or dissenting cultural posture, he is probably correct. But
"historical" sense cannot objectively rule out that possibility. "Common
sense" might, but *whose* intuitions control? Norman Lear's? Harry
Blackmun's? Jimmy Swaggart's? The point is, it takes just a little
memory (if that) to sense a *deep* anti-Catholic bias in prevailing cultural

and legal notions of religious liberty and of the proper relation of church to state. But Murray's aim is to forge an account of the American regime that Catholics *can* accept, and so he cannot recommend the dogmatic account. We may profitably view his thought here as something like asking what the religion clauses would *have to mean* to be compatible with Catholic faith commitments. But Murray, we should remember, was not a constitutional lawyer. He was a Catholic theologian whose intent was to project Catholic thought forcefully onto the American national stage. And it simply does not follow from an effective Catholic appropriation that Murray identified what they actually mean. (As we shall see, Protestant definitions and premises determined the "original intent" of the clauses, and we have already noted that their elaboration is now controlled by liberal individualism.) It might follow that other faith commitments (Protestant, Jewish, Mormon) would rightfully produce different sectarian accounts of the clauses. But Murray insists that his is the *only* acceptable account.

No "theological" account can delegitimate other "theological" accounts. To do that, one needs "neutral" ground. Hence, Murray argues historically, even though he dismisses the "genesis" of the religion clauses as a matter of separate interest. Murray was also no historian. I submit that his history was controlled by his objective — namely, to depict a regime acceptable to Catholics. By ruling out as an "Article of Faith" a "Protestantized" constitutionalism, Murray imposed an arbitrary constraint on historical investigation. With such a constraint, he can get the history right only by accident. He is not vouchsafed such good luck.

Murray adduces four specific arguments to show that, as a historical matter, the clauses came into being "under the pressure of their necessity to the public peace" (p. 58). Indeed, this *was* a settlement among contending religious groups. I would go one step further. With historian R. L. Moore, I would conclude that

> the full extension of religious tolerance, if indeed full tolerance describes the present state of religious affairs in the United States, was more the product of conditions of pluralism which no one sect had the power to overcome as of an abstract belief in the value of pluralism. Contemporary studies that point to a strong correlation between religious affiliation and prejudice should remind us that religious tolerance was not the free gift of a dominant religious group, the Constitution notwithstanding, but the product of uneasy

arrangements made between groups that did not much like one another.[16]

But this seemingly auspicious insight does not serve Murray's argument well. First, there are the demographics of it. That a "Protestant" settlement in the America of 1790 was coterminous with an "American" settlement — in a nation of 4,000,000 there were no atheists, perhaps 3,500 Jews, and 35,000 Catholics — does not make the "Protestant" component accidental, either then or now (not now, at least, if we do not dogmatically rule out some "originalist" account of constitutional law). A persuasive case can be made that Protestant faith commitments rather than Enlightenment rationalism or any form of protoliberalism controlled the early national settlement. In this view, "nonestablishment" represents a conclusion by Protestants that what distinguished Protestants sects was unimportant to political unity. This did *not* imply that what distinguished Protestantism from, say, Catholicism was similarly unproblematic. The flip side is that pan-Protestant ecclesiology, spirituality, and morality *were* essential to political solidarity. Free exercise in this scenario would be understood as a limited immunity for "worship." But again one can — and I think the framers did — arrive at such "liberty of conscience" from Protestant premises. They had Protestant worship in mind, and many believed regular public worship essential to political unity. But almost all eventually agreed that the particular style of Protestant worship — its sectarian form — was a matter of political indifference. By virtue of their understanding of God, man, grace, Spirit, and church, they were religiously obliged to abstain from civil interference with it.

"Nonestablishment" *was* historically an agreement among Protestants concerning sect equality.[17] In important respects and as Murray indicates, this "settlement" left unresolved some important questions. It appealed to many as a way to get on with other business — such matters as seeking political unity and concerted pragmatic action. Concretely, "nonestablishment" in the states was mostly a matter of enlisting nonsectarian loyalty to the revolution. At the national level, it assured all manner of believers that they could support the new

16. Moore, *Religious Outsiders and the Making of Americans* (New York: Oxford University Press, 1986), p. 205.

17. For the original meaning of the religion clauses of the First Amendment, see Bradley, *Church-State Relationships in America* (Westport, Conn.: Greenwood, 1987).

nation. But this half-empty glass is also half full. The positive view highlights the conditions of homogeneity that permitted agreement on the essentials of religious liberty. For instance, Protestants, and Catholics have *never* in our history agreed upon the meaning of religious liberty. Now, secularized liberals provide a coherent third view.

Murray neglects in the "two articles" piece what he so often elsewhere emphasized: the worldview shared by the founding generation's limited partnership in the settlement. Catholics, or "Papists," were largely second-class citizens in the thirteen original states and were barred from public office in New Hampshire as late as 1877.[18] Nor did these "articles of peace" prevent the U.S. Supreme Court in the late nineteenth century from sanctioning persecution of Mormons by treating Mormonism as no religion at all and thus no party to the First Amendment settlement.

Murray's work on the whole supports such a nonliberal account of the founding. He allows that it rests upon some substantive agreement about the good of man, and not simply a formal consensus agreed to by Rawlsian egos. He often describes this consensus about the good of men as "natural law." In view of the overwhelmingly Protestant character of our heritage and the nominalism that so often characterizes the Reformers, that conclusion is probably off the mark. That the common law carried notions coincident with natural law — specifically, that individuals possess rights antecedent to government — does not mean that common law is applied natural law. Indeed, equity has served more than common law as the carrier of "natural law" in Anglo-American legal history. There has been in America a "higher law" tradition, but that has drawn principally on "divine law" as revealed in Scripture. The effect has been, until recently, a common traditional morality, not natural law.

Nowhere does Murray welcome "moral pluralism," nor did he think American institutions could survive it. Put differently, and present moral pluralism notwithstanding, Murray recognized that the regime presupposes a certain kind of person. He did *not* agree that it presupposes only a Protestant person. He was concerned (properly, if one views his work as mediating the regime to Catholics) to expand religious pluralism to Catholics. But this was still a fairly modest ecumenical movement, and the move is consistent with claiming that the

18. *Federal and State Constitutions of the United States,* vol. 2, ed. Benjamin Perley Poore (New York: Lenox Hill, 1972), p. 1309.

regime presupposes Christians, or at least Christianity. Murray did not thereby promote any exclusivism as a component of citizenship. Nor do I. But it remains the case that Murray's work suggests that our institutions are Christian, and that is incompatible with what he characterizes as "articles of peace."

III

At the heart of Murray's meditation on church and state — and at the center of his conception of the American regime — is the differentiation of the spiritual and temporal authorities in the one society. "Dyarchy" is Murray's term of choice, and Pope Gelasius provided the seminal expression. In 494 he wrote to the Emperor Anastasius that "two [swords] there are, august emperor, by which this world is chiefly ruled, the sacred authority of the priesthood and the royal power."[19]

Let us assume with Murray both that this dyarchy permits Catholics to cleave to the regime and that the regime honors it. We must still insist that it is culturally contingent and that its host culture is Christian. The dyarchy is not some spiritual meteor that dropped out of the sky, nor is it found in nature. Indeed, as Tocqueville saw long ago, man's natural propensity is to live monistically — that is, by a single set of norms governing the whole of life.[20] The Christian insight is counterintuitive and historically unique.

So what is this "dyarchy"?

It has been formulated in a number of familiar ways. Believers should be "in" the world but not "of" it. Believers live "between the times," in the "already but not yet." Life is a "sojourn" or "pilgrimage." Ultimately the last shall be first, and the first last. One gains life by dying. The meek shall inherit the earth. These and many equivalent "symbols" express the same reality: the permanent tension in Western societies between the exigencies of pragmatic existence in history and the consciousness of divine order arising in the human soul. The reality so constituted is, most precisely, a field of tension bordered by two pulls, denoted "world" and "divine." When individuals who have ex-

---

19. Gelasius, quoted by Harold Berman in *Law and Revolution* (Cambridge: Harvard University Press, 1983), p. 92.

20. See Robert Flanders, *Nauvoo: Kingdom on the Mississippi* (Urbana, Ill.: University of Illinois Press, 1975), p. 241.

perienced this tension form a cultural matrix, the tension is channeled into two authorities within their society: spiritual and temporal. The matrix, by transmitting the underlying experiences via symbols, lays the foundation for a political community characterized by a distinction between "church" and "state." Like all ideas, if the idea of a distinction between church and state it is torn from its engendering experiences, it loses not only its proper meaning but any meaning at all. This is the core of what we call "the problem of church and state."[21]

"State" and "church" are the polar pulls in a field of tension. The Christian tradition provides many cognate symbolizations: the "sacred" and "profane," Augustine's two cities, medieval two-sword imagery, Roger Williams's garden and wilderness, and the Lutheran concept of the two kingdoms. All point to the tension between our experience of the attraction of the transcendent and the inescapable demands of pragmatic existence.

But separation of church and state, by means of a wall or otherwise, is thinkable only where men inhabit a particular historical context. That context includes the experiences issuing in the tension we have just discussed and an institutional milieu comprising a political organization that is territorial and national (a notion of "state" that begins only with the sixteenth century) and a religious organization taking the form of some concrete body properly denoted a "church." All these factors effectively coalesce only in modern Western societies. If they were not present in late eighteenth-century America, the First Amendment would never have been written. Put differently, the religion clauses are a Christian artifact. This is not to suggest that only Christians can enjoy the liberty they promise but rather that a Christian worldview produced them. Since that observation is the pivot of my own analysis — and Murray's — let me explain and defend it at length.

It is routinely though not widely remarked in the nonlegal literature that Christianity, as a historical fact, causes or gives rise to the church-state distinction. That is, I think, basically true. By "basically" I mean that the main trajectory of Christianity in the postapostolic era exhibits the problematic and that it is difficult to detect it anywhere

---

21. For a fuller discussion of this topic, see Bradley, "Church Autonomy in the Constitutional Order: The End of Church and State?" *Louisiana Law Review* 49 (1989): 1057-87. My treatment of these matters is greatly influenced by the work of Eric Voegelin, especially *Plato and Aristotle* (Baton Rouge: Louisiana State University Press, 1957) and *The New Science of Politics* (Chicago: University of Chicago Press, 1952).

else. To establish the warrants for such a hypothesis, we must begin by
investigating historical situations not measurably penetrated by Christianity to see whether the church-state problematic is there unob-
served. If not, why not?

In most such situations there is no church-state difficulty or
conflict — not because it has been "solved" but because it does not
exist. In the absence of the necessary experience or required verbal
symbols (or both), speaking of "church and state" is like lecturing a
blind man on color.

Eric Voegelin provides the first example in his interpretation of the
Platonic corpus. He asserts that Plato, like religious prophets and saints,
was pulled by "the divine chord." The problem for Plato was that the
available conceptual apparatus — that of classical philosophy — forced
him to locate the quest for human perfection, which saints pursue
through the church and beyond death, entirely within the political
community. The only available form of community was the polis. Put
differently, Plato experienced the divine pull and was surely aware of the
exigencies of pragmatic existence, but in his work the tension issued in
the truncated symbolism of a "perfect" political community. The result
in *The Republic* is a polis under the rule of mystic philosophers. Voegelin
concludes that the Republic represents an attempt to dissolve the tension
by making the order of the soul the order of society.[22]

May we then say that Western monotheism produced the "dyarchy"? No. Muslims, for instance, see their scripture much as Christian
fundamentalists see the Bible: as the literal word of God, verbally
inspired in toto and therefore inerrant. Completely lost in each case
is the distinction between divine truth and a time-conditioned expression of it, implying that scripture contains contingent elements rooted
in a particular cultural milieu. There is no room in Islam for a "critical"
appropriation of the Word, which might moderate the political problem that resurgent Islam presents — transnational violence claiming
divine sanction. In our time the Islam of most Muslims *is* an enormous
political problem, at least for infidels. Nevertheless, Islamic societies
do *not* experience the church-state tension. Why not?

The content of Shari'a dissolves the tension that might otherwise
surface in a monotheistic tradition that purports to be a faith that can
be lived in this world. Daniel Pipes explains the effect of Islamic law
as follows:

22. See Voegelin, *Plato and Aristotle,* and *The New Science of Politics,* pp. 61-75.

Islam, unlike Christianity, contains a complete program for ordering society. Whereas Christianity provides grand moral instructions but leaves practical details to the discretion of each community, Islam specifies exact goals for all Muslims to follow as well as the rules by which to enforce them. If Christians eager to act on behalf of their faith have no script for political action, Muslims have one so detailed, so nuanced, it requires a lifetime of study to master. . . . However diverse Muslim public life may be, it always takes place in the framework of Shari'a ideals. Adjusting realities to the Shari'a is the key to Islam's role in human relations.[23]

In other words, the law's completeness determines the relation between God and man. God's continuing demands are supposed to be fully (if implicitly) contained in a fully intelligible deposit of revelation. New questions arise, but, in principle, ancient scripture contains the solution. This confidence in the scrutability of an ahistorical "perfect" revelation perhaps also resonates within certain segments of Protestant fundamentalism, but nowhere in the bulk of Christian tradition. It has the effect of substituting for an ongoing and inherently unresolvable tension the challenge of completing a large jigsaw puzzle. There remains only the "tension" of wondering whether human ingenuity will be able to decipher the instructions encoded by Mohammed.

In Islam, the second pull — that of successful mundane existence — is quieted by the law's detailed prescripts for public life. An enduring political problem for Christian societies — how to deal with unbelievers and heterodoxy (which is to say, the problem of "pluralism") — does not arise in Islam: there is no such thing as a "pluralistic Islamic society." Muslims are either in power, in which case the Shari'a tells them how to deal with infidels, or they are out of power. If they are out of power, the law directs them to acquire it, by violence if necessary. The purpose of jihad, or so-called "holy war," as Pipes explains,

is not to spread the faith. Non-Muslims commonly assume that jihad calls for the militant expansion of the Islamic *religion;* in fact, its purpose is to spread the rule of Islamic *law.* The logic behind law being the central concern of jihad has special importance for the topic of Islam and political power: to approach God properly, man

23. Pipes, *In the Path of God* (New York: Basic Books, 1983), p. 76.

must live by the Shari'a, because the Shari'a contains provisions which can only be executed by a government, the state has to be in the hands of Muslims; Muslims must therefore control territory; to do this, they need to wage war — and thus, the provision for jihad. If Muslims do not rule, kafirs do; by definition, the latter do not see the Shari'a as a sacred law. For expediency's sake, to minimize Muslim antagonism toward their rule, non-Muslims may enforce some Islamic precepts, especially private ones, but they would never go to the effort of implementing Shari'a public regulations. For these reasons, Islam requires the expulsion of non-Muslims from power and their replacement by believers, by force, if necessary.[24]

Other examples of cultural systems in which the tension we are discussing is not found include those constructed on animistic and "pagan" belief systems. *Pagan* is perhaps the better-known term. Colloquially it designates a crude unbeliever, an atheist lacking table manners. But historically "pagans" were believers: they believed in what Christians called the religion of the Greeks and Romans, best rendered as "polytheism," a plurality of gods. "Animism" is technically the attribution of consciousness and (usually) spiritual powers to inanimate things and verges on paganism in generating a multitude of "gods" or "spirits," each deserving some part of human spiritual attention. A contemporary example of a cultural system that lacks the tension we have been discussing is that of the Native American, proponents of which are increasingly initiating church-state litigation. In *Bowen v. Roy* (476 U.S. 693 [1986]), for instance, a Native American asserted that her "spirit" was diminished when she was assigned a social security number. While accommodation of a lone litigant's spiritual needs may politically be the preferred course, the Supreme Court in *Bowen* properly sought a principled resolution of her claim.

The plaintiff lost her case, in an opinion that generally weakened the protection of conscientious objectors. The Court did not say as much, but I think (on the basis of the most recent Indian belief case, *Lyng v. Northwest Indiana Cemetery Protection Association,* 108 S.Ct. 1319 [1988]) that the perceived impossibility of sustaining our regime in an analytical matrix determined by Native American belief caused a reevaluation of earlier, sweeping statements on religious liberty. Where Indian spirituality prevails, "spiritual liberty" is incompatible with the

24. Pipes, *In the Path of God,* pp. 44-45.

existence of a secular state. *Bowen* makes clear that the spirit and the state cannot simultaneously roam where they will.

The opinion of the three dissenters in *Lyng,* written by Justice Brennan, frankly recognizes this, even as it supports the Native American claim. The opinon notes that for Native Americans, religion cannot be distinguished from social, cultural, political, and other aspects of Indian life. This is so because the Native American concept of nature (unlike that in other Western religious systems) does not presume that the universe has an intrinsic, regular order that can be discovered through scientific investigation; instead, it calls on man to participate in an ongoing process of creation. This approach to experience holds that "land, like all other *living* things, is unique and specific sites possess different spiritual properties and significance."[25] It is easy to agree with the dissenters that radically different categories are at work here, although by contrasting "Western" with Native American they betray a slippery grip on the priority of habitation in this hemisphere. After all, Columbus brought Christianity *to* the New World. But neither the dissenters nor the majority quite drew the inevitable conclusion: the contrast (at a minimum) is to Western monotheism, particularly Christianity, which provides the "categories" that make separation of church and state not just desirable but conceivable. The opinion really says that religious freedom as we know it is drawn from that same set of categories.

Simple observation of separatist groups such as the Amish and the Hasidim confirms an observation applicable to Native American spirituality: cultural isolation, and perhaps political sovereignty as well, is essential for maintenance of some religious commitments. Indeed, the importance of a geographic location to Old Testament Judaism (the Temple at Jerusalem) suggests that even that faith was largely dependent upon a certain political autonomy. The itinerant and difficult experiences of Mormons up until the 1890s strongly suggest that Mormonism too required political independence in order to be itself.

Murray would, I think, dispute none of this. In the "Articles of Faith" or "Articles of Peace" essay he recognizes the dyarchy as "Christianity's cardinal contribution to the Western political tradition" (p. 64). It provided the "artisans of the Constitution" a "clear grasp of the distinction between state and society" (p. 66). He also says that while

---

25. *Lyng v. Northwest Indiana Cemetery Protection Association,* 108 S.Ct. 1331 (1988).

the government has not "undertaken to represent transcendental truth
. . . it does indeed represent the commonly shared moral values of the
community" (p. 74). Thus, a certain morality translated into popular
virtue undergirds the regime. The burden of his "two articles" analysis
is to argue *for* Catholic acceptance of the clauses. In other words,
Catholics need not derive their political allegiance from "internal"
Catholic criteria.

This much establishes that Murray is no liberal in the theoretical
sense represented by John Rawls, and not just because Rawls characterizes Ignatius as a "fanatic."[26] The hallmark of such liberalism is
construction of political institutions and principles of justice to govern
them completely independent of religious belief. Rawls's method is to
prescind from virtually all moral and religious commitments in the
"original position" of choice. Murray sees that this stance is neither
religiously neutral nor "areligious"; he recognizes that it implicitly
involves the privatization of religion. It is my belief that this liberal
individualism has in fact taken over church-state jurisprudence since
Everson and that the judicial corpus since has been one big privatization
campaign. For this reason we must conclude that however we characterize Murray's position (and I believe that it is closer to his articles of
faith than he would have it), it is at odds with that of the Supreme
Court. Murray, by his own admission, would now be a dissenter.

IV

I have already indicated how precarious Murray's distinction is. I
should now like to add that it is indistinct, that the two positions he
articulates are not crisp alternatives. They simply do not constitute the
sharp dichotomy Murray proposes. To recast Murray's thinking, let us
unpack his rendering of "articles of faith." It has many possible denotations. Some are alternatives Murray rejects; others actually coincide
with his own commitments. This suggests that a more supple terminology could convey Murray's thought to us more effectively, regardless of the utility of his typology in the polemical environment
within which he wrote.

Viewing the religion clauses as an "Article of Faith" may mean,
among other things, that

26. Rawls, *A Theory of Justice* (Cambridge: Belknap Press, 1971), p. 553.

1. they fuse religious triumphalism and political messianism by col-
   lapsing the tension between worldly existence and divine reality,
   thereby immanentizing the Christian eschaton and monistically
   fusing church and state;
2. they are principles of the rightly ordered polity, the best political
   regime humans can conceive, but they retain a distinction between church and state;
3. they presuppose for their intelligibility a distinct worldview, such
   as the basic Christian differentiation of experience conveyed by
   Murray's dyarchy;
4. they presuppose for effective operations a certain kind of person,
   as Murray suggested by noting that our government has traditionally "represented" a common morality; or
5. they are regarded by the viewer with a reverence akin to that
   evoked by human encounters with the divine.

The fifth possibility is the easiest to handle, because it is unimportant. A veteran might cry as the flag passes during the Fourth of
July parade, or snap to attention, or demand that it not be desecrated,
and do so without implying anything more than that he is an emotional
patriot. And statesmen — even ordinary citizens — *ought* to take the
Constitution very seriously. As long as this reverence does not deify
the polity, this poses no theoretical difficulty.

The first option is clearly not Murray's view. It is not a Christian
idea; indeed, few people believe it at all. The second option may be a
Christian idea, but it is not Murray's. He considered the First Amendment to be good because it is well suited to a pluralistic society, but he
considered pluralism itself to be lamentable, against the will of God.
It is not the sinew of the "best" regime. "The United States is a good
place to live. . . . But it is not a church. . . . It is simply a civil community" (p. 54). One should respect it but not revere it. Reverence should
be reserved for higher things. This is probably the locus of Murray's
proffered distinction between Articles of Peace and Articles of Faith.
On the one side, he may have wished to deflect the tendency among
many Protestants to draw a straight, unbroken line from their own
religiously grounded conceptions of the best polity to the First Amendment and, indeed, to the entire regime. Murray saw this as virtually
the type of religious imperialism the Amendment was supposed to
forestall. On the other hand, he also quite perceptively recognized the
dominant thrust of secularist intellectuals who reasoned backward

from the contours of a proto-Rawlsian liberal polity to the only compatible role for religion: privatization. In each case there is a coincidence, lacking in Murray's own thought as a Catholic, between religious aspirations for society and the principles of the historical regime. I think Murray quite rightly warned that only a more modest, prudential, and even "temporal" approach to the question could work with fairness in a pluralist society. This approach he dubbed "Articles of Peace."

But Murray's analysis immediately collides with its own criterion. Because Murray subscribed to the third and fourth options listed above, it follows that the parties to his armistice *do* share cultural convictions in some decisive way and do draw from similar religious traditions. The breakdown of our common morality that has largely taken place *since* Murray's death has laid bare the cultural assumptions — now not shared — of his account. The result is that even that prudential account is now open to charges of religious and cultural imperialism.

The key here is the question Murray suppresses: What does the First Amendment *mean?* It states legal principles, but what are they? Murray does not answer that question in his "Two Articles" piece. In my view, he fails to do so because the question is unanswerable in that context. His argument can succeed only by holding definition at bay, because, aside from an originalist account, any answer can and must rest upon presuppositions peculiar to some, but not all, faith commitments. But "Articles of Peace" are supposed to rest upon no such grounds.

Law characteristically depends on sources external to itself for its descriptions. In this case, "establishment," "religion," and "free exercise" are the descriptors. Their broader heritage includes such terms as "separation of church and state," "liberty of conscience," "spiritual liberty," and "religious liberty." Any definition of such terms inevitably presupposes a set of descriptions. As the descriptions vary, so will the definitions. There are Protestant definitions, liberal secular definitions, Catholic definitions, and so on. There might as well be Jewish and Islamic accounts of some, but not all of them. In many systems of thought, the terms are unintelligible. This is the "pluralism" that Murray actually describes and that has been the stuff of controversy in our history.

Three illustrations may assist us here. The basic differentiation of authority in society into two orders *is* common Christian property, but there are very different conceptions of it within Christianity, even within the different branches of Protestantism. Luther's "two king-doms" cannot be equated with Calvin's two spheres, they both differ from Roger Williams's "the garden and the wilderness," and all three are different from the Gelasian "two swords," which in turn is different from Augustine's nearly contemporaneous conception of "two cities." In the "two swords" doctrine, "the priesthood administered the sacred mysteries, but the emperors made the laws, including the ecclesiastical laws."[27] In its struggle for freedom from imperial domination, the medieval church swung all the way to claim a spiritual superiority over the political realm. The debate over "superiority" eventually gave way to a better question: If each authority is supreme in its own sphere, how are we to coordinate the authorities within one society. The liberal secularist entertains his own dyarchy. It is a most peculiar construction in which all "value" judgments are ostensibly private and where the public sphere encompasses "policy goals" served by rational technique.

Protestants and Catholics have contended in America over the definition of two other critical terms: "liberty of conscience" and "spir-itual" or "religious" liberty. Protestants contend that the former has always meant, positively, individual interpretation of Scripture and the direct unmediated encounter of the soul with God through grace. It has also commonly, and negatively, been used to express hostility to the Catholic Church, especially the priesthood, and (in a related fash-ion) to endorse Bible reading in the public schools.[28]

"Spiritual" or, less commonly, "religious" liberty has always meant to American Catholics about the same thing as "ecclesiastical" liberty — not the Protestant individual liberty of conscience but the immunity and freedom of the church, of an effectively organized religious body, in society. Protestants, especially Calvin, associated the "spiritual" in its earthly manifestation with the individual and his conscience.[29] The church was a more ephemeral teaching instrument, not the ark of salvation. Indeed, Protestant Americans have traditionally viewed the "ecclesiastical" as the enemy of the "spiritual." Catholics more typically view them as not only harmonious but practically identical. The mod-ern mind, both inside the church and out, defines "liberty of con-

27. Berman, *Law and Revolution*, p. 92.
28. See Michael Holt, *The Political Crisis of the 1850's* (New York: Wiley, 1978), pp. 178-79.
29. See Elwyn Smith, *Religious Liberty in the United States* (Philadelphia: Fortress Press, 1972), pp. 167-70.

science" quite differently. It maintains that "conscience" is bound to a relativist or subjectivist epistemology, that it amounts to something like creation and mastery of one's own moral universe and the "right" to act on its urgings so long as others are not "harmed." Respect for conscience means the sanctity of individual moral "autonomy," and its currency is "sincerity." Unlike both Protestant and Catholic accounts, it has no transcendent referent. It is a practical monism. It has no place in the Christian tradition.

One way out of *this* "pluralism" is available at least to constitutional law. One might simply retrieve what the First Amendment meant in its originating context. "Nonestablishment" would then mean an equality among religious groups (but imply no hostility toward fostering religion generally), and free exercise would privilege *worship* (but not all conscientious behavior). This would have the effect of halting "judicialization" of church-state issues and simultaneously halting the imposition of the liberal individualist orthodoxy of privatization under the auspices of judicial interpretation. We would then be forced to move the question of the nature of American pluralism foursquare into the center of the American public argument. Underlying the different understandings of the nature of American pluralism embodied in the different interpretations of the religion clauses are nothing less than different definitions of the key terms of the discussion reflecting widely divergent ways of conceiving the universe.

What we need do is bring these "universes" and their discrepant accounts of religious liberty into some sort of dialogue. That will not be possible so long as we persist in the "judicialization" of church and state and pretend that the religion clauses can be interpreted in such a fashion as to avoid the presuppositions of any particular worldview. By establishing originalism as the guiding principle of judicial interpretation in this area, we would, in short, make room for the genuine political discourse we need.

Murray on Economics:
Liberal or Conservative?

John C. Cort

M Y FIRST AND LAST IMPRESSION of John Courtney Murray is of
him sitting in our living room, surrounded by some of the best
minds on the Harvard and Boston College faculties, discoursing on a
subject of his own choosing — namely, "How much unity do we need,
and how much pluralism can we stand?"

This was a meeting of a group that Sam Beer, chairman of the
government department at Harvard, and I organized and which met
for several years during the late fifties in an effort to bridge the chasm
that even then yawned between Stevenson Democrats at Harvard and
Stevenson Democrats at Boston College.

After this particular meeting one member pointed out that it took
a good man to hold the floor without interruptions after the group
had passed the two-beer mark, but that night, whenever Father Murray
spoke, all present listened in silence and respect.

He was a most impressive man with a most impressive mind, and
one of my own first-rank personal heroes. His being silenced by the
Ottaviani clique at the Vatican was cause for grief and bitterness, and
his vindication and triumph at Vatican II was an occasion for great joy
and thanksgiving. He was the leader, the champion in one of the most

EDITORS' NOTE: The argument in this essay is based on a thesis propounded by
the author in *Christian Socialism: An Informal History* (Maryknoll, N.Y.: Orbis Books,
1988).

significant struggles in the history of the Church, and his victory was a magnificent vindication of our faith in that Church.

That being said, one must add that his understandable fixation on the value of freedom did lead him at times to pass over, or at least *seem* to pass over, to slight, to underestimate the value of justice. This tendency has been seized upon by such busy defenders of capitalism as Michael Novak and John Rohr to claim Murray as one of their own. There is something to be said for their claim, and there are also some significant things to be said against their claim. I shall try to say both.

The topic of Murray's talk that night in our living room was a variation on the theme that dominated almost all of his writing: "As much freedom as possible; as much coercion as necessary." Sometimes the second part came out "as much government as necessary." If we keep this theme, this formula clearly in mind at all times, it will be easier to conclude that Messrs. Novak, Rohr, et al. must be denied the pleasure of claiming John Courtney Murray as a true-blue apostle of free-market economics.

Robert McElroy has written that "economics was one area which the intellectually far-ranging Murray assiduously avoided in his writings and speeches."[1] But this is not entirely true. There are occasional references, usually brief, to the subject of economics in his writings. Perhaps the most sustained discussion of the subject can be found in one of his five articles on Leo XIII that appeared in *Theological Studies* during the years 1953 and 1954. The article of which I speak is entitled "Leo XIII: Two Concepts of Government."

The article is a carefully reasoned argument for the aforementioned formula, and in fact the formula itself makes an appearance: "If one wished to sum up Leo's political concept of government in its relation to the socio-economic order, one might well use the phrase, 'As much freedom as possible, as much government as necessary.' " Murray adds that "the phrase has a good American ring, whatever one's judgment may be on the manner and success with which the U.S. has applied it."[2]

Let us now analyze the formula as Murray discusses it and then consider how both Novak and those who disagree with Novak interpret

1. McElroy, *The Search for an American Public Theology: The Contribution of John Courtney Murray* (New York: Paulist Press, 1989), p. 63.

2. Murray, "Leo XIII: Two Concepts of Government," *Theological Studies* 14 (December 1953): 559.

what Murray has to say. And let us begin not with his article on Leo XIII but with the foreword to the only book Murray published, *We Hold These Truths,* which is not so much a book as a collection of the more important among his sixty-nine articles. I start with it not only because it illuminates "the good American ring" that he attributed to his formula but also because it brings us immediately to the point of controversy: how would Murray really place himself on the liberal/conservative economic spectrum in the last decade of the twentieth century in the United States of America?

We can begin to answer the question if we turn to the foreword of *We Hold These Truths,* where Murray defends "the American Proposition." Says Murray, "it is classic American doctrine, immortally asserted by Abraham Lincoln, that the new nation which our Fathers brought forth on this continent was dedicated to a 'proposition'" — the proposition that "all men are created equal."[3]

The American Proposition, grounded in the Declaration of Independence, holds certain truths to be self-evident — specifically, "that all men are created equal, that they are endowed by their Creator with certain unalienable Rights, that among these are Life, Liberty and the pursuit of Happiness." Murray thus identifies the proposition with concepts and persons that strike a responsive chord among most Americans: the Declaration of Independence, the notion of self-evident truths, God the Creator endowing people with inalienable rights, Abraham Lincoln, the whole concept of natural law that was so dear to Murray's heart and mind, and, finally, liberty.

But he also mentions equality, and as a measure of what equality should mean, we have rights not simply to liberty but to life and the pursuit of happiness. In other words, he is getting into the area of justice. For several pages in the foreword he seems to abandon this theme in favor of the questions of the nature of a free society, of pluralism and civility and reasoned argument. But he quickly brings us back to the second part of the formula, to the realm of necessity, to government, to equality, and to justice when he says,

> ideally, I suppose, there should be only one passion in the City — the passion for justice. But the will to justice, though it engages the

3. Murray, *We Hold These Truths: Catholic Reflections on the American Proposition* (New York: Sheed & Ward, 1960), p. vii. Subsequent references to this volume will be made parenthetically in the text.

heart, finds its measure as it finds its origin in intelligence, in a clear
understanding of what is due to the equal citizen from the City and
to the City from the citizenry according to the mode of their equality.
This commonly shared will to justice is the ground of civic amity as
it is also the ground of that unity which is called peace. This unity,
qualified by amity, is the highest good of the civil multitude and the
perfection of its civility. (P. 8)

There is an echo here of an old Latin (and Christian) aphorism, *pax
opus iustitiae,* "peace is the work of justice" — an aphorism to which I
shall return in another context.[4]

Besides the dichotomy between freedom and justice, we come
upon at least one other dichotomy in Murray's thought, a dichotomy
that is relevant to the contest between freedom and justice in his mind
as it relates to economic affairs — the dichotomy between civility and
barbarism in modern society. Irving Babbitt reminded us that "barbarism is as close to civilization as rust to the most highly polished
steel." Murray reminds us of a more genteel sort of barbarism: "the
barbarian need not appear in bearskins with a club in hand. He may
wear a Brooks Brothers suit and carry a ball-point pen with which to
write his advertising copy" (p. 12).

How does barbarism arise? "Society becomes barbaric . . . when
economic interests assume the primacy over higher values" (p. 13).
There is a strong connection between barbarism and original sin,
between barbarism and "the decadence of moral corruption and the
political chaos of formlessness or the moral chaos of tyranny" (p. 13).
Murray's remedy for barbarism has a disquieting whiff of elitism:
"society is rescued from chaos only by a few men, not by the many. . . .
It is only the few who understand the disciplines of civility and are
able to sustain them in being and thus hold in check the forces of
barbarism that are always threatening to force the gates of the City"
(p. 13).

Who are these "few men"? In a discussion of how we arrive at
"the public consensus," Murray cites Adolf Berle's *Power without Property*

---

4. *We Hold These Truths* is an important starting point for any study of Murray's
thought not only because it is representative of his thought up to the year 1960
but also because it represents a kind of midpoint between the greater emphasis
placed on justice in the Leo XIII article of 1953 and the more insistent emphasis
on freedom in his writings during and after 1960 — when Vatican II was dealing
with religious liberty and Murray was naturally absorbed by that question.

with approval. We must rely on "the conclusions of careful university professors, the reasoned opinions of specialists, the statements of responsible journalists, and at times the solid pronouncements of respected politicians. . . . These, and men like them, are thus the real tribunal to which the American system is finally accountable" (p. 103).

Whatever happened to democracy? Whatever happened to natural law as defined by Thomas Aquinas, whom Murray quotes only a few pages later: "since the rational soul is the proper form of man, there is in *every* man a natural inclination to act according to reason, that is, according to virtue" (p. 119; italics mine). Must we depend for all our political and economic wisdom on this mostly white, male, comfortable middle- and upper-middle-class elite? E. B. White would seem to have been closer to St. Thomas, and also to the true spirit of democracy, when he gave voice to his modest but "recurrent suspicion that more than half the people are right more than half the time."[5] We have plenty of evidence that more than half the comfortable types are wrong more than half the time. Marx was wrong about a lot of things, but he was right about the fact that the comfortable folks have a very dominant tendency to think that the maintenance of their comforts is the only sound policy. And they can always find plenty of "careful university professors, specialists, responsible journalists and respected politicians" to agree with them.

I would not imply that Father Murray was guilty of this sin, but I like the comment of his fellow Jesuit Fr. Dan Berrigan, when he remarked about "careful university professors" and some theologians:

> their outcome in a given instance is nothing like a unitive conscience, political sense or passion, wisdom. None of these. But a small-minded, cold-fish attitude toward the world, any world but one's own; and one's own world tight and small as a worry bead in the palm. The above is commonly referred to as "value free" intellectual life. Value free, if one is allowed comment, only in the sense that it is an invitation to self-interest, fastidious, even disdainful toward the common life of people.[6]

Murray's faith in the fortunate few reached a sort of apogee of

---

5. White, *Wild Flag* (Austin: Houghton-Mifflin, 1954), p. 31.
6. Berrigan, *Daniel Berrigan: Poetry, Drama, Prose*, ed. Michael True (Maryknoll, N.Y.: Orbis Books, 1988), p. 334.

academic naivete a few pages after his tribute to the elite when he extended it to the lords and captains of industry:

> here, finally, is the key to the most curious aspect of the whole matter, namely, that the economic powers in society accept the judgments, directions, and corrections of the public consensus, at times to their own disadvantage, even when those moral dictates are not backed by the coercive force of the supreme public power.
>
> There is in men, even when they are powerful, some natural inclination to act according to reason in what concerns their power. . . . They do not want their economic action to be judged "evil." . . . Or, if this moral inclination fails, as it is likely to fail, in the face of the contrary imperatives of self-interest, these men of power are at least "natural" enough to submit to the just interventions of the public power in support of the public consensus. (Pp. 120-21)

We catch a clue to the mystery of where Michael Novak picked up his favorite oxymoron — "democratic capitalism" — in this section of Murray's book, where he writes, "finally, because concentrated economic power is checked by, and responsible to, the public consensus, the American economy qualifies as 'democratic'" (p. 104).

This is a novel definition of *democratic* — or it is a highly inadequate definition of *democratic,* given that there is a woeful absence of reassuring detail as to how, specifically, that awesome "concentrated economic power" of the lords and captains of U.S. industry, commerce, and finance is to be checked and held responsible to the public consensus.

And what about that public consensus? In other passages Murray himself is highly dubious about it and also about those "wise and learned" men who bring it forth from the test tubes and retorts of their intellectual laboratories. "I think . . . that the American university long since bade a quiet good-bye to the whole notion of an American consensus, as implying that there are truths that we hold in common," he says (p. 40). Or, as he argued in a speech to the John Carroll Society in 1961, "the fact of the matter is that there is a problem here. . . . It's the vacuum . . . that intellectual forces have created by their corrosive scepticism and positivism and pragmatism and relativism."[7]

McElroy highlights three powerful influences in our U.S. culture

7. Murray, cited by McElroy in *The Search for an American Public Theology,* p. 68.

that Murray himself laments and excoriates: technological secularism, practical materialism, and philosophical pluralism — influences that reduce the public consensus to confetti.[8] Murray is bitter about them, too. "What is our contemporary idiocy? What is the enemy within the city: If I had to give it a name, I think I would call it 'technological secularism.' The idiot today is the technological secularist who knows everything" (p. 49).

So this is the "wise and learned" or "wise and honest" community that is going to hold the rich and powerful to account and protect us all from their economic and financial shenanigans? Murray made these arguments in the fifties and early sixties, perhaps the most prosperous and upbeat period in the history of this country. Even such progressive economists as John Galbraith could at that point write such optimistic books as *The Affluent Society*. Perhaps Murray could not anticipate the publication of Michael Harrington's *The Other America: Poverty in the United States* in 1962, which revealed the continuing reality of misery and injustice even in that golden era of this fortunate, affluent society. In any event, Murray paid sanguine tribute to the U.S. economy: "our 'free institutions,' in their procedural aspects, are working today as well as they ever have worked or ever will work. Some tinkering with them may be needed" (p. 198).[9] One assumes he included our free economy among these institutions. With the wisdom of hindsight and our knowledge of the ever-increasing gap between rich and poor, we must label Murray's view of the U.S. economy as rose-colored indeed.

As Murray got caught up in the debate over religious liberty within the Church during the sixties, his obsession with freedom intensified. In 1964 he wrote that "truth, justice and love assure the stability of society; but freedom is the dynamism of social progress toward fuller humanity in communal living. The freedom of the people ranks as the political end, along with justice; it is a demand of justice itself. Freedom is also *the* political method whereby the people achieve their highest good, which is their own unity as a people."[10] And again,

8. See McElroy, *The Search for an American Public Theology*, pp. 44-53.

9. When one considers the fact that Murray's tribute to American society was written when segregation was still an ugly reality in the United States, when blacks were still terrorized and prevented from voting in much of the South, his confident optimism can only be regarded as embarrassing. Far more than tinkering was needed to make America a just society.

10. Murray, "The Problem of Religious Freedom," *Theological Studies* 25 (December 1964): 556.

"that which is primarily due in justice to the human person is his freedom — as much as freedom as possible. Finally, love of the human person and love among human persons require that the freedom of each and all should be respected as far as possible, and not curtailed except when and insofar as necessary.[11]

Friedrich Engels once wrote in glowing terms of "the ascent of man from the kingdom of necessity to the kingdom of freedom."[12] Unlike Engels's man, Murray's stands on the mountaintop in the kingdom of freedom, occasionally giving a wave of the hand to the poor folks down below in the kingdom of necessity. But there is a grace note that rescues Murray from falling into the reactionary camp: he does affirm that freedom ought not to be curtailed "except when and insofar as necessary." Despite his emphasis on freedom, he recognizes the existence of the kingdom of necessity.

So let us visit that kingdom again as it is reflected in Murray's thought, and for this purpose perhaps it will be helpful to go back to the article entitled "Two Concepts of Government." In this article, there is a strong emphasis on freedom, and in particular on the principle of subsidiarity, which appeared more prominently in Pius XI's *Quadragesimo Anno* and received one of its most succinct formulations in a *New Yorker* piece by Richard Goodwin: "the general rule should be to transfer power to [or retain it in] the smallest unit consistent with the scale of the problem."[13]

Nevertheless, from the very first page of his article, Murray recognizes the significance of Leo's famous labor encyclical *Rerum Novarum*, a significance that forever separates Leo and, by proxy, Murray from the economic conservatives. Writes Murray,

> as the Social Question pressed more and more urgently upon the Christian conscience in the latter half of the nineteenth century, two general schools of thought developed in Catholic circles with regard to the role of government in its solution. In Germany, where discussion was most active, the so-called Minimalists came to be led by

11. Murray, "The Declaration on Religious Freedom," in *Vatican II: An Interfaith Appraisal,* ed. John H. Miller (Notre Dame, Ind.: Association Press, 1966), p. 574.

12. Engels, in *The Marx-Engels Reader,* ed. Robert Tucker (New York: W. W. Norton, 1972), p. 838.

13. Goodwin, "The Sources of the Public Unhappiness," *New Yorker,* 4 January 1969, p. 50.

Bishop Freppel. The other school, so-called Interventionists, came under the more vigorous leadership of Bishop Ketteler. When Leo XIII finally issued *Rerum Novarum* in 1891, he firmly took his stand with Ketteler. This was a bold move, not pleasing to many Catholics. But when the initial resistance had been dissipated, the move was seen to be providential. By it, as someone has remarked, Leo XIII took the revolutionary flavor out of a strong program of government intervention in the socio-economic order; this was a necessary step toward a solution of the social Question.[14]

It is important to realize that Archbishop William Emmanuel Ketteler of Mainz was about as close to a Christian socialist as a Catholic archbishop could get in 1891. He was a not-too-secret admirer and supporter of Ferdinand Lassalle, founder of the first German socialist party and principal rival to Marx for leadership of the whole European socialist movement. Unlike Marx, who favored nationalization of industry, Lassalle was a strong promoter of worker-owned producer cooperatives, and this appealed to Ketteler, who actually wrote Lassalle for advice on how to set up some cooperatives. Although he had originally been opposed to state intervention in the economy, Ketteler eventually became one of its strongest advocates and was a cofounder of the Catholic Center Party, which favored state support for producer cooperatives and most of the other items in the Gotha program of the German socialists.

Leo XIII often referred to Ketteler as "my great predecessor" and once told Ketteler's former secretary that the archbishop was "the first openly to declare that employers *and* government had a responsibility and a duty to the workers of our time."[15]

Murray quotes the key passage in *Rerum Novarum:* "if therefore any injury has been done, or threatens to be done to the interests of the community *(rebus communibus)* — the kind of injury which cannot otherwise be repaired or prevented — it is necessary for public authority to intervene."[16] He quotes three other "classic texts" in the encyclical, the fourth and final of them concerning "the special duty of

14. Murray, "Leo XIII: Two Concepts of Government," p. 551.

15. See William Hogan, *The Development of Bishop Wilhelm Emmanuel von Ketteler's Interpretation of the Social Problem* (Washington: Catholic University Press, 1946), p. 18.

16. Murray, "Leo XIII: Two Concepts of Government," p. 552.

government to come to the aid of 'the unhappy multitude, which has no security through resources of its own' *(miserum vulgus, nullis opibus suis tutum)*." Murray comments that "Leo XIII has especially in view the growing urban proletariat, the new social phenomenon brought forth by the Industrial Revolution."[17]

It is unfortunately symptomatic of Murray, however, that he does not highlight the more striking and progressive statements of Leo. In the original document, the pope sets down a firm and explicit statement of the Church's "preferential option for the poor," *which he then insists must also be the state's preferential option:*

> rights indeed, by whomsoever possessed, must be religiously protected, and public authority, in warding off injuries and punishing wrongs, ought to see to it that individuals may have and hold what belongs to them. In protecting the rights of private individuals, however, special consideration must be given to the weak and the poor. For the nation, as it were, of the rich, is guarded by its own defenses and is in less need of governmental protection, whereas the suffering multitude, without the means to protect itself, relies especially on the protection of the state.[18]

This defense of the preferential option for the poor is one of the most significant statements made by any pope or council in modern times. This option, and the principle of subsidiarity, form the very heart, kernel, nub, and summary of Catholic social teaching. Almost every other principle fans out from it like spokes on a wheel, or ripples moving out concentrically from a stone thrown in a millpond.

Typically, I regret to note, Murray seems to prefer another quotation from Leo, not from the encyclical but from an allocution delivered to a group of French workers in 1887, four years before *Rerum Novarum.* The statement anticipates the interventionism of the encyclical, but it does so with a cautionary prelude that especially appeals to Murray's laissez-faire tendency:

> without a doubt the intervention and action of these [public] powers are not indispensably necessary, when conditions in labor and in-

17. Murray, "Leo XIII: Two Concepts of Government," p. 553.
18. Leo XIII, *Rerum Novarum: The Condition of Labor* (1891; rpt., Washington: National Catholic Welfare Conference, 1942), no. 54, 32.

dustry reveal nothing which offends against morality, justice, human dignity, the domestic life of the worker. But when any of these values is managed or compromised, the public powers, intervening in proper fashion and in just measure, are to do a work of salvation; for it falls to their charge to protect and safeguard the true interests of the citizens under their obedience.[19]

This is what Murray does with this quotation:

> If one could legitimately speak of "ideals" in the matter, the ideal would be a socio-economic order that would be entirely self-governing and free ("Without a doubt, the intervention and action of these [public] powers are not indispensably necessary . . ."). In other words, interventionism is not of the essence of government. . . . In principle, therefore, the essential function of government is not intervention, but the promotion, protection, and vindication of a truly free, self-governing, and ordered economic life.[20]

What Murray has done is to turn a preferential option for the poor into a preferential option for a free economy. And he has done it in the name of an ideal, a utopia that could not begin to exist — namely, one in which, as Leo put it, there are "conditions in labor and industry [that] reveal nothing which offends against morality, justice, human dignity, or the domestic life of the worker." This is by no means to deny for one minute that there is in *Rerum Novarum* and in Catholic social teaching generally an emphasis on the value of freedom and the principle of subsidiarity — "no intervention unless necessary," granted; but human nature and real life being what they are, intervention is always necessary, not everywhere at every moment, but somewhere at every moment.

However, Murray does again pull himself up short of joining the Reaganite free-marketeers. He does acknowledge the kingdom of necessity, the essential need for justice, the duty of the state to intervene in the interests of justice and the *miserum vulgus*, "the unhappy multitude," even though he seems to express, at the same time, a preferential option for freedom. "Freedom, of course, continues to be what

19. Leo, quoted by Murray in "Leo XIII: Two Concepts of Government," pp. 553-54.
20. Murray, "Leo XIII: Two Concepts of Government," p. 560.

Lord Acton said it was," writes Murray, "the highest political end." But
he adds a moral dimension to that freedom when he cites Lord Acton
again: "freedom is 'not the power of doing what we like, but the right
of being able to do what we ought'" (p. 36). The second quotation
brings Murray back to justice and the kingdom of necessity.

There are many references to the value of justice in Murray's
writings — references that separate him from those who would invoke
his name in support of free-market economics. I will cite three examples.

1. The special function of government with regard to the disin-
   herited masses remains a political function. . . . Its proper motive
   is justice — social and distributive. Its proper end is the end of
   justice, which is equality — not indeed the illusory 'equality' of
   Marxist or Socialist theory, but the real equality which lies in the
   intentions of nature as promoted by just laws which enforce rights
   and responsibilities, promote an equitable distribution of property, achieve a rightful harmony of particular social interests, and
   look to a just balance of that power within society which is related
   to property.[21]

It would be nice to have a little more detail on what Murray means by
"the intentions of nature . . . a rightful harmony of particular social
interests . . . [and] a just balance of that power within society which is
related to property." Moreover, he fails to distinguish the socialist
theory of equality from the Marxist theory. And, in light of the fact
that there are at least a hundred socialist theories and another hundred
that claim to be Marxist, his facile dismissals are a little off-putting.
Still, it is not a bad statement about the need for distributive justice
and "an equitable distribution of property."

2. Democracy is more than a political experiment; it is a spiritual
   and moral enterprise. And its success depends upon the virtue
   of the people who undertake it. Men who would be politically
   free must discipline themselves. (Pp. 36-37)

True, men must discipline themselves, but if they do not discipline
themselves, the state must provide that minimum of discipline which

21. Murray, "Leo XIII: Two Concepts of Government," p. 559.

is required by the demands of justice and "real equality." Real equality demands "as much government [coercion] as necessary."

Libertas opus iustitiae — "freedom is the work of justice" — just as much as *pax opus iustitiae.* Justice is not a higher political end than freedom, but it is prior. Not higher, but prior, an easy phrase to remember. Justice must come first, then freedom, morality, truth, love, and all those other good things. That is why Jesus, in Matthew 25, singled out our obligation to provide food, clothing, and shelter to the hungry, naked, and homeless as the single rock-bottom qualification without which there will be no ticket of admission to the kingdom of heaven, that ultimate kingdom of necessity. He knew which comes first. To rephrase another saying of his, "seek first the kingdom of God and his justice, and freedom shall be added unto you."

3. We have rejected that doctrine of modernity which asserted that government is the only enemy of freedom. We see that the modern concept of freedom itself was dangerously inadequate because it neglected the corporate dimension of freedom. We see too that modernity was wrong in isolating the problem of freedom from its polar terms — responsibility, justice, order, law. *We have realized that the modern experiment originally conceived only as an experiment in freedom, also had to become an experiment in justice.* We know that the myopic individualism of modernity led it into other errors, even into a false conception of the problem of the state in terms of the unreal dichotomy, individualism vs. collectivism. (P. 200; italics mine)

This is Murray at perhaps his most insightful on the subject of political economy. One might even say, "a plague on both capitalism and communism. What we need is a socialism that is grounded in both democratic and Christian values." But Murray, of course, could never bring himself to say that. It remained for Pope John Paul II to say something very close to it in his encyclicals *Laborem Exercens* and *Solicitudo Rei Socialis.* But we can say that in this third statement Murray does sign up as an economic liberal in the best sense of that much maligned word.

And yet we should note that Murray's economic liberalism is grounded not in Scripture but in the natural-law tradition. As Robert McElroy and John Coleman have pointed out, Murray does not care much for biblical references or even for appeals to Christian authorities, except for Leo XIII and, of course, Thomas Aquinas, who shared his own fondness for natural law. He would be uncomfortable making the kind of appeal noted above to Jesus' words in Matthew 25. McElroy agrees, observing that "biblical and religious claims which cannot be substantiated by independent recourse to natural law should have no place in a contemporary public theology."[22]

McElroy's point is valid, but where biblical and religious claims can be substantiated by natural law, why not make the most of it? As Coleman says, Murray's secular language is "chaste, sober and thin." It lights no bonfires.

But the appeal to Matthew 25 can be justified by natural law, at least if we hold to the natural law that Murray held to, which assumes the existence of a benevolent God who created all men and women equal and endowed them with certain inalienable rights.

St. Gregory the Great, following upon a tradition that goes back to the Old Testament prophets and to St. Basil and St. Ambrose, puts it about as well as anyone:

> Those who neither make after others' goods nor bestow their own are to be admonished to take it well to heart that the earth they come from is common to all and brings forth nurture for all alike. Idly then do men hold themselves innocent when they monopolise for themselves the common gift of God. In not giving what they have received they work their neighbors' death; every day they destroy all the starving poor whose means to relief they store at home. *When we furnish the destitute with any necessity we render them what is theirs, not bestow on them what is ours; we pay the debt of justice rather than perform the works of mercy.*[23]

St. Basil was more succinct: "The coat that hangs in the closet belongs to the poor."[24]

22. McElroy, *The Search for an American Public Theology,* p. 154. An emphasis on natural law and a shyness about making references to Scripture characterize a number of papal encyclicals, most notably those of Pius XI, Pius XII, and John XXIII. Pius XI's *Quadragesimo Anno* was written in large part by Oswald von Nell-Breuning, S.J., a pupil of Heinrich Pesch, who, with two other German Jesuits, Victor Cathrein and Gustav Gundlach, kept the natural-law tradition very much alive in Catholic social teaching.

23. Gregory, quoted by John C. Cort in *Christian Socialism: An Informal History* (Maryknoll, N.Y.: Orbis Books, 1988), p. 51; italics mine.

24. Basil, quoted by Cort in *Christian Socialism,* p. 44.

This tradition of equality and concern for the poor was not limited to the prophets, Jesus, and the more ancient Fathers and Doctors. Aquinas, Murray's primary mentor, not only revered it but insisted on it in his discussion of property and, as McElroy would say, substantiated it by recourse to natural law.

> For the well-being of the individual two things are necessary; the first and most essential is to act virtuously (it is through virtue, in fact, that we live a good life); the other, and secondary, requirement is rather a means, and lies in a sufficiency of material goods, such as are necessary to virtuous action. . . . Finally, it is necessary that there be, through the ruler's sagacity, a sufficiency of those material goods which are indispensable to well-being.[25]

In that section of the *Summa Theologica* in which Thomas explains that "if one is to speak quite strictly, it is improper to say that using somebody else's property taken out of extreme necessity is theft," he places the two aspects of his theory of property in their proper relationship and grounds them solidly in the teaching of Ambrose and Basil:

> The dictates of human law cannot derogate from natural or divine law. The natural order established by God in his providence is, however, such that lower things are meant to enable man to supply his needs. A man's needs must therefore still be met out of the world's goods, even though a certain division and apportionment of them is determined by law. And this is why according to natural law goods that are held in superabundance by some people should be used for the maintenance of the poor. This is the principle enunciated by Ambrose . . . , "It is the bread of the poor that you are holding back; it is the clothes of the naked that you are thwarting by burying your money away."[26]

The question then comes down to this: Can Judeo-Christian ethics justify the state in taking from the superabundance of the rich to supply the necessities of the poor? An answer certainly seems to be implied in Aquinas's assertion that the ruler is duty bound to supply

25. Aquinas, quoted by Cort in *Christian Socialism*, p. 56.
26. Aquinas, quoted by Cort in *Christian Socialism*, p. 56.

"a sufficiency of those material goods which are indispensable to [individual] well-being." In listing the duties of a prince, he is even stronger: "provision must be made so that no person goes in want, according to his condition and calling; otherwise neither city nor kingdom would long endure."

St. Thomas is not satisfied with the idea of welfare. He wants people to support themselves. He endorses the idea of full employment. "For the peace of the state it is necessary . . . that the legislator should think out remedies against these three reasons for injury done to others. In the case of those who are injured because they are unable to acquire what is necessary for subsistence, there will suffice the remedy of some modest possession, so that through their own labor they can earn their keep for themselves."[27]

In all probability Thomas was thinking of land, or perhaps a sum sufficient to start a small business. The equivalent today is, of course, a job. Note that Thomas is saying that if the government does not take care of this, then there is question of injury. Justice has been violated, not just charity.

It remained for Cardinal Tommaso Cajetan (1469-1534), an Italian theologian and papal legate who was one of the greatest commentators on St. Thomas, to spell out the implications of the Thomistic theory of property most clearly:

> Now what a ruler can do in virtue of his office, so that justice may be served in the matter of riches, is to take from someone who is unwilling to dispense from what is superfluous for life or state, and to distribute it to the poor. In this way he [justly] takes away the dispensation power of the rich man to whom the wealth has been entrusted because he is not worthy. For according to the teaching of the saints, the riches that are superfluous do not belong to the rich man as his own but rather to the one appointed by God as dispenser, so that he can have the merit of a good dispensation. The legal obligation [*legale debitum*] in this case is founded on the justice obligations of riches themselves. These belong in the classification of useful goods. And superfluity that is not given away is kept in a way that goes counter to the good of both parties. It is counter to the good of the one who hoards it, because it is his only so that he can preside at the giving away. And it is counter to the good of the

27. Aquinas, quoted by Cort in *Christian Socialism*, p. 57.

indigent because someone else continues to possess what has been given for their use. And therefore, as Basil said, it belongs to the indigent, at least as owed, if not in fact. And therefore an injury is done to the poor in not dispensing the superfluous. And this injury is something that the prince, who is the guardian of the right, should set to rights by the power of his office.[28]

It is interesting and ironic that Leo XIII, the pope whose economic theory Murray studied most closely, disagreed with the thought of the Fathers and Aquinas on the right and duty of the state to take superfluous wealth from the rich and give it to the poor. It is ironic because Leo was responsible for the renewal of Thomistic studies, and it appears that his own (or his advisors') studies of Aquinas left something to be desired. Note:

"No one is obliged to live unbecomingly." But when the demands of necessity and propriety have been sufficiently met, it is duty to give to the poor out of that which remains. "Give that which remains as Alms." These are duties not of justice, except in case of extreme need, but of Christian charity, which obviously cannot be enforced by legal action.[29]

It is impossible to reconcile this charity-but-not-justice tendency on Leo's part either with the Fathers or with Aquinas's statement that "provisions must be made [by the prince] so that no person goes in want, according to his condition and calling; otherwise neither city nor kingdom could long endure." Of course, we might reconcile Thomas and Leo by emphasizing Leo's conditional phrase "except in cases of extreme need." But that strikes me as too exceptional. The emphasis is wrong.

In any case, the ambiguity has been resolved and the proper emphasis restored by Paul VI in *Populorum Progressio:*

It is well known how strong were the words used by the Fathers of the Church to describe the proper attitude of persons who possess anything towards persons in need. To quote St. Ambrose: 'You are

28. Cajetan, quoted by Cort in *Christian Socialism*, p. 57.
29. Leo XIII, *Rerum Novarum*, no. 36, 16. The quoted material within the citation is from the *Summa Theologica*.

not making a gift of your possessions to the poor person. You are handing over to him what is his. For what has been given in common for the use of all, you have arrogated to yourself. The world is given to all, and not only to the rich'. That is, private property does not constitute for anyone an absolute and unconditioned right. No one is justified in keeping for his exclusive use what he does not need, when others lack necessities.[30]

Let us now consider some of those who have been pulling at Murray, as if in a tug-of-war, trying to pull him over to the left or the right to buttress their own liberal or conservative positions on economics. And let us begin with John A. Rohr, one of the contributors to a special issue of *America,* the Jesuit magazine, dated 30 November 1985, celebrating the twenty-fifth anniversary of Vatican II's *Declaration on Religious Liberty.* Rohr's piece is entitled "John Courtney Murray and the Pastoral Letters," and it speculates on what reaction Murray might have had to the letter on nuclear warfare and the first draft of the letter on Catholic social teaching and the U.S. economy, which had just been released by the U.S. bishops.

With extraordinary self-confidence Rohr writes that "Murray's most fundamental criticism of the economic pastoral" would be that it "does not take the state seriously."[31] The first draft of the letter reveals that Rohr is wrong. Among other things, the first draft states that

government has a positive moral function: that of protecting basic human rights, ensuring economic justice for all and enabling citizens to coordinate their actions toward these ends. While Catholic social teaching provides a positive affirmation of the role of government, it does not advocate a status approach to economic activity. The principle of "subsidiarity" is the primary norm for determining the scope and limits of governmental action.[32]

There are literally thousands of words devoted to the functions, responsibilities, scope, and limits of state action. I suspect that Rohr's

30. Paul VI, in *The Gospel of Peace and Justice: Catholic Social Teaching since Pope John,* ed. Joseph Gremillion (Maryknoll, N.Y.: Orbis Books, 1976), p. 394.
31. Rohr, "John Courtney Murray and the Pastoral Letters," *America,* 30 November 1985, p. 376.
32. "Catholic Social Teaching and the U.S. Economy," *Harvest,* December 1964, p. 16.

real grievance is that the bishops take the state *too* seriously, particularly with regard to its responsibilities.

Rohr's article does have one genuine distinction: it raises the preferential option for the middle class to new heights. Consider:

> government officials have a moral obligation to look first to the measures that will maintain and stabilize a society that is fundamentally just. This may lead them to give priority to the needs of the poor. However, it may also lead them to see an eroding middle class as a more dangerous political problem than the very genuine needs of unfortunate people who have never known anything but grinding poverty. This is hardly the teaching of the Gospel, but it is the sort of political morality that Murray would support. He has stated quite clearly that "the morality proper to the life of society and the state is not univocally the morality of personal life."[33]

Rohr has distorted Murray's distinction between private and public morality. Rohr seems to assume that because some people "have never known anything but grinding poverty," their needs are less urgent than those of an "eroding middle class." This reminds one of the classic remark of George Baer, leader of the mine operators during the coal strike of 1902; in response to those who appealed to him to settle the strike in view of the suffering of the miners and their families, he said, "they don't suffer. They can't even read."

Michael Novak is a more formidable and prolific member of the conservative team in the tug-of-war over Murray's true allegiance. Let us consider his argument, which he has a way of making with pontifical authority and reckless exaggeration. For example, "the extensive effort to commit the church to 'economic rights' has the potential to become an error of classic magnitude. It might well position the Catholic Church in a 'preferential option for the state' that will more than rival that of the Constantinian period."[34] And again,

> the concept of economic rights (to income, food, shelter, a job, etc.) flies in the face of what John Courtney Murray, S.J., called telegraphically "the American Proposition." That Proposition is in the form of

33. Rohr, "John Courtney Murray and the Pastoral Letters," p. 376.
34. Novak, "Economic Rights: The Servile State," *Catholicism in Crisis,* October 1985, p. 10.

a social experiment, boldly testing whether a system based upon
mature independence and self-reliance will produce more in the way
of social justice than any system based upon dependency upon the
state. . . . A regime recognizing economic (welfare) rights . . . will
irretrievably alter the nature of the American Proposition, setting
the United States upon a cause foreign to her own originality and
historic creativity, a course of tragic and ironical decline.[35]

Novak emulates Murray's cleverness by throwing in the Lincolnesque phrase "boldly testing whether a system . . . ," but this phrase
raises several questions. (1) Perhaps Jefferson and most of the founding fathers thought about the American Proposition in much the same
way that Novak does, but would they think the same way in 1990?
America was a very different country in 1776, when economic opportunity was only waiting to be seized. (2) Jefferson argued that "that
government governs best which governs least," and that is surely the
gospel that Novak has been preaching on behalf of American capi-
talists. But we know that Murray did not agree with that gospel,
because he says so explicitly. Still, this does not stop Novak from
arguing that Murray was equally an enemy of interventionism and
libertarianism: "Murray describes Leo XIII's vision as intermediate
between the Enemy on the left (the principle of interventionism) and
the Enemy on the Right ('free enterprise' alone, or libertarianism).
That is the same intermediate position that informs . . . all my own
work."[36] In his "Two Concepts" article, however, Murray not only did
not identify interventionism as "the Enemy on the left" but actually
applauded Leo's opting for interventionism as embodied in the radical work of Archbishop Ketteler. His response clearly refutes Novak's
interpretation:

in returning to his political concept of government, the next thing
to be noted is the way [Leo XIII] effectively dethroned the principle
which he took from the Enemy on the left — the principle of interventionism — from the status it had in the Enemy's camp, the status
of an absolute. Governmental intervention is not an absolute, any
more than free enterprise (as the Enemy on the right understood

35. Novak, "Economic Rights: The Servile State," p. 14.
36. Novak, "The Rights and Wrongs of 'Economic Rights,'" *This World,*
Spring 1987, p. 48.

the term) is an absolute. Intervention is relative to the proved social damage or danger consequent on social imbalance and disorder. At the same time Leo XIII was not captive to the doctrinairism latent in the pseudo-axiom, "That government governs best which governs least." . . . Leo XIII's relativist and realist concept of the political role of government in economic and social life preserves him from the doctrinairism of both the Right and the Left. It reveals a healthy distrust of government when it begins to infringe upon the freedom of society and its natural and free associational forms. At the same time it reveals a sound respect for government when it acts within the limits of social necessities by irresponsible uses or abuses of Freedom.[37]

A number of Catholic scholars and writers, led perhaps by David Hollenbach, S.J., one of the principal consultants to Archbishop Rembert Weakland and the committee that wrote the pastoral on the U.S. economy, have done a workmanlike job of roughing up Novak's argument in the aforementioned anniversary issue of *America*. Novak responded to Hollenbach in *This World* in an article entitled "The Rights and Wrongs of 'Economic' Rights: A Debate Continued."

A metaphor that might be used to describe Novak's attempt to refute Hollenbach is that of a military unit that lays down a smoke-screen and sends out small squads to distract the enemy with diversionary actions, all to conceal the main line of attack. For example, in his effort to refute the assertion made by Hollenbach, the U.S. bishops, and the popes that economic rights are "truly rights inhering in the nature of human persons," Novak describes six different kinds of rights — rhetorical, Catholic, legal, constitutional, Anglo-American philosophical, and Marxist-and-socialist, the last named turning out to be not one but two concepts.

Novak tries to make a significant distinction between what he calls "welfare rights" (an eighth category, or perhaps a subspecies of Catholic rights) and "economic rights" as both were defined by Pope John XXIII in *Pacem in Terris* in 1963. But Pope John lays it out so cleanly and neatly — even more cleanly and neatly than Hollenbach and the U.S. bishops — that one can do no better than quote the two paragraphs to which Novak refers and explain how Novak tries to reduce economic rights to insignificance.

37. Murray, "Leo XIII: Two Concepts of Government," pp. 558-59.

In paragraph 11 of *Pacem in Terris,* Pope John says,

> beginning our discussion of the rights of man, we see that every man
> has the right to life, to bodily integrity, and to the means which are
> necessary and suitable to the proper development of life. These
> means are primarily food, clothing, shelter, rest, medical care, and
> finally the necessary social services. Therefore, a human being also
> has the right to security in cases of sickness, inability to work, widow-
> hood, old age, unemployment, or in any other case in which he is
> deprived of the means of subsistence through no fault of his own.[38]

And in paragraph 18, in a section entitled "Economic Rights," Pope
John says, "when we turn to the economic sphere, it is clear that human
beings have the natural right to free initiative in the economic field
and the right to work."[39]

Novak makes six references to paragraph 11 and four to paragraph 18 in his article in *This World,* which is some indication of how
troublesome he finds them. He attempts to eliminate the trouble by
ignoring the first sentence of paragraph 11, which is the omnibus,
circus-tent, cover-all statement of natural human rights according to
Catholic teaching. He sees only the second and third sentences, which
he categorizes as "welfare rights" conditional on the inability of men
and women to make it on their own.

As for paragraph 18, he tries to take the sting out of that by
interpreting "the right to work" as "the freedom to work" and adds,
several times, that this is already guaranteed by the U.S. Constitution.
This reminds one of the antilabor legislatures, mainly in the South,
that interpret the right to work as the right to work without a union
shop. Novak displays an almost obsessive concern for freedom, while
displaying very little attention to what Murray would describe as its
polar opposite — the problem of justice. This concern is manifested
even in Novak's description of his immigrant family's poverty in north-
eastern Pennsylvania.

> My grandfather was out of work (my uncle had to quit the university)
> and gratefully accepted, although not as a "right," assistance in the
> form of the WPA. In the mills and mines of the Johnstown area

38. John XXIII, in *The Gospel of Peace and Justice,* p. 203.
39. John XXIII, in *The Gospel of Peace and Justice,* p. 205.

employment was then (as it is now) chronic. All of my relatives had come to these shores hungry, homeless, and unemployed. But they were now *free*.

Not only were these two realities distinct in their lives, they knew which one was the more fundamental, inviolable, and endowed in them by the Creator, and which one was first of all their own responsibility. Further, they knew that with freedom a healthy man and woman could find ways to work, to grow their own food, and to build their own shelter. Freedom is not only a more basic right. It is also the best means for meeting one's own responsibilities to earn one's own food, shelter and employment, thus achieving the dignity of financial independence.[40]

One naturally wonders if Novak's unemployed grandfather would have agreed with this statement as he saw his son quit the university. And how about those workers in Johnstown who are still unemployed? Would they agree that the right to work is no more than the freedom to grow their own food and build their own shelter?

To my old friend Michael Novak I can only say, "Give it up, Mike. You are backing a hopeless cause, clinging to a hopeless hope, that somehow you can change the clear meaning of the Church's teaching, that somehow you can transform Pope John and John Courtney Murray into rugged individualists. Pope John's argument is perfectly clear. Father Murray did lean more than was wise in your direction, but he was too smart and too sound in his thinking to go that far. Stop pulling at his coat sleeve." While Murray was certainly a defender of individual liberty, he never fell victim to Novak's myopic individualism.

And one further thought: justice is not higher than freedom. Just prior. And yes, more basic.

40. Novak, "The Rights and Wrongs of 'Economic Rights,'" p. 45.

Murray, American Pluralism, and the Abortion Controversy

Mary C. Segers

I T IS RISKY, AND YET TEMPTING, to speculate about the "what ifs" of history. In the case of John Courtney Murray, perhaps the preeminent American Catholic theologian of the twentieth century, such hypothetical speculation is especially inviting. Given Murray's knowledge of Catholic tradition and his analysis of the relation between law and morals, it is tempting to explore what Murray's position might have been on one of the most controversial issues in contemporary American politics, sound public policy on abortion.

Murray was a theologian first and a political theorist second. Yet his creative theologizing and careful, subtle interpretation of the history of papal teaching and Catholic thought made it possible for American Catholics to accept and embrace the American commitment to religious freedom and church-state separation in a pluralist society. A key to Murray's success was his use of historical method in reinterpreting Catholic tradition, his willingness to situate papal utterances within particular historical, social, political contexts. And so Murray would be the first to situate his own writing within its proper historical context.

Murray's work was a product of his time, a period (the 1950s and 1960s) in which American Catholics seemed to reach political maturity. The election of the nation's first Catholic president symbolized and

I acknowledge with gratitude the assistance of J. Leon Hooper, S.J., of the Woodstock Theological Center, Georgetown University, for access to material from the John Courtney Murray Archives used in the preparation of this essay. — M.C.S.

confirmed the increasing participation of Catholics in the mainstream of American society. At a time when the United States saw itself as the leader of the free world in the struggle against "atheistic communism," Murray was a staunch cold warrior in his foreign policy approach. In an age when American society grew concerned about "the population problem" and struggled with legal restrictions on contraception, Murray reminded Catholics of proper distinctions between law and morals and reminded non-Catholic Americans that many of the antiquated state statutes against birth control were the work originally of Protestants, not Catholics.

In the 1990s, however, the challenges confronting Americans have changed. The cold war is over, and communism does not pose the threat to the free world it once did. The intellectual climate of the nineties is different from that of the forties, fifties, and sixties. Were Murray living today, he would be challenged by the new "communitarian" critique of liberalism, especially the historicist, particularist, and relativist emphases in the work of contemporary philosophers such as Alasdair MacIntyre and Richard Rorty.[1] Murray was, after all, a strong defender of political liberalism; his political philosophy was a curious blend of Burkean social conservatism and a natural-law liberalism based on conceptions of human rights and limited government. Were he alive today, Murray would also be intrigued and challenged by recent developments in theology ranging from the political theology of such Europeans as Johann B. Metz and the development of liberation theology in Latin America to the public theology of Americans such as John Coleman and the major strides in feminist theology made during the past twenty years.

On a more practical level, Murray would probably be intrigued by the American Catholic bishops' assumption of a new role during the seventies and eighties, as they sought to influence public debate and policy on war and peace, economic affairs, and U.S. foreign policy in Central America. And undoubtedly Murray would have been challenged profoundly by the abortion issue, since it, perhaps more than any other contemporary issue, poses fundamental questions about his

---

1. For more on the critique of liberalism and the communitarian challenge, see MacIntyre, *After Virtue: A Study in Moral Theory* (Notre Dame, Ind.: University of Notre Dame Press, 1981), and *Whose Justice? Which Rationality?* (Notre Dame, Ind.: University of Notre Dame Press, 1988); Rorty, *Contingency, Irony, and Solidarity* (New York: Cambridge University Press, 1989); and *Liberalism and the Moral Life*, ed. Nancy Rosenblum (Cambridge: Harvard University Press, 1989).

view of an American public philosophy based on rational deliberation and consensus.

In order to determine what Murray might have said about the dilemma of public policy in a pluralist American society deeply divided over the morality of abortion, I propose to examine what Murray had to say about birth control in the 1960s. Contraception and abortion are not exactly analogous, but there are enough similarities between them historically to suggest that a comparison might be profitable. For one thing, Catholic moral teaching considers both artificial contraception and abortion to constitute serious violations of natural law and the procreative purpose of human sexuality. Second, some contraceptives (the intrauterine device, RU-486, and some forms of the anovulent pill) may be termed abortifacients, since they operate after conception to prevent implantation of a fertilized ovum in the uterine wall. Thus the actual medical-biological distinction between conception and abortion is not all that clear. Third, there is the historical fact that, just as the American Catholic bishops have undertaken a major political effort to reverse *Roe v. Wade* and bring back abortion restrictions, so an earlier American Catholic Church, during the period from 1920 to 1960, conducted major political campaigns in various states to prevent the reform of birth control laws.

During the fifties and sixties, John Courtney Murray served occasionally as adviser and consultant to individual members of the American Catholic hierarchy on birth control policy in the states. Although the Church's moral teaching opposed artificial contraception, Murray did not argue that Roman Catholic moral theology on this point should automatically be translated into civil law. Instead he relied on traditional jurisprudential distinctions between law and morals to suggest that contraception is a matter of private morality and that liberalization of highly restrictive birth control statutes is permissible. In at least two cases, Connecticut and Massachusetts, Murray left written analyses of what sound law and policy might be in the matter of contraception. I propose to examine these analyses for possible clues to what Murray, were he alive today, might advise in the abortion controversy of the eighties and nineties.

To do this systematically, I shall first discuss briefly the reform of birth control laws during the 1960s. I shall then consider Murray's views of the Connecticut birth control statute invalidated by the U.S. Supreme Court in its 1965 *Griswold* ruling and his evaluation of the effort by Massachusetts to change its laws in 1965. Based on these actual cases and on Murray's many writings on religious freedom and the relation between law and morals, I shall then discuss how I think Murray might address the question of abortion policy in the United States.

Changes in Birth Control Laws in the 1960s

Between 1873 and 1965, many American state legislatures enacted birth control statutes banning the sale and distribution of contraceptives and contraceptive information. In one state, Connecticut, the law even prohibited the *use* of contraceptives. Initially, enactment of such laws was due in large part to the political lobbying of Protestant moral reformers (such as Anthony Comstock); as Murray himself once remarked, the 1879 Connecticut birth control statute was passed by the Protestants, not Catholics. However, in the early twentieth century, as Protestant support for birth control laws began to wane, organized Catholic influence replaced it. From the 1920s through the 1960s, the Roman Catholic Church in the United States vigorously opposed legislative modification or repeal of birth control statutes — largely at the state and local level.[2]

These efforts of Catholic churchmen were most effective in states and cities with large Catholic populations: New York, Massachusetts, Illinois, Connecticut, and Pennsylvania. Clergy pressured Catholic hospitals to dismiss Protestant doctors who dared to become affiliated with Planned Parenthood. Catholic charitable organizations pressured community funds and welfare councils to exclude Planned Parenthood. In small communities, private birth control clinics were sometimes closed by the police; in large urban centers such as New York and Chicago, municipal hospital physicians were prohibited from prescribing contraceptive devices for any patient, regardless of the religious beliefs of doctor or patient. Throughout her long career as a public health nurse and birth control advocate, Margaret Sanger encountered stiff opposition from American Catholic churchmen. In fact, church leaders opposed women's suffrage partly because of the early

2. For more on the history of birth control legislation in the United States, see C. Dienes, *Law, Politics, and Birth Control* (Urbana, Ill.: University of Illinois Press, 1972); Thomas Littlewood, *The Politics of Population Control* (Notre Dame, Ind.: University of Notre Dame Press, 1977); and Norman St. John-Stevas, *Life, Death and the Law* (Bloomington, Ind.: Indiana University Press, 1961).

association of Sanger's birth control movement with aspects of feminism and the suffrage movement.[3]

Nevertheless, despite Catholic opposition, changes in social mores and the behavior of Americans indicated an increasing acceptance of birth control. In 1955 a national survey of married women in their childbearing years (18-39) showed a strong majority approval of family planning: 83 percent of those interviewed had adopted some means of birth control. By 1959 Planned Parenthood operated centers in twenty-eight states and the District of Columbia. As for state law, by 1960 twenty of the fifty American states had no legislation on the subject of contraception, while another seventeen states prohibited traffic in contraceptives but exempted physicians and pharmacists from the statutory prohibition. Five states, including Connecticut and Massachusetts, prohibited the sale and advertising of contraceptives with no exceptions, while thirty states prohibited advertising.[4] In general, birth control devices were considered medical remedies, and dispensation was controlled by doctors and health clinics. Perhaps the moral and social acceptability of birth control was reflected most clearly in the fact that, by 1959, most of the Protestant churches in America had rescinded their initial views of contraception as immoral and had either approved it as a proper method of family planning or decreed that contraceptive use was a matter to be decided according to individual conscience.[5]

In the 1960s several major developments signaled continued changes in attitudes toward birth control. Innovations in the technology of contraception (development of the pill and intrauterine devices) made birth control cheaper, more effective, and relatively safer and easier. Concerns about overpopulation in Third World countries and, later, in the United States itself led to heated debate among demographers, planners, and environmentalists about appropriate population policy. In 1965, the Supreme Court in *Griswold v. Connecticut*

3. The opposition of Catholic clergy to women's suffrage is chronicled in several sources. See James Kenneally, "Catholicism and Woman Suffrage in Massachusetts," *Catholic Historical Review* 53 (1967): 43-57; and James Hennessey, *American Catholics: A History of the Roman Catholic Community in the United States* (New York: Oxford University Press, 1981).

4. For a concise legal history and analysis of birth control policy in the United States from passage of the Comstock legislation in 1873 until 1960, see St. John-Stevas, *Life, Death and the Law*.

5. For a discussion of changes in churches' views of the morality and legality of contraception, see St. John-Stevas, *Life, Death and the Law*.

invalidated a Connecticut statute that prohibited the use of contraceptives. That same year, the federal government began to dispense contraceptives to poor women as part of its "war on poverty." By 1970 Congress had passed and President Nixon had signed the Family Planning Services and Population Research Act (familiarly known as Title X of the Public Health Service Act) to make family planning services available to all who wanted but could not afford them. In a few short years, Congress had formally changed birth control services from the roster of politically forbidden activities to the agenda of important social issues.

For American Catholics, the 1960s were no less momentous than for American society as a whole. In addition to the election of the first Catholic president, the decade saw a new pope convene the Second Vatican Council (1962-1965) to reform Church life and reorient the Church toward more engagement with the world. In theological circles, a lively debate on the morality of artificial contraception continued throughout the 1960s. In 1968, Pope Paul VI published the encyclical *Humanae Vitae*, which reaffirmed the Church's traditional ban on artificial contraception. Catholics in the United States and Europe reacted with consternation and dismay at the papal refusal to change Church teaching.

Murray died in 1967, shortly after the culmination of his theological work. His portrait graced the cover of *Time* magazine in December 1960 to mark the publication of *We Hold These Truths*. He had emerged from a period of Vatican-imposed silence to be present at the later sessions of Vatican II and to draft the Council's *Declaration of Religious Liberty*. Although Murray's attention was focused on Vatican II, members of the American Church hierarchy consulted him for advice regarding an appropriate Catholic response to changes in birth control policy. Murray's wise counsel in these cases provides useful insights concerning the proper relation between law and morals in a pluralist democracy.

The Connecticut Birth Control Law

The Connecticut statutes invalidated in *Griswold v. Connecticut* provided as follows:

> Any person who uses any drug, medicinal article or instrument for the purpose of preventing conception shall be fined no less than fifty

dollars or imprisoned not less than sixty days nor more than one year or be both fined and imprisoned.

Any person who assists, abets, counsels, causes, hires, or commands another to commit any offense may be prosecuted and punished as if he were the principal offender.[6]

Prior to the *Griswold* ruling, there were a number of unsuccessful attempts to have these statutes repealed or declared unconstitutional. They were challenged on at least five different occasions in the period from 1940 to 1965. In *Griswold,* the Supreme Court finally held both statutes unconstitutional on the grounds that, by prohibiting the use rather than merely regulating the sale of contraceptives, they constituted invasions of the right of privacy.

It is clear from his comments in *We Hold These Truths* that Murray could find little to defend in the Connecticut birth control law. In his view, the Connecticut statute exemplified a tendency of American Protestant moral reformers to confuse law and morals. Noting that the statute was passed in 1879 under Protestant pressure during the notorious "Comstock Era," Murray wrote,

the text reveals a characteristic Comstockian-Protestant ignorance of the rules of traditional jurisprudence. In general, the "free churches," so called, have never given attention to this subtle discipline, at once a science and an art, that mediates between the imperatives of the moral order and the commands or prohibitions of civil law. In fact, so far from understanding jurisprudence, these sects have never really understood law but only power, whether they wield the latter in the form of majority rule or of minority protest. In any case, the Connecticut statute confuses the moral and the legal, in that it transposes without further ado a private sin into a public crime. The criminal act here is the private use of contraceptives. The real area where the coercions of the law might, and ought to, be applied, at least to control an evil — namely, the contraceptive industry — is quite overlooked. As it stands, the statute is, of course, unenforceable without police invasion of the

6. Connecticut General Statutes (1958 Revised), title 53, ch. 939, sec. 53-32, and title 54, ch. 959, sec. 54-196, as cited in *Family Planning and the Law,* 2d ed., ed. Roy D. Weinberg (Dobbs Ferry, N.Y.: Oceana Publications, 1979), p. 35.

bedroom, and is therefore indefensible as a piece of legal draught-manship.[7]

Murray criticized Protestant moral theory for failing to grasp the distinction between private and public morality as well as the difference in order between moral precepts and civil statutes. He believed that moral reformers reacted to social evils by legislating against them without ever asking "whether this is the sort of good or evil that law can, or ought to, cope with" (p. 156). Moreover, he argued that this confusion of law and morals led in turn to a second fallacy — namely, that if what is moral ought by that fact to be legal, it follows that what is legal is also moral. But Murray was quick to point out that the legality of an action is *not* conclusive evidence of its morality. "From the foolish position that all sins ought to be made crimes," he wrote, "it is only a step to the knavish position that, since certain acts (like the private use of contraceptives) are obviously not crimes, they are not even sins" (p. 158).

Of importance here is the fact that Murray, by insisting on the distinction between sin and crime (in the case of artificial contraception), reserved to private citizens the right to decide whether birth control is moral. The fact that a practice is *legally permissible* does not necessarily mean that it is *morally desirable* or good. Murray thus created space for groups such as Catholics to respect their Church's teaching against artificial contraception and yet refuse to impose through civil law that conviction of private morality on non-Catholic Americans.

Murray further justified his jurisprudential separation of law and morals in the matter of the Connecticut birth control statute by invoking a consequentialist approach to sound lawmaking. In the tradition of Aquinas, he concluded that the unenforceability of the Connecticut law was a telling indication that it was imprudent, unwise, and unsound.

Murray's natural-law jurisprudence was grounded in a Realist epistemology, but it was politically realistic in the sense that he did not expect law to create perfect men and women in ideal societies. He refused to equate law with morality or crime with sin. He recognized that lawmaking involves balancing competing values and that sound

---

7. Murray, *We Hold These Truths: Catholic Reflections of the American Proposition* (New York: Sheed & Ward, 1960), pp. 157-58. Subsequent references to this volume will be made parenthetically in the text.

public policy must meet at least minimal standards of consent in order to be enforceable. This awareness of the complexity of the law in a religiously diverse democracy is also evident in his approach to the repeal of highly restrictive birth control laws in Massachusetts in the mid-1960s.

Reforms of the Massachusetts Birth Control Law

The Massachusetts birth control law prohibited the manufacture, sale, and distribution of contraceptives and permitted no exceptions to this rule. The statute applied to drugs and devices intended to prevent pregnancy or to cause or procure miscarriage and thus considered contraception and abortion as related crimes. Sections 20 and 21 of Title I, Chapter 272 of Massachusetts Annotated Laws (1956) were the relevant provisions. They are cited here because Murray commented upon them directly.

> Section 20: Whoever knowingly advertises, prints, publishes, distributes or circulates, or knowingly causes to be advertised, printed, published, distributed or circulated, any pamphlet, printed paper, book, newspaper, notice, advertisement or reference, containing words of language giving or conveying any notice, hint or reference to any person, real or fictitious, from whom, or to any place, house, shop or office where any poison, drug, mixture, preparation, medicine or noxious thing, or any instrument or means whatever, or any advice, direction, information or knowledge, may be obtained for the purpose of causing or procuring a miscarriage of a woman pregnant with child or of preventing, or which is represented as intended to prevent, pregnancy, shall be punished by imprisonment in the state prison for not more than three years or in jail for not more than two and one half years or by a fine of not more than one thousand dollars.

> Section 21: Whoever sells, lends, gives away, exhibits, or offers to sell, lend or give away any instrument or other article intended to be used for self-abuse, or any drug, medicine, instrument or article whatever for the prevention of conception or for causing unlawful abortion, or advertises the same, or writes, prints or causes to be written or printed a card, circular, book, pamphlet, advertisement

or notice of any kind stating when, where, how, of whom or by what means any such article can be purchased or obtained, or manufactures or makes any such article, shall be punished by imprisonment in the state prison for not more than five years or in jail or the house of correction for not more than two and one-half years or by a fine of not less than one hundred nor more than one thousand dollars.[8]

By the 1960s there was widespread noncompliance with and nonenforcement of the Massachusetts birth control law. Nevertheless, its explicit legal norms constituted a negative public policy that seriously impeded acceptance of publicly supported birth control and effectively thwarted attempts to operate private birth-control clinics. The impact of this was, of course, class-differential: poor people, dependent on free medical services, were effectively denied assistance.

Efforts to change the Massachusetts law dated to the 1920s. In 1942 and again in 1948, the state had been the scene of bitterly contested campaigns in which the Catholic Church, led by Cardinal William O'Connell of Boston and later by Archbishop Richard Cushing, successfully opposed legal change. However, the Boston Archdiocese of the 1960s under Cardinal Cushing was a different place. Cushing had come to recognize the importance of tolerance and mutual respect in a pluralist society, and he was a leader in the effort to secure adoption of the *Declaration of Religious Liberty* at Vatican II. Commenting on the Massachusetts Comstock law, he said that "it is important to note that Catholics do not need the support of civil law to be faithful to their religious convictions, and they do not seek to impose by law their moral views on other members of society."[9]

From 1963 until 1966, when the Massachusetts law was finally changed, Cardinal Cushing indicated in a variety of public forums (on television, in testimony before congressional and state legislative committees, and in private correspondence) that he did not feel obligated to oppose a change in the law. He had consulted Father Murray in the matter, and, in a "Memorandum to Cardinal Cushing" (undated, but probably written in 1964 or 1965, judging from internal evidence), Murray stated that "in my opinion, Catholics may and should approve amendment of Sections 20 and 21 of Chapter 272 of the *General Laws* of Massachusetts." As Murray understood proposed changes to the

8. Cited in *Family Planning and the Law*, pp. 37-38.
9. Cushing, quoted by Dienes in *Law, Politics, and Birth Control*, pp. 149-50.

Massachusetts statute, "the necessary amendment would permit doctors and responsible agencies to give contraceptive information to those who request it, and hence permit the sale of contraceptives."[10] Murray offered two general lines of argument to support his recommendation: (1) arguments based on the differential character of law and morality and on the distinction between public and private morality, and (2) arguments derived from the concept of religious freedom.

Appealing first to traditional notions of jurisprudence, Murray maintained that it is not the function of civil law to prescribe everything that is morally wrong. As an instrument of social order, the scope of law is limited to the maintenance and protection of public morality. Matters of private morality lie beyond the scope of law and are properly left to personal conscience. Issues of public morality arise, however, "when an act or practice seriously undermines the foundations of society or gravely damages the moral life of the community, in such a way that legal prohibition becomes necessary in order to safeguard the social order as such. So, for instance, offenses against justice must be made criminal offenses, since justice is the foundation of civil order."[11]

Even in cases of public morality, however, Murray did not think that civil law should automatically reflect all moral norms. He offered four significant qualifications concerning the use of positive law to enforce standards of public morality. First, the scope of law is limited to the protection and maintenance of relatively minimal standards of public morality. A minimum of public morality is a social necessity; moreover, the force of law is coercive, and people can normally be coerced into the observance of only minimal standards. Second, this minimalist approach to the use of law to enforce moral norms holds with particular force in the case of a free society, in which government is not paternal and the jurisprudential rule obtains: as much freedom as possible; as much restriction and coercion as necessary. Third, the measure of public morality that can and should be enforced by law is necessarily a matter of public judgment, especially in a democratic society. Consensus is crucial: the people whose good is at stake have a right of judgment with regard to the measure of public virtue that is to be enforced and the manner of public evils that are to be repressed. Fourth, Murray emphasized issues of legal efficacy and enforceability.

10. Murray, "Memorandum to Cardinal Richard Cushing," Murray Archives, Languiner Library, Georgetown University, n.d., p. 1.
11. Murray, "Memorandum to Cardinal Richard Cushing," p. 1.

He stressed that there must be a reasonable correspondence between the moral standards generally recognized by the conscience of the community and the legal statutes concerning public morality. Otherwise laws will be unenforceable and ineffective, and they will be resented as undue restrictions on civil or personal freedom.

According to Murray, the central issue was whether contraception was an issue of public morality or private morality, and he acknowledged that the question was disputed among Catholics. Nevertheless, he found the case for affirming contraception a matter of private morality to be sufficiently conclusive.

> It is not merely that the practice is widespread, as a matter of fact, or that so many people do not consider it to be wrong. The more decisive reason is that practice, undertaken in the interests of "responsible parenthood," has received official sanction by many religious groups within the community. It is difficult to see how the state can forbid, as contrary to public morality, a practice that numerous religious leaders approve as morally right. The stand taken by these religious groups may be lamentable from the Catholic moral point of view. But it is decisive from the point of view of law and jurisprudence, for which the norm of "generally accepted standards" is controlling.[12]

Murray thus concluded on grounds of valid tradition and theory of law and jurisprudence that the amendment of the Massachusetts birth control statutes "was permissible and even advisable." He found additional support for this conclusion in a second set of arguments derived from the concept of religious freedom. Here Murray held that the concept of religious liberty includes a twofold immunity from coercion. "First, a man may not be coercively constrained to act against his conscience. Second, a man may not be coercively restrained from acting according to his conscience, unless the action involves a civil offense — against the public peace, against public morality, or against the rights of others."[13]

Murray argued that since the practice of contraception involves no civil offense, the principle of religious freedom should obtain. On this reading, the Massachusetts birth control statutes were contrary to

12. Murray, "Memorandum to Cardinal Richard Cushing," p. 1.
13. Murray, "Memorandum to Cardinal Richard Cushing," p. 2.

religious freedom. Thus, from the perspectives of traditional jurisprudence and religious liberty, the Massachusetts statutes could not pass
muster as sound law.

In his memo to Cushing, Murray next addressed what he called
"issues of prudence" — that is, points for Massachusetts Church officials and ordinary Catholics to bear in mind as they changed from
opposing to supporting legalized contraception. First, in an attempt
to avoid another bitter referendum, Murray advised legislating change,
urging that an amendment should be passed by the state legislature
with as little public agitation as possible. Second, Murray advised
Catholics to make publicly known the grounds of their approval —
namely, that they, like all citizens, are bound by the principles of law,
jurisprudence, and religious freedom. Third, Murray suggested that

> Catholics themselves must be made to understand that, although
> contraception is not an issue of public morality to be dealt with by
> civil law, it remains for them a moral issue in their family lives, to
> be decided according to the teaching of the Church. Because con-
> traception is made legal, it is not therefore made moral, any more
> than it should be made illegal simply because it is immoral.[14]

Murray's concluding point addressed what Church authorities
should say publicly about the proposed amendment to the Massachusetts statutes. "In a sense, it is a pity that they should have to say
anything," he wrote. "The authority of the Church declares the moral
law — that contraception is contrary to the moral law. But the authority
of the Church does not decide what the civil law should be. This
decision rests with the civil community, its jurists and legislators."
Nevertheless, Murray recognized that Cardinal Cushing had to state
publicly that the proposed amendments to the Massachusetts statutes
were acceptable to the Catholic Church, and he therefore summarized
his advice to Cushing as follows:

> Perhaps the essential thing is to make clear: (1) that from the stand-
> point of morality Catholics maintain contraception to be morally
> wrong; and (2) that out of their understanding of the distinction
> between morality and law and between public and private morality,
> and also out of their understanding of religious freedom, Catholics

14. Murray, "Memorandum to Cardinal Richard Cushing," p. 2.

repudiate in principle a resort to the coercive instrument of law to enforce upon the whole community moral standards that the community itself does not commonly accept.[15]

It took almost two years to reform the Massachusetts birth control law in a manner acceptable to the Catholic Archdiocese of Boston. During legislative committee hearings on proposed bills, Cardinal Cushing's representatives indicated general acceptance of statutory reform provided the new law included adequate safeguards to protect the morals of the young. Such safeguards as restrictions on advertising, prohibition of vending machine sales, restriction of contraceptives to married persons, and requiring a doctor's prescription to obtain contraceptives were deemed necessary by the Catholic Church. In public statements at committee hearings, Cardinal Cushing affirmed the traditional Catholic position on the immorality of birth control but also asserted that the demands of public morality are not coextensive with private morality. "In the present case," he stated, "especially in the light of the position taken by other religious groups in our plural society, it does not seem reasonable for me to forbid by civil law a practice that can be considered a matter of private morality."[16] It seems that Cushing followed Murray's advice in making what he judged to be a necessary change in the Church's public policy stance on birth control.

Murray and Public Policy on Abortion

How is Murray's advice to Cushing relevant to the contemporary abortion debate? And, were Murray alive today, how would he approach the controversial question of appropriate abortion policy in a pluralist society?

Murray would undoubtedly defend the right of the Roman Catholic Church and other churches to address the moral dimensions of public policy officially and to contribute to the public debate about the morality and legality of abortion. He would also defend the efforts of Catholics, fundamentalists, Mormons, Orthodox Jews, and other religiously minded citizens who seek to restrict abortion in the United States. However, Murray would be cognizant of the plurality of re-

15. Murray, "Memorandum to Cardinal Richard Cushing," p. 2.
16. Cushing, quoted by Dienes in *Law, Politics, and Birth Control,* p. 201.

ligious and secular views on the morality and legality of abortion, and he would be particularly mindful of the fact that no single view currently commands a majority of American public assent. Murray's continuing hope, of course, was that a *consensus iuris,* an agreement about what is right and just, would emerge from rational deliberation about public affairs. When a consensus does not emerge, agreement on sound law and acceptable public policy is difficult if not impossible.

While Murray would surely defend the Catholic Church's right to advance its view in the policy debate, he would also probably insist that a responsible Catholic social ethics in a pluralist, democratic society is obliged to make its case on grounds acceptable, in principle, to both the Catholic (and larger Christian) community and to the larger secular society. Moreover, the Church's case has to be made in the language of reason and natural law, not in the language of biblical ethics or gospel norms. In *We Hold These Truth,* Murray argues that in a pluralist society, any minority group has the right to work toward the elevation of standards of public morality through the use of the methods of persuasion and pacific argument. Conversely in such a society, no minority group has the right to impose its own religious or moral views on other groups through the use of methods of force, coercion, or violence. Thus, if Catholic Church officials wish to shape public consensus on abortion policy, they can do so only through appeals to reason in the language of secular, nontheistic ethics. Threats of hellfire and eternal punishment for citizens and politicians who do not agree with the policy preferences of the bishops would be inappropriate, probably unpersuasive, and possibly counterproductive.[17]

Murray described the dilemmas of a religiously diverse democracy in these terms:

> the problem of popular consent to the order of law and to its manifold coercions becomes critical in a pluralist society, such as ours. Basic religious divisions lead to conflict of moral views; certain

17. Murray made a similar point about the *Declaration on Religious Liberty.* Speaking of conciliar documents, he stated that the *Declaration on Religious Liberty* "is the only conciliar document that is formally addressed to the world at large on a topic of intense secular as well as religious interest. Therefore, it would have been inept for the *Declaration* to begin with doctrines that can be known only by revelation and accepted only by faith" ("The Declaration on Religious Freedom," in *War, Poverty, Freedom: The Christian Response,* Concilium 15 (New York: Paulist Press, 1966), pp. 3-16.

asserted "rights" clash with other "rights" no less strongly asserted. And the divergences are often irreducible. Nevertheless, despite all the pluralism, some manner of consensus must support the order of law to which the whole community and all its groups are commonly subject. . . . What is commonly imposed by law on all our citizens must be supported by general public opinion, by a reasonable consensus of the whole community. (Pp. 167-69)

Murray's statement here could qualify as an apt description of the abortion dilemma in contemporary American society. This invites us to pose two questions: (1) Were Murray with us today, would he favor the use of coercive law to prohibit or severely restrict abortion? and (2) How might he advise American Catholics to approach the question of abortion policy in the United States? Based on his approach to the relation between law and morals and to the question of religious freedom, as outlined in the memorandum to Cardinal Cushing and developed in numerous other articles and books, I think Murray might emphasize the following considerations.

First, much depends on whether abortion is categorized as a matter of public or private morality. Is abortion an act or practice that seriously undermines the foundations of society or gravely damages the moral life of the community, in such a way that legal prohibition becomes necessary in order to safeguard the social order as such? Is it an offense against justice that must be made a criminal offense, since justice is the foundation of civil order? The answer to this question depends in part on how one regards fetal life. If the fetus is defined as a human being from conception, then abortion is an other-regarding action that raises questions about justifiable killing. On this view, abortion is a public issue, a matter of public morality, because it affects another party, a human being who cannot be consulted but whose interests deserve protection as a matter of justice. Defined in this way, as an issue in the ethics of killing, abortion would properly become a subject of governmental regulation and restriction — although even in this relatively clear case, issues of enforceability and legal efficacy would still influence the degree of governmental regulation.

It should be noted that Catholic moral teaching does not hold this clear, compelling position. The 1974 *Vatican Declaration against Procured Abortion* holds that we cannot be certain whether the fetus is human from the moment of conception; and since we are operating in a situation of doubt and uncertainty, it is wrong to risk the killing of innocent human life.[18] This softer formulation of the Catholic position invites moral theologians, social ethicists, and others to explore the conditions under which taking risks with killing is permissible or impermissible. Moral theologians weigh such questions in matters of just war and the administration of capital punishment, for example.

On the matter of automatically translating Catholic moral teaching into civil law, Murray would be cognizant, I think, of the fact that the Catholic position on the absolute impermissibility of direct abortion is a minority position in American society. Public opinion polls have shown consistently that less than 20 percent of the citizenry wants to outlaw abortion in all circumstances. This means that any attempt to make public law conform to the strict Catholic moral position is probably unrealistic and, moreover, risks infringing upon the rights and liberties of non-Catholic Americans in our religiously diverse society. Murray's jurisprudence and his great work on religious freedom suggest that he would be loath to use the force of coercive law to impose a distinctly minority view on the citizenry.

Other considerations would temper Catholic willingness to use public law to impose the Church's moral theology on non-Catholic citizens. These include the distinction between state and society that Murray emphasized, the role of the church in a pluralist society, the presence or absence of consensus concerning the morality and legality of abortion, the duty of tolerance and respect for the religious liberty of nonbelievers, and consequentialist considerations about the efficacy of abortion laws.

Even if abortion is a matter of public morality and therefore subject to possible legal enforcement, Murray, if you will recall, offered several important caveats regarding use of civil law to enact and enforce standards of public morality. First, in a free society, the law is limited to maintenance of relatively minimal standards of public morality, since people can normally be coerced into the observance of only minimal standards. Second, the jurisprudential rule is: as much freedom as possible; as much restriction and coercion as necessary. Third, there must be a reasonable correspondence between the moral standards generally recognized by the conscience of the community and the legal

18. The Vatican *Declaration* states, "from a moral point of view this is certain: even if a doubt existed concerning whether the fruit of conception is already a human person, it is objectively a grave sin to dare to risk murder" (Sacred Congregation for the Doctrine of the Faith, *Declaration on Abortion* [Washington: United States Catholic Conference, 1974], p. 6).

statutes concerning public morality. In the absence of such a correlation, such laws will be ineffective, unenforceable, and resented as undue restrictions on civil or personal freedom. This points to the obvious fourth factor: consensus is crucial in the matter of sound public policy on abortion; the measure of public morality that can and should be enforced by law is necessarily a matter of public judgment.

Murray hoped that a consensus about what is right and just might emerge from rational deliberation about public affairs. But in American society the abortion issue has provoked dissensus rather than consensus. Initially, the issue polarized activists into extremes on both sides of the issue. Now several "middle-ground" positions have emerged. Some analysts identify in public opinion surveys a large centrist group that opposes abortion on demand while supporting some abortions in the difficult circumstances of rape, incest, fetal deformity, and threat to the mother's life or health. Another consensus has developed more recently around the view that law and public policy should preserve a woman's right to decide such matters as abortion. On this view, each individual woman should be allowed to act according to her moral beliefs regarding the rightness or wrongness of abortion, and the state ought not to coerce or restrict her conduct or moral decision making. This position maintains that it is not the province of the government to dictate what should be done in cases of involuntary pregnancy. The emergence relatively recently of these two possibilities for policy consensus in the United States illustrates another problem for Murray's approach to law and policy — namely, what approach ought to be taken if the emerging consensus is different from the moral teaching of the Church? Should law and public policy reflect that consensus? And what should the Church do in such a case?

Recall that, in his memorandum to Cardinal Cushing, Murray argued that much depended on whether contraception was a matter of public or private morality. Matters of private morality lie beyond the scope of the law and should be left to personal conscience. Matters of public morality concern the basic foundations of society or threaten grave damage to the moral life of the community, and so legal prohibition is necessary to safeguard the moral order. Those who would argue that society is being undermined by the incidence of abortion would have to define their terms precisely and, more especially, provide some empirical evidence to substantiate their claim. It is not self-evident that abortion fits Murray's first definition of public morality. And it should be noted that Murray gave additional criteria for

establishing whether an act or practice should be classified as an issue
of public or private morality. He argued that contraception was a
matter of private morality because (1) the practice is widespread;
(2) many people do not consider it to be wrong; and (3) numerous
religious groups approve it as legally permissible and morally right in
many if not most circumstances. The same criteria apply to the issue
of abortion: (1) the practice is widespread now and was widely practiced before 1973, when it was illegal; (2) many people do not consider
it to be wrong; and (3) numerous religious groups approve it as legally
permissible and morally acceptable in many instances as part of a moral
duty of responsible parenthood. Like artificial contraception in the
sixties, abortion in the nineties is arguably a matter of private morality
by these criteria. The decisive point is the fact that most Episcopalians,
Methodists, Presbyterians, Lutherans, Baptists, Reform Jews, and other
religious groups regard abortion as morally permissible, while most
Catholics, Mormons, fundamentalists, evangelical Christians, and Orthodox Jews regard it as morally impermissible.

This kind of religious pluralism suggests that, in a free society, a
permissive public policy is appropriate. This is especially the case
because the religious diversity reflects a lack of moral consensus on
abortion. Public morality consists essentially of agreed-upon moral
standards applicable to all. It is very much a function of consensus. It
refers to ethical norms that command the assent of others, are publicly
acknowledged, and may be incorporated into the public law. Currently,
these conditions do not obtain regarding abortion; indeed, public
debate has produced dissensus rather than consensus. By all of Murray's criteria, abortion may more properly be categorized as an issue
of private morality. Since this is the case, public policy may relegate
abortion to the private sphere of moral decision making by individual
women who best know their own circumstances and who are directly
affected by involuntary pregnancy.

I also suspect that in his approach to abortion policy, Murray
would be cognizant of the moral duty of the citizen in a pluralist
democracy to respect the religious and civil liberties of non-Catholics
and nonbelievers. Murray's work on religious freedom suggests that
while error does not have the same rights as truth, persons in error,
consciences in error, do have rights that should be respected by both
church and state. Again, the decisive point is the diversity of religious
opinion in the United States on the morality of abortion. The duty of
American Catholics to respect and tolerate the religious freedom of

non-Catholic citizens should give pause to Catholic efforts to reenact legal restrictions on abortion. The question is whether restrictive laws against abortion would unjustifiably restrain the religious freedom of other non-Catholic Americans who believe they have a duty in conscience to resort to abortion, if necessary, as a means of fulfilling their obligation to be responsible parents.

If it would be imprudent and possibly intolerant for the American Catholic Church to use the coercive power of the law to enforce its moral teaching against abortion, what role might it appropriately play in the abortion controversy? Here Murray's distinction between state and society is relevant. Murray maintained that government's proper function is to attend to public order and to maintain the conditions necessary for its survival. Society's role, on the other hand, is to work toward the common good of all. On this view, society consists of all the many individuals, groups, and associations that constitute the body politic — corporations, trade unions, interest groups, civic associations, churches, and schools. Together these various groups work for the good of all in society. Government itself has a more limited function — to attend to the public order, which is just one part (although a major part) of the common good. (If government tries to exceed this limited function, if it tries to realize the complete good of all groups in society, it becomes totalitarian.)

The distinction between state and society is relevant for a consideration of the role of the Catholic Church in the abortion controversy. Were Murray alive today, I think he would stress the Church's positive role in society rather than its political role in shaping a more restrictive abortion policy. Murray would hold that prudence dictates that the Church should not focus primarily on using coercive law to restrict abortion; rather, the Church's role in this controversy should be to exemplify Christian charity by using its resources to assist women who are involuntarily pregnant. If we assume that the Church's goal is to reduce the incidence of abortion without coercing women, then as a practical matter it would be less advantageous to endorse coercive laws and policies, the effectiveness of which is dubious, than to provide the social and economic support that many women need in order to bear and rear their children. It is possible, even probable, that in taking such measures, the Church and indeed individual Catholic Christians would play a more prophetic role and set a more convincing example of genuine respect for life than they would by using political pressure to pass coercive abortion laws.

Conclusion

The world has changed in major ways since the 1950s and 1960s, when John Courtney Murray did his major work. And so my analysis of how Murray would approach the question of abortion policy today is admittedly conjectural and may be wide of the mark. Murray was, after all, a loyal, faithful Jesuit, and it is possible that if he were alive today he might be leading the charge of Catholic antiabortion activists seeking to make the nation's laws reflect Catholic moral opposition to abortion. But I don't think so. Murray knew that American Catholics had to recognize that law seeks to establish and maintain only that minimum of morality necessary for a stable, functioning society. His sophisticated jurisprudence led him to recognize that not every sin need or should be made a crime. He stressed legal efficacy and enforceability in approaching the question of legislating morality. Above all, he was respectful of religious liberty and tolerant of religious differences in a free society.

Moral Orthodoxy and the Procedural Republic

Robert P. Hunt

I T HAS BEEN ARGUED in recent times that the enemy of the pluralist society is the proponent of a public or political orthodoxy, the person who argues that the American regime is grounded in an ensemble of substantive moral truths that define the nature and limits of our experiment in self-government. This person poses an unrivaled danger to our American way of life, so the story goes, precisely because he believes that his truths are normative for society. He believes, wrongly, that his conception of the good life is grounded in objective moral reality and concludes, even more wrongly, that he is entitled to impose that conception on others. If we are to avoid the imposition of such an orthodoxy, we must find some alternative to it, and the alternative that is typically offered is the "procedural republic." Given the sheer multitude of religious, ethnic, racial, and social groups that constitute our pluralist community at both the national and state levels — and the variety of "interests" that those groups represent — it is both impossible and undesirable to reach substantive agreement at the level of moral principle. We must strive for a procedural, rights-oriented, neutral foundation that eschews a public orthodoxy.

Anticipating these arguments against "orthodoxy" in 1960, John Courtney Murray contended that "no society in history has ever achieved and maintained an identity and a vigor in action unless it has had some substance, unless it has been sustained and directed by some body of substantive beliefs."[1] Murray contended that a truly moral

1. *We Hold These Truths: Catholic Reflections on the American Experiment* (New

public philosophy was needed if America was to recapture its roots in the Western constitutional tradition. Moreover, the public philosophy would have to be defended articulately by those trained in the art of civil discourse, defended as "an ensemble of substantive truths, a structure of basic knowledge, an order of elementary affirmations that reflect realities inherent in the order of existence" (p. 9). And it would have to be defended even at the risk of being branded with the anathema of "orthodoxy."

The battle lines between Murray and the proceduralists seem to be clearly drawn, but they have been obfuscated in contemporary historical circumstances by those who would appropriate Murray under the banner of "neutralism." Some would argue that although Murray might not have agreed with the "neutralists" in principle, he would have concurred with them in practice because of his argument that politics is limited to maintaining public peace and order — a concept that drastically limits the power of government in a pluralist society. For example, on 6 June 1989, the editors of the Los Angeles *Times* commended

> the great Jesuit theologian and exponent of religious liberty, John Courtney Murray, [who] once argued that "The law, mindful of its nature, is required to be tolerant of many evils that morality condemns."
>
> In our pluralistic society, as Father Murray's discerning remark suggests, the boundary between church and state is not always a clear line one can walk with sure-footed confidence. More often, it is a kind of social precipice approached across treacherous, shifting soil that may give way at any moment. Prudent people stay well back from the edge.[2]

The editorial was written in response to Los Angeles Archbishop Roger Mahoney's statement on the relationship between Roman Catholic

---

York: Sheed & Ward, 1960), p. 84. Subsequent references to this volume will be made parenthetically in the text.

2. "A Response to Mahoney: Zeal and Politics," Los Angeles *Times*, 6 June 1989. The editorial implies that Murray's argument regarding the prudential limitations on human positive law is grounded in a distinction between church and state. By interpreting Murray in this fashion, the editors manage to collapse moral issues into religious issues. But much of Murray's effort in *We Hold These Truths* is devoted to preventing this collapse and ensuring that a moral public consensus can be sustained in the absence of agreement on matters of religious belief.

moral teaching and the consequent obligation imposed on Catholic public officials in America to seek the repeal of laws permitting abortion. The implications of the editorial are clear: Archbishop Mahoney fails to realize that in a pluralist society a public official must often tolerate what he personally believes to be morally wrong, especially when we are discussing a particularly neuralgic issue (i.e., abortion) about which there is little moral concord. The "prudent" public official must not press his moral claims too far in the public square, for when he does so, he upsets the pluralist nature of American society, attempts to "impose" his own religious and moral views on those who do not share those views, and consequently violates the cherished American distinction between church and state. And, in support of this philosophy, the editorial cites Murray approvingly.

We are left to infer that Murray would have approved of the *Times*'s logic. Albert J. Menendez pushes this logic even further, seeing an affinity between Murray's "church-state" argument and Mario Cuomo's perspective on the Roman Catholic public official's role in the abortion controversy. "Father John Courtney Murray dealt with [the issue of the separation of church and state] and related themes in his remarkable 1960 book, *We Hold These Truths*. More recently, New York Governor Mario Cuomo resurrected this concept in an important address at the University of Notre Dame in 1984."[3] Just as Murray argued for religious pluralism as an article of peace in a religiously divided America, so Murray, we must assume, would have accepted moral pluralism (that is to say, he would not have pushed his claims too far) in a morally divided America. The *Times* editorial and Menendez's article imply that Murray's "prudent" (i.e., careful) church-state perspective can be extended into the moral arena to resolve the issues that threaten to divide us as a nation — the most volatile issue, of course, being that of abortion.[4] On the issues that divide us, it seems, "neutrality" is the key, and Murray justifies such neutrality in practice.

A fundamental question remains unanswered for those who

3. Menendez, "Why Strict Separation of Church and State Is Good for Catholics," *Crisis*, July-August 1988, p. 34.

4. Cuomo argued for "consensus morality" on the abortion issue in a speech entitled "Religious Belief and Public Morality: A Catholic Governor's Perspective," delivered at the Univeristy of Notre Dame, Notre Dame, Indiana, 13 September 1984. By emptying the term "public consensus" of objective substantive content, Cuomo approached an endorsement of the sort of contentless proceduralism that Murray criticized throughout the 1950s and early 1960s.

would invoke the name of John Courtney Murray to discern the proper
relationship between religion, morality, and politics: How might Murray have responded, in principle, to several contemporary attempts to
redefine America in neutralist terms? It will be argued that those who
would appropriate Murray as a principled or practical defender of the
"neutral" state fail to consider seriously Murray's commitment to the
American polity as an inevitably moral enterprise. This failure is
grounded in a desire, on the appropriator's part, to collapse moral
issues into the private realm of autonomous selfhood — as evidenced
by the "pro-choice" argument in the contemporary abortion debate in
America. Furthermore, the appropriator loses sight of the nature of
Murray's philosophical antagonist — the "neutralist" who harkens
back to the nineteenth-century laicist tradition, a tradition excoriated
by Murray in his study of the thought of Pope Leo XIII. If the philosophical foundation for "neutralism" is recognized for what it is — an
alternative political orthodoxy that would comprehensively reorder
America's spiritual, moral, and political life — it becomes more difficult
to portray Murray as an indifferentist who would be willing to sacrifice
moral principle at the altar of expediency or a truncated view of civil
peace.

The Early Proceduralists: Interest-Group Liberalism

The very notion of a substantive political orthodoxy does not sit well,
as has been noted, with many persons who subscribe to what they
believe to be the principles of liberal democracy. In fact, these persons
contend that a liberal democracy can avoid constitutional decay only
to the extent that it takes no substantive view of human nature or the
goods that actualize that nature. As early as 1951, David Truman
articulated the principles of what has since come to be called "interest-group liberalism." The only way in which the United States could
avoid the maw of totalitarian politics, Truman argued, was for it to
eschew all notions of a mythical "common good" that might serve as
the lodestar by which public policy judgments could be made. Truman
held that the assertion of an "inclusive 'national' or 'public' interest"
was "part of the data of politics," but he argued that it did not "describe
any actual or possible situation within a complex modern nation" such
as the United States. There can be no "totally inclusive" national
interest because there are no attitudes shared by all persons within the

nation. And it would be wrong to foster such attitudes, because "the differing experiences and perceptions of men not only encourage individuality but also . . . inevitably result in differing attitudes and group affiliations."[5] The remedy for totalitarianism lies in the ability of a multiplicity of interest groups to have input into the policy-making process, and the only agreement that should exist between and among an inevitably divided American citizenry is on the rules of the game — the procedures through which every interest is able to stake its claim to some portion of the national pie. According to Truman, the republic of common aims (the harbinger, in his eyes, of totalitarian politics) is being replaced by the procedural republic (which reifies a diversity of "interests" in the political realm), and it is the procedural republic that should command our loyalty and respect.

Michael Sandel has noted, however, that Truman and other "interest-group liberals" have not eliminated the need for consensus. Rather, they have grounded the consensus (i.e., the society's political orthodoxy) in a contentless formalism. They have found "a different sort of legitimating ethic" and have caused the nation to engage in a "gradual shift, in our practices and institutions, from a public philosophy of common purposes to one of fair procedures, from the national republic to the procedural republic."[6] Despite their protestations to the contrary, the interest-group theorists have grounded their philosophy of governance in a legitimating ethic that moves from the empirical fact of diversity to the moral judgment that such diversity is not only necessary but also desirable. In making this moral leap of faith, the interest-group liberals have transcended their own positivist/behavioralist perspective and endorsed a formalistic view of the political good.

In *We Hold These Truths,* John Courtney Murray addressed himself directly to the moral problems that arise under the proceduralist's vision of the *civitas,* and his analysis of this early form of proceduralism gives us a foundation upon which it might be possible to discern what he would say about later variations on the same theme. Murray held that for the Trumanite liberal, the constitutional "consensus is . . . purely procedural. It involves no agreement on the premises and

5. Truman, *The Governmental Process* (New York: Alfred A. Knopf, 1951), pp. 50-51.
6. Sandel, "The Political Theory of the Procedural Republic," in *Constitutionalism and Rights,* ed. Gary C. Bryner and Noel B. Reynolds (Albany: State University of New York Press, 1987), p. 152.

purposes of political life and legal institutions; it is solely an agreement
with regard to the method of getting things done, whatever the things
may be. The substance of American society is our 'democratic institutions,' conceived as purely formal categories" (p. 84). Murray asserted
that "any kind of content may flow . . . under [such] punctilious regard
for correct democratic procedures" (p. 84), even a content that undermines the moral foundation of a democratic regime. The proceduralist
has not conquered the monistic tendencies of the modern totalitarian
state; he has not managed to prevent the absorption of society into the
state. Rather, he has elevated a process to the status of demigod. He
is all too willing to accept the verdict of the *demos* as expressed through
the process, even if the verdict clearly erodes the substantive consensus
that originally grounded the American people's willingness to abide
by certain procedures. The proceduralist's attempt to create a legitimating ethos absent substantive agreement about normative ends is
doomed to fail because procedures alone provide no sufficient warrant
for communal allegiance. Murray argues that America must transcend
such an eviscerated notion of consensus, must adopt a vision of the
civitas that invokes "one supreme interest, the essential human interest,
which is that man should do good and avoid evil" (p. 116). At the heart
of the proceduralists' "empirical" argument is a philosophical disposition to turn men into moral ciphers, to dignify the pursuit of individual
and group self-interest above considerations about what constitutes the
common good. Under such a system, it should come as no surprise
when the *demos* churns out decisions that are devoid of moral principle.
Murray's solution for this potential moral vacuum was not a recipe of
accommodation or a call for the further privatization of moral values;
to the contrary, he advocated reviving a substantive moral consensus
through civil conversation.

The proceduralist, according to Murray, finds himself at an impasse that cannot be resolved within the framework of his own truncated view of "the governmental process." Whatever essential value
might be found within the proceduralist's worldview (e.g., his desire
to avoid totalitarianism) is destroyed by his value-free approach to the
public arena. The proceduralist believes that men of principle are
dangerous, for they would push their claims to the point at which
political accommodation is impossible. Men of principle must be replaced, therefore, by men of "interests" — men who understand that
their values are grounded in subjective judgments, that their preferences are little more than rationalizations for self-interest. Once those

who engage in the governmental process understand this fact, political accommodation and compromise is more likely to occur.

Under such a scheme, the cutting of a deal becomes a good in and of itself, regardless of the substance of the deal that is cut. The political virtue of prudence — the ability to relate ends and means within a complex realm of human choices, to choose the greater good or the lesser evil in given historical circumstances — is replaced by a pragmatism that, ironically, cannot work because it refuses to recognize the moral nature of democratic politics. The proceduralist engages in a systematic cutting off of debate when the participants dare to raise larger questions about the objective, substantive moral reality that lies at the heart of democratic politics.

The victor in the procedural republic, according to Murray, must inevitably be that individual or group which has the strongest political muscle, and the will of the *demos* becomes the greatest good. But we have no ground for supposing that the *demos* will be anything other than what Madison, in *Federalist* paper #10, describes as a faction — "a number of citizens, whether amounting to a majority or minority of the whole, who are united and actuated by some common impulse of passion, or of interest, adverse to the rights of other citizens, or to the permanent and aggregate interests of the community."[7] Murray maintains that interest-group proceduralism cannot save us from the maw of totalitarian politics. We must oppose it in both principle and practice.

Contemporary Proceduralism: The Liberal Neutral State

Is the proceduralist really satisfied with "letting any content flow" in his punctilious regard for procedures? Or does he realize that "going with the flow" might well destroy the multiplicity of lifestyles and conceptions of the good that are the hallmark of contemporary American society? Recognizing this theoretical difficulty and the practical possibility of majoritarian tyranny, the contemporary proceduralist becomes a defender not of contentless proceduralism but of the liberal neutral state.

This liberal neutral state receives its most compelling justification in the academic writings of figures such as Ronald Dworkin and Robert

7. *The Federalist Papers* (New York: New American Library, 1961), p. 78.

Nozick, but its precepts have directly influenced the American political system through the constitutional arguments of public officials such as Supreme Court Justices William Brennan and Harry Blackmun.

Dworkin lays out the principled foundation for the neutral state in his claim that "government must be neutral on what might be called the question of the good life. . . . Each person follows a more-or-less articulate conception of what gives value to life. . . . Since the citizens of a society differ in their conceptions, the government does not treat them as equals if it prefers one conception to another, either because the officials believe that one is intrinsically superior, or because one is held by the more numerous or more powerful group."[8] Dworkin denies that his defense of "neutrality" is grounded in skepticism about theories of the good or that it is based on a radically individualistic conception of the human person. He claims that "neutrality" is based on no theory of the human person whatsoever but, rather, on an implicit and a priori assumption about the limits of governmental power in a pluralist society. "Its constitutive morality provides that human beings must be treated as equals by their government, not because there is no right and wrong in political morality, but because that is what is right. . . . The liberal conception of equality is a principle of organization that is required by justice, not a way of life for individuals."[9] Individuals should be freely and equally able to live out their personal and social existence as they see fit, as a matter of right. They might choose to be orthodox Roman Catholics or Jews, liberal Protestants, secular humanists, radical individualists, or anything else; and government ought not to tell them which conception of social reality is superior. But those individuals, clearly, must not be free to impose their own conception of social reality on others. Notions of objective goodness must be left at the door of the public square, for it is only by doing so that each individual maintains equal dignity in the eyes of others and equal respect for others. Thus, the neutral state recognizes, according to Michael Sandel, "that we are separate, individual persons, each with our own aims, interests, and conceptions of the good, and seeks a framework of rights that will enable us to realize our capacity as free moral agents, consistent with a similar liberty for others."[10] The

8. Dworkin, "Liberalism," in *Liberalism and Its Critics*, ed. Michael Sandel (New York: New York University Press, 1984), p. 64.

9. Dworkin, "Liberalism," p. 77.

10. Sandel, Introduction to *Liberalism and Its Critics*, p. 4.

argument that there is no single, governmentally enforceable conception of the good leads, paradoxically, to the idea that there is a good regime — a regime based on the equal recognition of rights and fundamental moral autonomy.

John Arthur has taken Dworkin's "neutralist" perspective and inserted it back into the thought of the framers of the American Constitution, arguing that our founding Federalists were early proponents of the neutral state. Relying on a radically individualistic reading of *Federalist* paper #10, Arthur contends that the Federalists knew that "society is composed of diverse, pluralistic factions" and that "government should strive to remain neutral with respect to society's competing factions."[11] Recognizing the danger that political majorities might attempt to impose their own conception of the good on others and thus undermine the freedom of the morally autonomous individual, the framers, according to Arthur, created an extended republic in which the sheer multiplicity of interests would make it impossible for government to do anything other than "define the political rights of citizens and establish the tax, contract, and property laws forming the background against which citizens pursue their own ends."[12]

If we accept Arthur's reading of the Federalist perspective, then we can assume that the framers anticipated, and Dworkin recognized, the dangers implicit within Trumanite proceduralism, that both the framers and Dworkin would reject contentless proceduralism *for the same reason*. Moreover, they would concur with Murray's practical rejection of the Trumanite perspective on the grounds that it fails to recognize, as Arthur notes, that "governmental power is not absolute and that moral rights are not defined by the state."[13]

But if, as the neutralist claims, "moral rights are not defined by the state" but must be recognized and upheld by the state, what is the substantive foundation for those rights? Upon what conception of human nature does the neutralist rely to support his defense of individual rights? Strangely enough, the answer seems to be: upon no conception of human nature at all. At least that is the claim made by the neutralist. Arthur expresses the Dworkinian perspective on this

11. Arthur, *The Unfinished Constitution: Philosophy and Constitutional Practice* (Belmont, Calif.: Wadsworth Publishing, 1989), p. 21.

12. Arthur, *The Unfinished Constitution*, p. 202.

13. Arthur, *The Unfinished Constitution*, p. 4.

matter when he claims that "moral rights need not be part of the furniture of the universe, in the sense that they are discovered rather than created; nor must those who reject skepticism hold to the idea that moral statements are 'true' in ways resembling statements of scientists or everyday claims about trees and tables."[14] In other words, rights might be discovered or they might be created. They might exist as valid truths within the moral furniture of the universe or there might not be any moral furniture of the universe. What persons cannot disagree about, if they are to be true participants in the American experiment, is the a priori validity of "rights" — "rights" which, as Michael Sandel has noted, trump the claims of any political majority.

It seems that neutralists are willing to admit that natural or human rights might be fictitious, but, as Alasdair MacIntyre notes, they are willing to invest those "fictions with highly specific properties."[15] They would frame a public order on the principle that government ought not to promote any conception of the good life. Those who believe otherwise are entitled to their beliefs, but they seem to fall beyond the pale of legitimate public discourse.

What neutralists cannot admit is that their whole project is grounded in a particular conception of human nature that disposes them to view "rights" in a particular way and to defend those rights against all those who would legislate some aspect of personal morality. The substantive properties of these rights, and the conception of human nature upon which they are based, are best discovered when we turn to the "constitutional" perspectives of Supreme Court Justices William Brennan and Harry Blackmun, particularly as those perspectives impact on their defense of a constitutional right to privacy. Justice Brennan, for example, respects the American Constitution less for its specific and manifest commitment to democratic and moral self-government than for its general "sublime oration on the dignity of man, a bold commitment by a people to the ideal of libertarian dignity protected through law."[16] According to Justice Brennan, the

14. Arthur, *The Unfinished Constitution*, p. 4.

15. MacIntyre, *After Virtue: A Study in Moral Theory* (Notre Dame, Ind.: University of Notre Dame Press, 1981), p. 67.

16. Brennan, "The Constitution of the United States: Contemporary Ratification," in *Civil Liberties and Civil Rights Debated*, ed. Herbert M. Levine and Jean Edward Smith (Englewood Cliffs, N.J.: Prentice-Hall, 1988), p. 63. Brennan provides an extended discussion of his constitutional vision in an address he delivered at Georgetown University address on 12 October 1985.

dignity of man is protected in large part by a constitutional right to privacy.

To whom does the right to privacy accrue? To married couples? To couples ordered together in a particular fashion for particular ends? No, it accrues to *individuals,* and individuals can invoke the right to privacy to trump legislative action. Moreover, they can trump legislative distinctions based on a legislative body's moral preference for one type of relationship (e.g., marriage) over another (e.g., cohabitation). In *Eisenstadt v. Baird,* in which the Supreme Court struck down a Massachusetts law that prohibited the distribution of contraceptives to single persons except by a physician or pharmacist, Justice Brennan's majority opinion for the Court invokes a radical individualism that has profound political consequences.

> The marital couple is not an independent entity with a mind and heart of its own, but an association of two individuals with a separate intellectual and emotional make-up. If the right to privacy means anything, it is the right of the individual, single or married, to be free from unwarranted governmental intrusion into matters so fundamentally affecting a person as the decision whether to bear or beget a child.[17]

The Dworkinian, neutralist implications of Brennan's argument are clear: the Constitution protects individuals in matters that fundamentally affect their person. The Massachusetts law banning the sale of contraceptives to unmarried couples introduced an unconstitutional intrusion into the individual's exercise in self-definition. Furthermore, any state law regarding contraceptive use that favors married over unmarried couples violates the "equal dignity and respect" of the unmarried couple. And, finally, what are couples anyway if they are not "individuals" united by choice and living a life free from governmental restraint?

Justice Brennan has gone a long way to read the notion of the unencumbered self into the Constitution. His dissent in *Labine v. Vincent,* in which the Court upheld state regulations that favored legitimate children over "nonmarital children," decried the "moral prejudice" that oppressed "bygone centuries" of human beings.[18] According to Justice Brennan, it seems, the "equal protection" and "due process"

17. *Eisenstadt v. Baird,* 405 U.S. 438, 440-55 (1972).
18. *Labine v. Vincent,* 401 U.S. 532, 541-59 (1971).

clauses of the Fourteenth Amendment preclude state governments from making moral distinctions between human beings or life-styles. State governments that engage in such an enterprise violate the libertarian dignity accorded to human beings by the Constitution.[19]

Justice Harry Blackmun — best known, of course, for his intellectual fathering of the abortion right — has gone farther than even Justice Brennan in his critique of conventional morality, as evidenced by his dissent in *Bowers v. Hardwick* in 1986. What aroused Justice Blackmun's vitriolic dissent was the Court's upholding, by a narrow 5-4 majority, of a Georgia statute that prohibited the act of sodomy. Blackmun argued that the case was not about "a fundamental right to engage in homosexual activity" but was rather about the right to be let alone. And it is important for individuals to be let alone, because "individuals define themselves in a significant way through their intimate sexual relationships with others." The variety of such attempts at self-definition suggests, for Justice Blackmun, that "there may be many 'right' ways of conducting those relationships, and that much of the richness of a relationship will come from the freedom an individual has to choose the form and nature of these intensely personal bonds."[20]

Whatever merit might be contained in Justice Blackmun's dissent regarding the prudential need for limited government is subsumed into a larger and by no means neutral perspective on the relationship between the Constitution, the courts, and the self-defining individual. The Supreme Court, according to Blackmun, does not protect the privacy of the home, marriage, or the family because of "a preference for stereotypical households." To protect them for this reason is to endorse a substantive, communitarian view of the good and, thus, to inhibit self-definition. The sole basis for protecting any societal institution is that "it contributes so powerfully to the happiness of individuals."[21] Justice Blackmun is correct: *Bowers v. Hardwick* has little to do with homosexual sodomy and everything to do with the morally autonomous self whose norms are right not because they conform to some external moral standard but because they are freely chosen. Or at least Justice Blackmun is correct given his

19. For an extended critique of Brennan's (and Harry Blackmun's) apparent animus toward traditional notions of morality and family, see Robert K. Faulkner, "Difficulties of Equal Dignity: The Court and the Family," in *The Constitution, the Courts, and the Quest for Justice*, ed. Robert A. Goldwin and William A. Schambra (Lanham, Md.: University Press of America, 1989), pp. 93-114.

20. *Bowers v. Hardwick*, 106 S.Ct. 2851 (1986).

21. *Bowers v. Hardwick*, 106 S.Ct. 2851 (1986).

own radically individualist perspective and his desire to read that perspective into the Constitution.

If we accept the constitutional vision of Dworkin, Arthur, Brennan, and Blackmun, we impose onto the Constitution, through a neo-Kantian gloss in support of "equal dignity and respect," a Nietzschean view of the morally autonomous self. We are left to wonder about how John Courtney Murray might respond to this contemporary "neutralist," "proceduralist" view.

Murray contra the Procedural Republic

Richard John Neuhaus has argued that the neutral state establishes a public orthodoxy that misunderstands the nature of democratic society in general and the moral foundation of the American regime in particular. The state that is committed to the relativization of all values, says Neuhaus, elevates the principle of relativity to the level of the absolute. Neuhaus contends that "without the counter-claims of 'meaning-bestowing institutions' of religion" (which have been duly privatized in the procedural republic), "there is not an absence of religion but, rather, the triumph of the religion of relativity."[22] Just as the relativists of the 1930s and 1940s perceived a danger to their agenda in the meaning-bestowing institutions of religion and hence called for the privatization of religion, so our contemporary relativists perceive a danger to their agenda in any substantive conception of the moral good and hence seek to empty the public square of moral content. They would rely instead on the self-reliant, unencumbered individual who transcends the limitations and "moral prejudices" of prior generations. Our contemporary neutralists thus express a preference for two substantive values above every competing social or moral good: (1) civil peace, which can be obtained only if participants in public dialogue do not "impose" their own conception of the good on others, and (2) the rights of the autonomous individual, which are best protected under the neutralist regimen, under the safeguards of the procedural republic. The advocate of the procedural republic is, in short, a modern incarnation of nineteenth-century Continental laicism.

John Courtney Murray did not live to engage in debate with the

22. Neuhaus, *The Naked Public Square* (Grand Rapids: William B. Eerdmans, 1984), pp. 86-87.

later proceduralist, but he did provide, in his masterly analyses of the social and political thought of Pope Leo XIII, a scathing critique of laicism. And it is to those analyses that we must turn if we are to discern how contemporary friends of Murray should react to the phenomenon of proceduralism/neutralism.

Whether Murray, like Neuhaus, would describe the modern neutralist as religious is debatable, but he would clearly have rejected the argument that government can ever be morally neutral. Just as all action is directed to some end, so the action of government must, by its nature, be directed to some end. To deny the moral function of government, says Murray, would be to "imply a concept of government that is altogether unhistorical; all governments have stood in the service of some truth, some morality, indeed some God, even though the god may have been an idol. . . . The political and legal action of government is inevitably in some moral direction."[23] Neutralists are necessarily engaged in an impossible enterprise; their very use of such phrases as "equal dignity and respect" and "libertarian dignity under law" betrays the theoretical impossibility of "neutrality" as a guiding moral principle. Unless these terms are to be absolutely meaningless or hopelessly abstract, they must be filled with some moral content. The question that Murray would ask of the neutralist is not "Is your government truly neutral?" but rather, "In what moral direction would your government take us, given the substantive arguments that underlie your supposed neutrality?"

Murray assures us that government cannot and ought not be neutral regarding fundamental moral issues. It must take the side of those who would "protect the human heritage against those who would dissipate it by the corrosion of doubt, denial, or cynicism."[24] For Murray, the true human heritage does not rest on the mere imposition of power but on a true order of rights and duties that carefully balances the need for freedom and authority. In endorsing the aphorism "As much freedom as possible, as much government as necessary," Murray believes that he is avoiding the immoral extremes of libertarianism and statism.[25] But the aphorism itself is of little assistance to us in the political realm, Murray assures us, unless we properly understand the

23. Murray, "Leo XIII: Government and the Order of Culture," *Theological Studies* 15 (March 1954): 12.

24. Murray, "Leo XIII: Government and the Order of Culture," p. 13.

25. Murray, "Leo XIII: Two Concepts of Government," *Theological Studies* 14 (December 1953): 559.

corporate dimension of human freedom and the intrinsic limitations placed on government by the Western constitutional tradition — a tradition that is itself properly grounded in the natural moral law.

Just as the human heritage is not protected by the omnicompetent monistic state, so it is not protected by an a priori defense of the morally autonomous or unencumbered self. The danger of modernity lies in its unwillingness to accept the concept of "true order" as discernible in the nature of things. It reduces all connections between and among individuals and groups to "power" relationships — relationships grounded in will, not reason. Having reached the conclusion that a public defense of the right ordering of things is abysmally anachronistic and epistemologically flawed, the modernist supplies a new justification for the obstinate fact of power. Power, seen as the imposition of will, is the new principle of order, but this "power" has no implicit moral limitations placed upon it. The modernist regime, if it is left to its own devices, swings wildly from an abstract defense of the will of the *demos* to an abstract defense of the isolated individual. Or, as Murray puts it, "society, trapped in the false antithesis of unlimited freedom vs. unlimited power, will swing helplessly between the extremes of individualistic anarchy and totalitarian tyranny."[26]

The proceduralists' arguments have evolved over the course of the past forty years, but the course of that evolution is a living testament to the inadequacy of proceduralism as a foundation for a viable public philosophy: the early interest-group liberals (e.g., Truman) desired to avoid tyranny at all costs, but their remedy for tyranny was an arid proceduralism that reduced "authority" to "power," blurred the distinction between legitimate and illegitimate interests, and permitted any content to flow as long as the rules of the game were followed. The later "proceduralists" recognized that contentless formalism posed a danger to individual rights and so endorsed a regime that would protect each individual's pursuit of his own conception of the good. But their philosophy of limited government is undermined by a radical individualism that, in common with early proceduralism, sees governance as nothing other than the imposition of will. If a will is to be imposed, they argue, let it be the individual who imposes his own moral values on himself alone. Because of the absence of a substantive notion of the common good under all forms of proceduralism, the regime is left to swing wildly

26. Murray, "Leo XIII: Government and the Order of Culture," p. 5.

in the direction of an anarchic individualism in which "self-definition" becomes the norm.

For John Courtney Murray, the proper political question is not whether the state has the right to legislate morality, for the state always moves in some moral direction when it enacts legislation. The proper political question is: "How far and in what circumstances" does the state's power to meet "the requirements of public morals, public health, public safety, public order, and the general comfort of society" extend (p. 159)? This question should be answered not through assumptions about moral autonomy or self-definition but through the use of prudential reasoning grounded in the natural-law tradition. This tradition supplies us, in principle, with a clear understanding of the proper relationship between morality and positive law. And this understanding allows us to avoid the extremes of political Puritanism and political indifferentism.

Because it distinguishes between society and the state, between the common good in all of its societal aspects and the more limited requirements of public order, the tradition avoids a Puritanical politics that turns every private sin into a public crime. The Puritanical position is foolish (i.e., imprudent) because it fails to recognize that any "legal code will always be imperfect from the standpoint of truth and justice," that the positive law must often tolerate what morality condemns.[27] Civil law, Murray assures us, must lead man to manhood, not to sainthood.

On the other hand, the tradition manages skillfully to avoid an even more "knavish position that, since certain acts . . . are obviously not [civil] crimes, they are not even sins. Upon a foolish disregard of the distinction between private and public morality there ensues a knavish denial that there is any such thing as public morality" (p. 158). To engage in this "knavish denial" is to reject the principle "that human law finds its ultimate norm and the primary source of its obligation in the higher law of God," not in the will of the *demos* or the will of the autonomous individual.[28]

Having criticized both Puritanism (for its imprudent inattention to the limits of politics) and indifferentism (for its principled inattention to the moral foundation of human law), Murray admits that he has not provided a detailed legal code for society. He leaves the application

27. Murray, "Leo XIII on Church and State: The General Structure of the Controversy," *Theological Studies* 14 (March 1953): 26.
28. Murray, "Leo XIII on Church and State," p. 25.

of moral principles to concrete circumstances "to the prudence of the legislator and the [reasoned] will of the people."[29]

Advocates of proceduralism/neutralism will have little regard for Murray's argument precisely because they have little regard for political prudence. The questions "How far?" and "By what means?" have little or no place in their political vocabulary. They want to remove difficult moral issues from the public square, to privatize morality so thoroughly that the state has no ability to "impose" any conception of the good on autonomous moral actors. In their desire to restrict the state's ability to legislate against perceived "immoral actions," they have elevated "normlessness" itself to the level of the norm and charged government with the duty of upholding this "normless" orthodoxy. Murray would concur with Francis Canavan, who contends that "normlessness . . . turns out to be itself a norm. It is a steady choice of individual freedom over any other human or social good that conflicts with it, an unrelenting subordination of all allegedly objective goods to the subjective good of individual preference."[30]

The theory of freedom to which the neutralists adhere is eerily reminiscent of the theory of freedom propounded by the nineteenth-century laicist — a theory that was excoriated by Pope Leo XIII and dismissed by Murray himself as "shallow" and "appallingly thin." It is the theory of "the outlaw individual conscience" (*exlex uniuscuiusque conscientiae iudicium*) — a conscience that makes itself the arbiter of truth and error, of right and wrong, with no reference to anything higher than its own sense of justice. The nineteenth-century laicist operated in a self-created moral vacuum. He believed that he had the right to say something because he believed himself to be right. He thought he was free to say what he thought simply because he thought it. He inverted a traditional maxim of Thomist philosophy and held that "the truth does not make the mind free; rather the free mind makes the truth."[31]

If the nineteenth-century laicist went too far in applying his voluntarist notion of truth in the area of speech and ideas, his twentieth-century "proceduralist" compatriots go even further: they extend the voluntarist argument into the realm of action. They argue that the individual has the right to do something because, when he acts according

29. Murray, "Leo XIII on Church and State," pp. 25-26.
30. Canavan, "The Pluralist Game," *Law and Contemporary Problems* 44 (Spring 1981): 34.
31. Murray, "Leo XIII: Government and the Order of Culture," p. 3.

to his own conception of the good, he is engaged in "self-definition"; he has disencumbered himself from traditional codes of morality and is living out the Rousseauean dream — abiding by that morality which he has imposed on himself. Government's role is twofold: to protect those who have already disencumbered themselves and to disencumber those who have not yet been fortunate enough to do so on their own. Thus, the proceduralism of Dworkin and Arthur shapes itself into the moral egalitarianism of Brennan and Blackmun — an egalitarianism that bears an instinctive and self-righteous hostility toward all notions of objective morality.

Murray contends that any public orthodoxy grounded in the theory of the outlaw conscience is inadequate:

> we see that the modern concept of freedom itself was dangerously inadequate because it neglected the corporate dimension of freedom. We see too that modernity was wrong in isolating the problem of freedom from its polar terms — responsibility, justice, order, law. . . . We know that the myopic individualism of modernity led it into other errors, even into a false conception of the problem of the state in terms of the unreal dichotomy, individualism vs. collectivism. (P. 200)

If the nineteenth-century laicist was myopic, it might well be argued that the modern proceduralist/neutralist, grounding his conception of freedom in the absence of external restraint and the positive affirmation of self, is myopic with a vengeance. The neutralist reifies "the self-conscious free individual, armed with his subjective rights, whose ultimate origins he may have forgotten but whose status as legal certitudes he cherishes" (p. 210). And, in reifying the self-conscious free individual who asserts his "rights" against all antagonists (even the antagonist of higher moral obligation), the neutral state "creates the ethos of society, embodies it, imparts it to its citizens, and sanctions its observance with rewards and punishments" (p. 209). The defenders of the neutral state have indeed clothed what Neuhaus describes as the naked public square, but the garments are threadbare and provide no adequate intellectual, moral, or political protection for democratic society. A regime that absolutizes the autonomous self weakens the "natural" intermediary institutions (e.g., the family, the community, the churches) that limit the pretensions of the state. These natural institutions are seen in a new light — as "voluntary" associations whose chief merit lies in the fact that autonomous individuals choose to accept their "values" not because these "values" are true but because they are freely chosen by the self-defining individual.

In short, what Murray argued in 1953 — namely, that "the brittle and contracted universe in which such a theory [of the outlaw conscience] could attract the thinking mind has long since been shattered"[32] — was overly optimistic. The brittle and contracted universe of the outlaw conscience has not been shattered at all. It has been reconstituted in the groves of modern academe and, occasionally, imposed upon the American people by a Supreme Court that would free individuals from the impediments of law and morality.

According to Murray, the framers of the American Constitution were not operating in a brittle and contracted universe. While they recognized the necessity and desirability of religious freedom, they also recognized the corporate and moral dimension of human freedom. They believed that "the freedom toward which the American people are fundamentally orientated is a freedom under God, a freedom that knows itself to be bound by the imperatives of the moral law" (p. 164). Thus, if man's "use of freedom is irresponsible, he is summoned after the fact to responsibility before the judgment of the law" (p. 165). The framers avoided the monism of the modern totalitarian state and the excessive individualism implicit in the neutralist argument by adopting a vision of freedom that incorporates "the freedom of the Church, the freedom of sacred things from profanation at the hands of political power, the freedom of association that is the condition of political freedom to share in the direction of the *res publica,* and even the freedom of the human mind itself to search for truth and embrace it when found."[33] The proceduralist, to the extent that he abstracts the individual from his social responsibilities and prevents truly democratic and moral self-governance, endangers both freedom *and* order.

Murray and the Realm of Practical Politics

Having rejected the notion of the procedural republic/neutral state in principle, is it still possible that Murray would endorse it in practice? Given Murray's recognition of the need for limited government, for civic

32. Murray, "Leo XIII on Church and State," p. 19.
33. Murray, "On the Structure of the Church-State Problem," in *The Catholic Church in World Affairs,* ed. Waldemar Gurian and M. A. Fitzsimons (Notre Dame, Ind.: University of Notre Dame Press, 1954), p. 25.

amity amid our differences, might he not accept the arguments of those who would privatize morality on particularly divisive social issues such as abortion? After all, the Los Angeles *Times* editorial and the Menendez article cited earlier defend the proposition of "moral neutrality" in a pluralist society and use Murray to advance their arguments.

The manifest difficulty of maintaining this position is that Murray was not a defender of moral neutrality. While Murray argued that government ought to be denied all competence in the field of religion, that "the area of state — that is, legal — concern was limited [by the framers of the Constitution] to the pursuit of certain enumerated secular purposes" (p. 66), he also argued that "sheer diversity" in the moral and political spheres leads to moral and political chaos.

> Granted that the unity of the commonwealth can be achieved in the absence of a consensus with regard to the theological truths that govern the total life and destiny of man, it does not follow that this necessary civic unity can endure in the absence of a consensus more narrow in its scope, operative on the level of political life, with regard to the rational truths and moral precepts that govern the structure of the constitutional state, specify the substance of the common weal, and determine the ends of public policy. (Pp. 72-73)

The various religious communities that originally constituted our national union were able to engage in civil conversation with each other precisely because they agreed with each other about the rational truths and moral precepts that govern the structure of the constitutional state. Both the Declaration of Independence and the U.S. Constitution allowed the participants in the American experiment in self-government to avoid the chaotic frenzy of sheer diversity. They affirmed the political truths of "constitutionalism, the rule of law, the notion of sovereignty as purely political and therefore limited by law, the concept of government as an empire of laws and not of men" (p. 32). And these political truths were grounded in an even deeper substantive consensus about the moral truths that would set us free as a people and give us the capacity for virtuous self-governance. In short, the framers of the Constitution affirmed the notion of ordered liberty, of free persons possessing the requisite virtues for a democratic experiment in self-government.

An essential attribute of moral self-governance is the people's capacity, through their elected representatives, to enact laws that express their disposition to protect the human heritage against dissipation. Ralph McInerny expresses the imperative and yet prudential aspect of the connection between law and morality and at the same time provides a Murrayite critique of the procedural republic and those who would employ Murray to serve their own ends:

> we regularly incorporate substantive views into the legal system — murder and theft and cigarette smoking and emitting noxious gases [are legislated against]. This is done, not because we have betrayed the spirit of the nation's founders, but because a purely procedural republic is logically impossible.
>
> One does indeed wish to legislate morality, not because it is one's own, but because it is true. There are loads of things in anyone's morality that do not have the necessary status for being enshrined in civil law, but killing the innocent is not one of them.[34]

If we accept McInerny's argument, we might well come to the conclusion that it is, at best, extremely imprudent to go along with those who would privatize morality and leave the innocent unprotected by civil law. The imprudence borders on moral indifference when, in the name of neutrality, "opponents" of abortion argue that government should do little or nothing to restrict or prohibit the taking of innocent human life. Murray himself was no moral indifferentist; nor was he a legal libertarian. Since the laicist/neutralist is willing to employ government (and, in particular, an unelected, unrepresentative elite — the Supreme Court) to impress his own moral vision of the autonomous self on others, his philosophical opponent must be willing to uphold the tradition of civility, the patrimony of constitutionalism and ordered liberty. Just as Pope Leo XIII was willing to defend the use of law to uphold that tradition, so must the modern friend of Murray be willing to defend the use of law to protect certain aspects of morality (e.g., respect for the sanctity of innocent human life) from erosion. But the modern friend of Murray must also recognize something that Leo XIII did not recognize in combatting Continental laicism — namely, that law alone cannot fill the moral vacuum. To surrender to an arid legalism, as Murray reminded us, is to ignore the fact that "the moral and spiritual forces of the popular conscience must first be awakened before human legislation can make for higher goals."[35]

34. McInerny, "Those Mothers on the Mall," *Crisis*, December 1989, p. 3.
35. Murray, "Leo XIII on Church and State," p. 26.

Those who would invoke the name of John Courtney Murray ought to commit themselves, as Murray did, to reawakening the moral and spiritual forces of the popular conscience. In doing so, they must avoid both the moral indifferentism that follows advocacy of the procedural republic and the confusion between morality and law that arises among puritanical legalists. At the present juncture, it would seem, the proceduralist poses the greater danger to the Western heritage. His constitutional and moral vision entails, ostensibly in the defense of limited government, a wholesale rejection of the principle of ordered liberty, of the corporate dimension of human freedom to which Murray himself appealed. What is needed, therefore, is a different sort of pluralism — a pluralism that the editors of *First Things* describe as "the civil engagement of our differences and disagreements about what is most importantly true." This pluralism, if successful, "revives and sustains the conversation about what really matters, which is the truth."[36]

The contemporary proceduralist/neutralist relies on academics and Supreme Court justices to impress his constitutional vision upon a typically reluctant American people, but those who would oppose him in principle and practice must recognize that the problem of the procedural republic cannot be solved by governmental fiat alone. They must help rebuild a stable public consensus around the transcendent moral and political truths about which Murray spoke, making government less necessary but, at the same time, more effective in upholding true public order and civility. As I have noted elsewhere, Murray's faith in the efficacy of public argument might be naive, for the theory of neutrality upon which many contemporary public arguments seem to be based has gained support precisely because it claims to be an alternative to orthodoxy.[37] The possibility of effective public argument is not improved by those who would, in Murray's name, cut off debate about moral truth lest others fear that someone might be trying to "impose" his values on others. The sooner the theory of neutrality, of the procedural republic, is recognized for what it is — not an alternative to orthodoxy but an alternative orthodoxy that "closes off" the public square to meaningful and spirited debate about the things that really matter to us — the greater the likelihood that Murray's faith in public argument on behalf of the tradition of civility will be rewarded.

36. "Putting First Things First." *First Things* 1 (March 1990): 8.
37. See Robert P. Hunt, "Murray, Niebuhr, and the Problem of the Neutral State," *Thought* 255 (December 1989): 375.

EPILOGUE

The Future of the
John Courtney Murray Project

George Weigel

JOHN COURTNEY MURRAY, a man of piquant humor, would doubtless be amused as well as pleased by the notion that his "project" would be enjoying a revival in the last decade of the twentieth century.

Readers of this volume may be surprised to learn that that didn't seem a likely prospect twenty years ago, shortly after Murray's death. Then, amidst the churnings set loose by the Second Vatican Council, the civil rights revolution, the Vietnam trauma, the rise of radical religion in America, and the emergence of the theologies of liberation to the south, Murray was deemed hopelessly passé — and by precisely those younger American Catholic scholars who might have been expected to take up and extend Murray's work.

John Coleman, S.J., argued, for example, that Murray's corpus was deeply flawed by a "bias toward liberty at the expense of justice in the American public philosophy," by a "theory of natural law that rests on particularistic Catholic theological principles and theories that do not command widespread allegiance," and by an inability "to evoke the rich, polyvalent power of religious symbolism, a power that can command depths of emotional commitment."[1] A less sophisticated commentator than Coleman summed up the successor generation's indictment in these terms: "but we know so much more than Murray did."

This hermeneutic of deprecation began to shift in the mid-1980s,

---

1. Coleman, "A Possible Role for Biblical Religion in Public Life," *Theological Studies* 40 (December 1979): 702.

in response to three hotly debated issues in American Catholic (indeed, American religious) social ethics. Critics of the Marxist-oriented political theory embedded in certain forms of the theology of liberation found in Murray a rich source of material and reflection for creating a religiously grounded defense of the liberal democratic state. In 1982-83, the debate over the drafting of the National Conference of Catholic Bishops' pastoral letter "The Challenge of Peace" led some scholars to look back into Murray's thought for the outlines of a theology and politics of peace and freedom that took the threat of totalitarianism seriously even as it acknowledged the dangers posed by nuclear weapons. Finally, in 1984, the vigorous debate over the public role of religion occasioned by the controversy between Archbishop John J. O'Connor of New York and Rep. Geraldine Ferraro, the Democratic vice presidential nominee, on the issue of abortion found combatants on all sides of the fray looking to Murray to buttress their arguments. The two most developed statements during that controversy, the speeches by Gov. Mario Cuomo and Congressman Henry J. Hyde at the University of Notre Dame, each made explicit reference to Murray's work on the church-state (better, religion-and-society) question, as did Cardinal Joseph Bernardin in a major statement at Georgetown University and non-Catholic commentators such as Charles Krauthammer of *The New Republic*.

In a contest strikingly similar to that for the legacy of his contemporary Reinhold Niebuhr (whose Christian Realism had also been deprecated by a successor generation that later found reason to reclaim the master), the rights to Murray's mantle were thus posthumously debated by religious and political intellectuals and activists covering a rather extraordinary range of the ideological landscape. Murray was no longer passé. Scholars — including those who once found Murray impossibly old hat — vied to fix an interpretation of his lifework that would sustain their own enterprises in the future.[2] Deepening and extending the "Murray Project" was no longer deemed quixotic or antediluvian but actually quite fresh and exciting.

There are, as the sociologist Peter Rossi once remarked, many ironies in the fire.

---

2. The most radical of these was J. Leon Hooper's *The Ethics of Discourse* (Washington: Georgetown University Press, 1986). Robert W. McElroy took a more self-consciously centrist cut at an overview of the Murray enterprise in *The Search for an American Public Theology: The Contribution of John Courtney Murray* (New York: Paulist, 1989).

A Project Defined

Since I believe I was the first to employ the phrase "The John Courtney Murray Project,"[3] it may not be altogether inappropriate for me to offer my own sense of the main thrust and the boundaries of Murray's work, as the prolegomena to a few suggestions as to where the project might be directed in the future.

In simplest form, the Murray Project may be summarized in the phrase used by Richard John Neuhaus to describe the public dimension of this possible "Catholic moment" in American history: the Murray Project involves "the culture-forming task of constructing a religiously informed public philosophy for the American experiment in ordered liberty."[4] A brief gloss on the key terms in that packed definition may help orient what follows.

The term "culture-forming" is drawn from Paul Tillich's understanding that politics is a function of culture and that the heart of culture is religion. Politics, in other words and as Murray understood well, is not simply a matter of who wins this or that vote. Politics is most basically a matter of those ideas, norms, and stories by which a people identifies itself, its task in history, and the means appropriate to the pursuit of that task.

The "public philosophy," a central concept in Murray's work, involves the reception and nurturing of a commonly acknowledged set of intellectual coordinates capable of disciplining and mediating the public discourse of diverse communities of conviction and concern on matters touching the right ordering of our common life. America's most serious difficulties, Murray argued, revolved around the fact that "the public philosophy" was in deliquescence in these United States — a judgment that has been thoroughly vindicated since Murray's death.

Were such a public philosophy to be re-created among us, it would have to take account of the incorrigibly religious character of the American people and the fact that the commitment of most Americans to democratic pluralism and civility rests on biblically grounded moral norms; that is to say, the public philosophy would have to be

3. See George Weigel, *Tranquillitas Ordinis: The Present Failure and Future Promise of American Catholic Thought on War and Peace* (New York: Oxford University Press, 1987), pp. 107-38.

4. Neuhaus, *The Catholic Moment: The Paradox of the Church in the Post-Modern World* (San Francisco: Harper & Row, 1987), p. 283.

"religiously informed." Conversely, and given what Murray recognized as the natively pluralist religious situation in the United States, that "religiously informed public philosophy" would have to be cast in a language and conceptuality that cut across what Murray thought of as the "interacting conspiracies" of our public life: Protestant/Catholic, Christian/Jewish, religious/secular.[5] Confessional admission tickets could not be required in the American public square. But the debate in the square would have to take account of the religious grounding of most citizens' convictions about the right ordering of society — hence Murray's call for a revivified natural-law ethic.

Murray knew that the argument about the ordering of our common life, even disciplined by a thick and culturally "received" public philosophy, would be an ongoing one. Thus, following Lincoln, he presented the notion of America as a never-finished project, an "experiment" in which each succeeding generation is a generation of founders and framers.

Finally, "ordered liberty," which is arguably the key phrase of the lot. Murray was fond of Acton's *mot* that freedom is "not the power of doing what we like, but the right of being able to do what we ought" (p. 47). The American republic, Murray insisted, is a matter of substance, not just of procedures. A free society must be a disciplined society. Rights must be understood to entail responsibilities, and the exercise of individual liberty must contribute to the achievement of the common good. On these matters, too, Murray's concerns in the 1950s about the state of public moral culture in America seem prescient indeed.

The John Courtney Murray Project, then, was not a matter of making Catholics "acceptable" in the United States (Murray always understood that the key issue was whether America was compatible with Catholic understandings of the human person and human community), nor was Murray simply the precursor of Catholic acculturation, an Ignatian John the Baptist to John Fitzgerald Kennedy.[6] Rather, the Murray Project was an incomplete but powerful attempt to define the purposes of what a later generation of theologians would call the

5. Murray used the term *conspiracy* in its classic sense of "unison, concord, unanimity in opinion and feeling" (*We Hold These Truths: Catholic Reflections on the American Proposition* [Garden City, N.Y.: Doubleday Image Books, 1964], p. 33), not in the debased, post-Watergate parlance of the American press. Subsequent references to *We Hold These Truths* will be made parenthetically in the text.

6. As, for example, John Murray Cuddihy charges in *No Offense: Civil Religion and Protestant Taste* (New York: Seabury, 1978).

"public Church" — the ministry, if you will, of the Church to the wider civic community precisely as civic community, as *polis*.[7] Perhaps more carefully than Niebuhr (and certainly more carefully than proponents of the earlier forms of the theology of liberation), Murray understood that the Church's nurturing of a morally informed public square, much less the Church's address to specific issues of public policy, was a secondary vocation, always subordinate to the Church's primary tasks of evangelization, sacramental worship, and charity.[8] Still, the tasks of the "public Church" are not insignificant, given the abiding significance of religion in American life and the affinity, as Murray understood it, between the American experiment and the classic tradition of Catholic political philosophy.

In sum, and to complexify the Neuhaus formulation a bit, the Murray Project may be understood as involving three concentric circles. The innermost circle is the issue of religious freedom and Murray's herculean effort to disentangle Catholicism from its traditional commitment to the altar-and-throne arrangements of the confessional state. The second circle is the question of Catholicism and American democratic pluralism, as evidenced in Murray's polemic against the "new nativism" of Paul Blanchard and his other attempts to counter the prejudice against his Church that Arthur Schlesinger, Sr. (in a phrase that might well be meditated upon by Arthur Schlesinger, Jr.), once described as "the deepest bias in the history of the American people."[9] The third, and most comprehensive, circle of the Murray Project reverses the polarities of the second circle. Here the defendant is not Catholicism but American democracy, and the question, again Lincolnesque, is whether this national experiment in government of, by, and for the people can survive, much less prosper, absent a far more thoughtful and disciplined public moral argument about its purposes, and the means to achieve them, than Murray discerned in his own time.

7. The phrase (if not the most satisfactory understanding of "the public Church") is Martin Marty's; see *The Public Church: Mainline-Evangelical-Catholic* (New York: Crossroad, 1981).

8. For a critique of Niebuhr's theology of the "public Church," see William Lazareth's comments in "The Story of an Encounter," in *Reinhold Niebuhr Today*, ed. Richard John Neuhaus (Grand Rapids: William B. Eerdmans, 1989), pp. 116-18 *passim*.

9. Schlesinger made this comment to John Tracy Ellis, the doyen of American Catholic historians; see Ellis, *American Catholicism*, 2d rev. ed. (Chicago: University of Chicago Press, 1969), p. 151.

In all three of the interlocking circles of the Murray Project there is considerable work to be done, as the years since Murray's death have amply illustrated. Doing that work — extending and developing the Murray Project — is not a matter of asking silly questions about what Murray would have said about the federal budget deficit, or the child care bill, or U.S. policy toward communist China, or aid to El Salvador, or the capital gains tax, or any other specific issue on the policy agenda. The Murray corpus is not a kind of children's encyclopedia, to be consulted for approved and simplified answers to confusing questions. Rather, extending the Murray Project involves a subtler and more difficult task — "putting on," if you will, the sensibility of John Courtney Murray, his ensemble of intellectual and political predispositions, the moral-intellectual framework through which he discerned the world around him and made his judgments on it. By "sensibility" here, of course, I do not mean to invoke Jane Austen, but rather Thomas Aquinas.

Putting on Murray Today

Three dispositions would, I believe, characterize the work of anyone who sought to extend the Murray Project in deliberate continuity with (or, at the very least, in profound sympathy with) Murray's own mind and spirit.

First, the Murray Project will be properly extended and developed by those who share, or respect, Murray's passion to live and think as a Christian intellectual, with the adjective being the word of greatest consequence here. In his magnificent sermon at Murray's funeral, Walter Burghardt, S.J., limned this dimension of Murray:

> Whether immersed in Trinitarian theology or the rights of man, he reflected the concerns of one of his heroes, the first remarkable Christian thinker, the third-century Origen. He realized with a rare perceptiveness that for a man to grow into an intelligent Christianity, intelligence itself must grow in him. And so his intellectual life reproduced the four stages he found in Origen.
>
> First, recognition of the rights of reason, awareness of the thrilling fact that the Word did not become flesh to destroy what was human but to perfect it. Second, the acquisition of knowledge, a sweeping vast knowledge, the sheer materials for his contemplation, for his

ultimate vision of the real. Third, the indispensable task that is Christian criticism: to confront the old with the new, to link the highest flights of reason to God's self-disclosure, to communicate the insight of Clement of Alexandria that Father Murray loved so dearly: "There is but one river of truth, but many streams fall into it on this side and that." And fourth, an intelligent love: love of truth wherever it is to be found, and a burning yearning to include all the scattered fragments of discovered truth under the one God and His Christ.[10]

Father Burghardt concluded his sermon by describing Murray aptly as "the embodiment of the Christian humanist, in whom an aristocracy of the mind was wedded to a democracy of love." I would simply add one further quality to this aspect of Murray's character as a Christian intellectual: his willingness to confront the new with the old. Whether the issue was national defense or federal support of independent schools, Murray knew that there were things that the classics of Western thought could still teach overly self-confident moderns. Murray believed that the American experiment, for example, stood "in fundamental continuity with the central political tradition of the West" (p. 40), as he believed that the Jacobin impulse (in the French Revolution and its contemporary heirs) constituted a fundamental break with that great tradition. But Murray was no simplistic acolyte at the altar of inevitable political progress. Things could get worse, as the harsh face of twentieth-century totalitarianism had revealed. Nor was America immune from the dangers of a kind of historical regression. The "noble, many-storeyed mansion of democracy" could, absent the reconstitution of a religiously informed public philosophy, be "dismantled, levelled to the dimensions of a flat majoritarianism, which is no mansion but a barn, perhaps even a tool shed in which the weapons of tyranny may be forged" (p. 53).

The generation of Catholic theologians trained since the Second Vatican Council needs little reminder of the truth in Clement of Alexandria's image, nor is the task of "Christian criticism" (or, at least, criticism) much underdeveloped these days. What may be missing, though, is that passion to bring old and new together in a dynamically orthodox synthesis of Christian understanding.

Murray, one of the intellectual architects of Vatican II, was also a churchman in the finest sense of the term: a man with a profound

10. Burghardt, "He Lived with Wisdom," *America*, 9 September 1967, p. 248.

love for the Church, rooted in a profound love for the Lord of the Church. Murray wanted to think in, and for, the Church, and he was quite aware of the fact that the truth of a proposition was not measured by its contemporaneity. Those who would extend Murray's project ought to evince a similar respect for the great tradition of Christianity, the *traditio* of the Gospels, the creeds, and the first seven ecumenical councils.

Second, the Murray Project will be advanced by those who share Murray's skepticism about fads — fads *à gauche*, and that faddish traditionalism which would freeze Christian self-understanding in patterns and practices that are, in truth, not much older than our grandparents.[11]

Religious social ethics has been beset by liberal faddishness in the generation since Murray: secular theology, the death of God, liberation theologies, Habermasian hermeneutics, and feminist deconstructions have followed each other at a dizzying pace (the common denominator among them being a profound dis-ease with the American experiment). Nor have the establishment guilds in the field (among them, the Catholic Theological Society of America and the Society of Christian Ethics) proven themselves altogether immune to the temptation to follow the fads in a kind of Gadarene rush toward "relevance."

Perhaps in reaction to this neophilia, and perhaps responding to other impulses, another cadre of Catholic social ethicists have defined themselves in soi-disant "restorationist" terms, the net result of which is another line of attack against the very possibility of constructing a "religiously informed public philosophy for the American experiment in ordered liberty." Here the classic Continental bias against the possibility of a genuine development of doctrine emerging from the New World has been reintroduced, this time by American scholars and publicists who might have been expected to know better.[12]

---

11. For my analysis of these two curiously parallel phenomena, see chaps. 3 and 4 of Weigel, *Catholicism and the Renewal of American Democracy* (New York: Paulist Press, 1989).

12. On this, see David Schindler, "U.S. Catholicism: A Moment of Opportunity?" *Thirty Days* (May 1989): 57-60; a response to Schindler's critique by Michael Novak, Richard John Neuhaus, and myself ("America Is Not a Secular Society," *Thirty Days* [June 1989]: 53-55), and Schindler's further reflection ("The One, True American Religion," *Thirty Days* [June 1989]: 55-59). See also the reviews of *The Catholic Moment* by Glenn Olsen (*Communio* 15 [Winter 1988]: 474-87) and J. Brian Benestad (*Communio* 16 [Winter 1989]: 488-96), and Richard Neuhaus's response (*Communio* 16 [Winter 1989]: 552-57).

What radicals and restorationists have in common is a deep distrust of pluralism and a preference for a monistic society, culture, and polity that would, in all its constituent parts, reflect the Truth as the monists understand it.

Neither of these monisms — the monism of the left or the monism of the right — seems adequate to the task that the Murray Project identified. A religiously informed public philosophy for the American experiment in ordered liberty will take far more seriously than either radicals or restorationists the natively pluralistic character of the American polity, but it will see this as, just possibly, an incarnation of the Clementine image cited above in Father Burghardt's homily. Murray's disposition, which was not so much "centrist" as *ahead* of the usual polemical barricades, is a badly needed ballast for the current discussion of the public Church. Against monisms of either ideological hue, those who would develop the Murray Project must insist that pluralism is neither the ignoring of our differences nor their melting in the furnace of revolutionary (or counterrevolutionary) zeal but rather serve as a context for the forthright engagement of our differences — including our religious differences — within the bond of democratic civility.[13]

Third, those who would extend and develop the Murray Project ought to "put on" Murray's mature patriotism. John Courtney Murray was no apologist for modern American culture, nor did he find much comfort in the ways in which the policy world addressed the public issues that most concerned him — church and state, war and peace, education. What was at stake beneath these debates, Murray argued, was no less than "America's understanding of itself." Unless the American people found "more reasoned grounds for their essential affirmation that they are uniquely a people, a free society," the republic was in serious trouble. For "the complete loss of one's identity is, with all propriety of theological definition, hell. In diminished forms it is insanity. And it would not be well for the American giant to go lumbering about the world today, lost and mad" (pp. 17-18).

It is hard to imagine a more stringent reading of the contemporary American reality coming from the pen of the most radical of

13. For a more extended discussion of this point, see Richard John Neuhaus, "Genuine Pluralism and the Pfefferian Inversion," *This World* 24 (Winter 1989): 54-63; and George Weigel, "Achieving Disagreement: From Indifference to Pluralism," *This World* 24 (Winter 1989): 71-86.

liberation theologians or feminist denouncers of "patriarchy." Yet Murray's critique was set within a fundamental affirmation of the rightness of the American experiment itself, an appreciation for the freedom that the Church enjoyed in the United States, and an intuition that the American quest for ordered liberty was an important paradigm of possibility in a world in which the dialectic of order and freedom was *the* contemporary issue, and the key question was "On what principles is the world going to be ordered?"[14]

Here too, then, Murray was a man of neither the conventionally celebratory right nor the conventionally deprecatory left. His conviction that the American experiment found its deepest taproots in Christian medieval understandings of the human person and human society sustained his positive appraisal of the intention of the founders and framers. Moreover, Murray's claim that the American Founding was misunderstood if it was taken to be the expression of a rationalist individualism has been buttressed by the post-Murray investigations of Alasdair MacIntyre (on the Augustinian and Aristotelian roots of the Scottish Enlightenment) and William Lee Miller (on the impact of the Scottish Enlightenment on James Madison and the Founding).[15] Conversely, Murray saw, with almost clairvoyant prescience, the *Kulturkampf* that was coming in American society, as the forces of radical autonomy and the proponents of the merely procedural republic challenged the concept of a substantive American experiment with foundational affinities to the Actonian concept of freedom-and-obligation. Nor was Murray convinced that the latter forces would necessarily prevail. Mature patriotism committed to a civilized argument over the nature of the republic characterized Murray's work and ought to inform those who would follow his path.

Adding to the Armamentarium

Because John Courtney Murray died a generation ago, the development of a "Murray sensibility" today will involve more than simply replicating Murray's own predispositions and intuitions. Those who

14. Murray, "Things Old and New in *Pacem in Terris*," *America*, 27 April 1963, 612.

15. See MacIntyre, *Whose Justice? Which Rationality?* (Notre Dame, Ind.: University of Notre Dame Press, 1988); and Miller, *The First Liberty: Religion and the American Republic* (New York: Alfred A. Knopf, 1986).

would put on Murray today should consciously strive to extend that sensibility in two directions.

First, the development of the Murray Project will be far more ecumenical and interreligious than Murray himself could have imagined.

The "pattern of interacting conspiracies" Murray discerned in the 1950s involved Protestants, Catholics, Jews, and secularists. Mainline Protestantism, in Murray's view, remained deeply concerned that Catholicism would prove an "instrument of tyranny" in public life; Catholics, conversely, were nervous about renascent nativism and were quite tired of being characterized as "among us but . . . not of us." Jews, rightly conscious of the history of their persecution at Christian hands, now allied themselves with "the secularizing forces," the triumph of which, they believed, would afford them a security they had never known before. Evangelical Protestants were simply off the radar screen. Then there were the secularists, able to concede the utility of "religion-in-general," yet alarmed by "religion as a Thing, visible, corporate, organized, a community of thought that presumes to sit superior to, and in judgment on, the 'community of democratic thought,' and that is furnished somehow with an armature of power to make its thought and judgment publicly prevail" (pp. 30-32).

The picture has become more complicated over the past generation. Mainline Protestantism has abandoned the culture-forming task it assumed as by divine right even as late as Murray's day; the churches of the mainline are now moribund, not least because they have conceded point after point, doctrinally and behaviorally, to the "secularizing forces" within their own communities.[16] Evangelical Protestantism, conversely, has returned from the cultural wilderness and is fully engaged in the public square — often in tactical alliance with Catholics on specific policy matters. The major Jewish organizations continue to defend the proposition that only a religiously naked public square is safe for Jews, but a younger generation of Jewish scholars is vigorously challenging that assumption, conscious not only of the Jewish experience under pagans such as Hitler and Stalin but also of countervailing currents supportive of a public role for religion in the early history of American Judaism.[17] The secularists, meanwhile, now march under

16. See Wade Clark Roof and William McKinney, *American Mainline Religion: Its Changing Shape and Future* (New Brunswick, N.J.: Rutgers University Press, 1987).

17. See Jonathan D. Sarna, "American Jews and Church-State Relations" (New York: American Jewish Committee, 1989).

the banner of "the American Way," and are if anything more strident in their insistence that only the highest possible wall of separation between religion and society will prevent the American republic from falling into the travails of Belfast, Beirut, and Amritsar.

Murray knew that the "barbarian . . . [wearing] a Brooks Brothers suit" (p. 23) was the greatest obstacle to the development of the public philosophy and thus the greatest threat to the flourishing of the American experiment. And in that judgment, as in so many others, Murray was prescient indeed. For it has now become quite clear that the basic fault line in American culture runs not between denominations or religions but rather between believers on the one hand and radical secularists (or barbarians, in Murray's pungent terminology) on the other. Put another way, the great divide in America today is between those who would hold the American experiment accountable to transcendent moral norms and those who insist that the purpose of the republic is to protect the exercise of autonomous, individualist reason in its quest for "fulfillment."

Contrary to the confident expectations of generations of sociologists, modernization has not equaled secularization in the United States. But there is one thoroughly secularized segment of the American population, and that is the country's cultural elite — in the academy, the prestige press, the popular entertainment industry. Here, at the chief cultural switchboards of American life, the consensus on the public role of religion is simple, direct, and propagated with great (some might say, fanatical) zeal: there is no place for religion in the public life of the American republic. The *locus classicus* for this position is Harvard law professor Laurence Tribe's textbook on constitutional law, in which he states that there is a "zone which the free exercise clause carves out of the establishment clause for permissible accommodation of religious interests. This carved-out area might be characterized as the zone of permissible accommodation."[18] Free exercise, in other words, has no public meaning or function; the free exercise of religious faith contributes nothing to the furthering of the American experiment.

In short, the *Kulturkampf* in contemporary America is not defined confessionally but rather is being contested between believers on the one side and unbelievers aggressively hostile to the public church (or synagogue, or mosque, or ashram) on the other. Those who would,

18. Tribe, *American Constitutional Law* (Mineola, N.Y.: Foundation Press, 1978), p. 823.

following Murray, engage in the construction of a *religiously* informed public philosophy thus find themselves by necessity in a new "conspiracy," comprising Catholics, evangelical Protestants, remnants of the Protestant mainline, and dissidents from the received wisdom in mainstream Jewish organizations on this business of religion-and-society.

The most potent ecumenical coalition within this larger conspiracy lies, quite probably, along the Catholic/evangelical axis — a situation that Murray could not have foreseen and might well have regarded as improbable in the extreme. But as evangelical Protestantism — aroused by a host of Supreme Court decisions on public religion and brought finally into electoral politics in a massive way by the abortion license defined in *Roe v. Wade* — has established itself over the past fifteen years as one of what Murray would have called the "growing ends" of American religion, a new ecumenical dialogue has commenced: first, on matters of tactics in the public arena but more recently in terms of a crucial dimension of the Murray Project — the creation of a mediating language and conceptuality to discipline public moral argument in America. Indeed, these days one finds younger evangelical scholars reading Murray with great interest and appreciation, while a considerable number of Catholics of the same generation turn to such as Jon Sobrino or Leonardo Boff for their "political theology."

Be that as it may, the Murray Project will be advanced today only if it becomes a thoroughly ecumenical enterprise. Happily, there are signs that that is already the case, and that the real issue now is the deepening of the ecumenical conversation. Murray, whose friend and Woodstock colleague Gustave Weigel, S.J., was an early Catholic ecumenical pioneer, might have found the new situation tinged with irony. But I don't doubt that he would have approved.

The second necessary development in the "Murray sensibility" will involve a conversation with those advocating a "narrative" approach to Christian moral theology and its public presentation of itself. The *odium philosophicum* of those pressing for this reconception of moral language, which carries with it a distinctive conception of the public church, is primarily directed toward those post-Enlightenment moral theorists who think of the moral enterprise as one in which autonomous selves reason their way to universalizable principles without the guiding force of any community or tradition. This, the narrativists insist, is simply self-delusion, for everyone lives "within a story," including those who deny they are doing so and express their dissent by inventing a new "story," that of the autonomous, unencumbered, posttraditional self.

But the narrativists are also nervous about natural-law approaches to moral reflection, judging them to be perhaps too dismissive of (or, perhaps better, less than fully attentive to) Christian particularity. Why should Christians, the narrativists ask, present themselves and their moral claims as anything other than distinctively, embeddedly, thoroughly Christian? Natural-law proponents, on the other hand, worry that even the most sophisticated of narrativists has not satisfactorily answered the question — and may even deny the possibility — of a "mediating" language through which and in which evangelical and mainline Protestants, Catholics of various theological hues, Jews, secularists, and others can contend reasonably and civilly in the American public square.

This is not the place to attempt a detailed commentary on this argument, but its unfolding will have serious repercussions for the Murray Project. The power of narrative approaches to moral theology, and their pastoral and catechetical fruitfulness within the Church, cannot be denied and must be reckoned with if the task at hand is the creation of a *religiously* informed public philosophy for the American experiment in ordered liberty. Conversely, some narrativists may now be willing to acknowledge that (in the jargon) there are thin and thick versions of the natural law and that the latter clearly arise out of theologically committed, fully encumbered selves — selves like Thomas Aquinas, for example. "Thicker" natural-law approaches can deal with the undeniable fact that they emerge from within traditions (or "story-lines") and thus may not involve so great a danger of decomposition into the perils of radical autonomy or false universalism as their "thinner" cousins. Natural-law ethics can, in short, be theological ethics.

The conversation between narrativists and natural-law theorists will likely be one of the most provocative, as well as one of the feistiest, theological contestations of the foreseeable future. Those who would advance the Murray Project had best take that conversation — and the possibility that it just may temper one's understanding of the Project — with great seriousness.

Continuing the Project: Three Agenda Items

Theorists of democratic change analyzing the cultural, social, and political upheavals in east central Europe and Latin America in the 1980s distinguished between "democratic transition" and "democratic consolidation" — the latter referring to the postrevolutionary strengthening of both the institutions of democratic governance and the habits of mind (the "virtues") of a democratically acculturated people. The distinction is a useful one, but the fuller truth of the matter, as Murray well knew, is that "democratic consolidation" is never completed in any final sense. Every generation of Americans, for example, must answer the question posed to the generation of 1863 by Lincoln — namely, whether this nation, or any nation so conceived and so dedicated, can long endure.

The 1990s in America seem likely to be a decade in which new and pressing questions of "democratic consolidation" — fundamental questions of American democratic culture — will come to the forefront of our public life. The abortion debate, the most urgent civil rights debate of the past twenty years, will continue to engage Americans in a protracted controversy over the boundaries of the community of the commonly protected. The return of eugenics — in the form of genetic engineering, technologically managed conception, issues of the treatment of severely handicapped newborns, and the whole array of hotly contested questions at the other chronological end of life (including definitions of death, "extraordinary" means of treatment, and so forth) — will challenge Americans' understanding of Jefferson's inalienable right to life in unprecedented ways.[19] Grave problems of drug abuse, marital and familial breakdown, and the urban underclass — all widely recognized now as having to do with basic questions of character formation — will put new pressures on churches, synagogues, schools, voluntary associations, and other "mediating structures" as the ineffectuality of government as a problem-solver in these areas becomes ever more apparent.

In short, the 1990s may well be a kind of postpolitical decade, in which questions of democratic culture take precedence over questions of "policy" narrowly defined.

Archbishop J. Francis Stafford provocatively defined our current circumstances in these terms in a 1989 pastoral letter entitled "Virtue and the American Republic": "the great division in America today is not between races, classes, or sexes, but between the responsible and the irresponsible — whether our focus is on the marketplace and the

---

19. See Richard John Neuhaus, "The Return of Eugenics," in *Guaranteeing the Good Life: Medicine and the Return of Eugenics*, ed. Richard John Neuhaus (Grand Rapids: William B. Eerdmans, 1990), pp. 1-28.

workbench, on interpersonal relationships, on reproductive technology, on the political process or the urban underclass."[20]

The responsible and the irresponsible: that division (and its ramifications in the public policy arena) will, in turn, intensify the debate
between those who conceive of America as a republic of procedures
and those who insist, with John Courtney Murray, that democracies
are, by their very nature, substantive experiments. Put another way,
the 1990s will see even sharper conflicts between those who define
freedom in terms of the autonomous individual (as that mythic beast
has been understood by certain currents in Enlightenment and post-
Enlightenment thought) and those who, with Murray, argue for Acton's
definition of freedom as "the right of being able to do what we ought."
In the former camp, "rights" are trumps, and the purpose of the state
is to protect that "untrumpable" status. In the latter camp, rights will
continue to be understood as the means by which responsibilities are
fulfilled. Few arguments in American public life are of greater foundational significance for the future life of the republic than this great
debate over the very nature of freedom.[21]

The importance of Murray's thought in this contest ought to be

---

20. Stafford, "Virtue and the American Republic: A Pastoral Letter to the
Church and Denver," Archdiocese of Denver, 14 September 1989.

21. Pope John Paul II had this debate in mind during his 1987 pastoral visit
to the United States, when he said the following:

> among the many admirable values of this nation there is one that stands out in
> particular. It is freedom. The concept of freedom is part of the very fabric of this
> nation as a political community of free people. Freedom is a great gift, a great
> blessing of God.
>
> From the beginning of America, freedom was directed to forming a well-
> ordered society and to promoting its peaceful life. Freedom was channeled to the
> fullness of human life, to the preservation of human dignity, and to the safeguard
> ing of all human rights. An experience of ordered freedom is truly a part of the
> cherished history of this land.
>
> This is the freedom that America is called to live and guard and to transmit.
> She is called to exercise it in such a way that it will benefit the cause of freedom
> in other nations and among other peoples. The only true freedom, the only
> freedom that can truly satisfy, is the freedom to do what we ought as human
> beings created by God according to his plan. It is the freedom to live the truth
> of what we are and who we are before God, the truth of our identity as children
> of God, as brothers and sisters in a common humanity. That is why Jesus Christ
> linked truth and freedom together, stating solemnly, "You will know the truth
> and the truth will set you free" (Jn. 8.32). All people are called to recognize the
> liberating truth of the sovereignty of God over them as individuals and as nations.
> ("Miami Meeting with President Reagan," *Origins,* 24 September 1987, p. 238)

clear from several of the preceding essays in this volume. What Americans face in the 1990s is, in fact, a heightened form of the dilemma that Murray presciently analyzed in the 1950s. Three issues in that great contest — suggestive, not exhaustive — may help to focus debate on the future of the Murray Project.

Church and State: Toward the Civil Public Square

Debate over the public role(s) of religion in America has intensified — and in some significant respects, deteriorated — since the appearance of Murray's pioneering studies on the relationship between classic Catholic political theory and the First Amendment. The annual jurisprudential water torture of Supreme Court opinions on the constitutionality of religious symbols on public property; school textbooks that describe Thanksgiving without mentioning its origins in religious conviction and that elaborate the biography of Dr. Martin Luther King, Jr., while failing to note that he was a Baptist minister; federal bureaucrats who try to strip Catholic AIDS hospices and shelters for the homeless of religious objects; the emergence of a high-tech politics of secularism in the organization "People for the American Way"; and the resurrection of what Murray once called the "new nativism" of Paul Blanshard on the editorial pages of the New York *Times,* the country's paper of record — these and other portents suggest that the "articles of peace" that Murray believed the First Amendment to contain are becoming tattered and thin, this time due to the aggressive attempts of some elements of our society to impose an orthodoxy of secularism in our public life.

Virtually everyone understands that John Courtney Murray was a great defender of the right of religious freedom and a great opponent of the notion that the coercive powers of the state ought to be put at the service of doctrinal or ecclesiastical claims. What is perhaps less well understood is that Murray was also a vigorous opponent of what Richard Neuhaus would later call the "naked public square." Murray, in fact, resisted monisms of every ideological stripe — the monism of the old altar-and-throne arrangements, the monism of Marxism-Leninism, *and* the monism of Blanshard's legally secularized public arena. His principled defense of pluralism, grounded in what he understood to be the authentic, "Gelasian" tradition of Catholic social thought, led him to reject both the sacred and naked public squares in favor of what might be termed the "civil public square," the *agora* of our common life in which creeds are "intelligibly in conflict."[22]

Creating a civil public square in the contemporary United States is thus one of the most urgent tasks in the extension of the Murray Project. At the level of ideas and values, that task of creation will require critical analysis of and debate on a number of issues.

It will require a new debate on (and a new understanding of) the relationship between the free-exercise and no-establishment clauses of the First Amendment. The current view of liberal legal scholars such as Laurence Tribe is, as we have seen, that free exercise is a concession from a government the primary responsibility of which is to enforce the most stringent possible conception of disestablishment. Those who would extend the Murray Project will want to argue that Professor Tribe has it precisely backwards, that the original (and subsequent) purpose of "no establishment" was to serve the end of the free exercise of religion.

Building the civil public square will also require serious attention to the new historiography of the American founding, which challenges both the Parrington/Beard reading of Locke and the progressivist historians' positioning of Locke as the *fons et origo* of the American revolutionary experience. More recent studies of the founding have emphasized the impact of the Scottish Enlightenment on James Madison and on the founders' and framers' understanding — entirely congenial to Murray — that only a virtuous people can be free. This claim, of course, immediately raises the question of the sources of personal and public virtue. And because the available survey research demonstrates beyond reasonable cavil that biblical religion remains the source of virtue, public and private, for most Americans, we have reopened, once again, the issue of the "public church" — though now at a far deeper level than that imagined by either Norman Lear or Laurence Tribe. Questions of tolerance, and of the relationship between tolerance and religious conviction, loom large here. But there is considerable evidence to suggest that the increasing religiosity of the American people over the past two generations has been paralleled by increasing tolerance of the religious views of others.[23] Further research on this

22. On the Gelasian tradition, see *We Hold These Truths*, pp. 196-204.

23. See Theodore Caplow, *All Faithful People* (Minneapolis: University of Minnesota Press, 1983). See also "The Williamsburg Charter Survey on Religion and Public Life" (Washington: Williamsburg Charter Foundation, 1988).

heartening phenomenon, complemented by further philosophical and theological reflection on the nature of tolerance (and its distinction from indifference) will provide another strand in the lengthening cable of the Murray Project.

Americans will debate "church and state" (or, better, religion and society) for so long as there are Americans. In the face of the new nativism of imposed secularity — which threatens evangelical Protestants, Jews, Muslims, and mainline Protestants as well as Catholics (targeted as the last may be at the moment) — an understanding of Murray's thought on these questions, and an ecumenical commitment to deepening and extending it in light of current realities, is essential if we are to "secure the blessings of liberty for ourselves and our posterity."

Catholic Identity and Higher Education

John Courtney Murray was no sectarian in matters of higher education; he invested a part of the waning energies of his later years in trying to arrange the transfer of his beloved Woodstock College to the campus of Yale University. On the other hand, Murray understood that Catholics would make their distinctive intellectual contribution to human wisdom and to the working-out of the American experiment if they thought and wrote and argued as . . . well, as Catholics.

This is not an idea very much in favor in elite American Catholic circles twenty-five years after Vatican II. Throughout the worlds of Catholic higher education, one senses an acquiescence to the prevailing norms (some might say, a surrender to the dominant intellectual and life-style fads) of the American university world. Issues of "academic freedom" are framed as though the "Catholic college" or university had nothing but a semantic connection to the Roman Catholic Church and its highest teaching authority.[24] Pro-abortion student organizations

---

24. During the trial of Fr. Charles Curran's lawsuit against the Catholic University of America, Fr. Richard McBrien, chairman of the theology department at the University of Notre Dame, testified that "only a review by academic peers could determine a theologian's right to teach. According to prevailing American standards of academic freedom, Father McBrien said, a university could not surrender such judgements to any outside body like the Vatican's Congregation for the Doctrine of the Faith, the body that censured Father Curran" (Peter Steinfels, "Academic Freedom Is the Key Issue in Suit," New York *Times*, 18 December 1988, p. 30).

flourish on some Catholic campuses. A feminist hermeneutic of Christian history, the purpose of which is nothing less than the radical deconstruction and dismissal of the classic Christian creeds, is accepted as one among many possible "models" of Catholic self-understanding.

The reaction to this and other concessions to the *Zeitgeist* has been the emergence of Catholic colleges that are, in truth, ghetto schools the administrators of which have set their teeth against modernity and all its works, and all its evil array. But this is surely no answer for those who, with Murray, cherish Clement of Alexandria's image of the multiple streams that feed into the one river of truth.

Extending the Murray Project in Catholic higher education today will require a multifaceted reformation in Catholic intellectual life in general.

One crucial element in that reformation will be a new reading of the intentions of the Second Vatican Council, a reading that does not ignore the Council as promoting the *aggiornamento* of the Church but that grounds this updating and reform in the Council's other imperative — that of *ressourcement,* the rediscovery and appropriation of the full history of Christian wisdom, with a special emphasis on the christologically centered anthropology of the Church Fathers. *Ressourcement* is the essential precondition to a revivified Catholic identity that challenges the sterile alternatives posed by today's Catholic deconstuctionists (Catholicism-as-high-church-humanism) and restorationists (Catholicism-as-Tridentine-legal-system). *Ressourcement* is also the intellectual lever by which the dull and patterned debate over "authority" and "authoritarianism" can be reconceived so that the most urgent question becomes not "Who's in charge here?" but "What is authoritative for the Church?"[25]

The reformation of American Catholic intellectual life that would, over time, yield a reformation of Catholic higher education will stand or fall on this question of whether Catholic scholars follow Murray's example in being modern scholars who are not modernists. Will Catholic intellectuals contribute to the debunking not of modernity per se but of the ideology of modernity, by opening themselves and their students to the full range of Christian wisdom? Will they embrace what Fr. George Florovsky called the "ecumenism of time"? Will they rediscover the classic Catholic "scandal of particularity" in terms of both the foundational Christian scandal of the incarnation and the

25. Cf. Neuhaus, *The Catholic Moment,* pp. 126-37.

particularity of the American experience of God's self-revelation in Christ? Here are three questions, the answers to which will tell us much about the future of the Murray Project.[26]

America and the World: The Quest for Peace and Freedom

In rather sharp contrast to time-value documents such as the American bishops' 1983 pastoral letter "The Challenge of Peace," John Courtney Murray's writing on international politics retains a remarkable freshness even as world-historical changes sweep the globe from Santiago to Vilnius. Murray did not write a great deal about international affairs, but what he did publish was rooted in his appreciation for the distinctive understanding of social ethics in the "tradition of reason," an understanding that allowed the Catholic social ethicist to work at the intersection of moral norms and international politics without torturing himself over the "pseudo-problems" that bedeviled others of his colleagues, such as the alleged "gulf between the morality of the individual and collective man," of "self-interest," and of "power" (pp. 272-73).

The question of self-interest, or national interest, will be the focus of considerable attention in the American 1990s, as the United States defines the ends and means of its foreign policy in a post–cold war world. Murray was, on these matters, a Christian realist, but of a distinctively Thomistic sort. He recognized the distinctive character of politics-among-nations but insisted that that distinctiveness did not absolve the statesman from participation in moral argument about the ends and means of power. In the "tradition of reason," even international politics is obliged to pursue the "fivefold structure of obliga-

---

26. There is nothing offensive to a true ecumenism in this insistence on the centrality of "Catholic identity" in Catholic higher education. As ecumenism moves beyond a negotiating model toward what some have called the "reconfessionalizing" of the ecumenical enterprise, it should be more and more widely understood that the keys to a true ecumenical dialogue are going to be found through the deepening, in ecumenical dialogue, of Lutheran identity, Methodist identity, Catholic identity, and so forth. What too often passes for ecumenical sensitivity in Christian intellectual circles today is actually a common acquiescence to the prejudices of the secular academy (which, it should be added, is unsurpassed as a rigorous imposer of orthodoxies in modern America).

For a more developed presentation of the points made in this brief section, see my essay "Secularism R.I.P.: Reclaiming the Catholic Intellectual Tradition," *Crisis* (October 1989): 22-31.

tory political ends," by which Murray meant the classic goals of "justice, freedom, security, the general welfare, and civil unity or peace." The boundaries of the achievement of those ends in world politics are narrower than within a given national community, but those boundaries can be extended by prudent statecraft. Thus, "the national interest, rightly understood, is successfully achieved only at the interior, as it were, of the growing international order to which the pursuit of national interest can and must contribute" (pp. 272-73).

The chief obstacle to that growing international order, as Murray saw it, was Marxism-Leninism, as an ideology and as a world-historical project. The implosion of communist ideology, the waning of Marxism-Leninism as a political force in the world, and the democratic revolution of the late 1980s have created new conditions for the possibility of the pursuit of a world order congenial to classic Western political values. A great debate on the degree to which America should take the lead in the pursuit of that world order is certain to unfold in the 1990s. Traditional isolationists of the right will make common cause with new left-influenced neo-isolationists in arguing, "Come home, America."[27] Against that seductive song, those who would extend and develop the Murray Project must continue to urge a rational and prudent internationalism, skeptical of present international legal and political organizations but committed, as a matter of moral principle, to the notion that there are duties beyond borders — and thus committed, as a matter of statecraft, to the development of a world-order politics answerable to democratic values and conducted according to nonviolent democratic procedures.

In the mid-1940s, Murray, commenting on the principles that undergirded Pope Pius XII's vision of a postwar peace, argued that public opinion must "grasp the fact that the juridical organization of the international community is an inescapable demand of social justice, a true and genuine moral imperative, laid upon the collective conscience of States and peoples by the moral law and sanctioned by the sovereignty of God."[28] At the same time, Murray cautioned, Pius's moral imperative involved, in its achievement, historical and technical

27. See Patrick J. Buchanan, "America First, Second, and Third," *National Interest* 19 (Spring 1990): 77-82; and Alan Tonelson, "A Manifesto for Democrats," *National Interest* 16 (Summer 1989): 36-48.

28. Murray, "World Order and Moral Law," *Thought* 19 (December 1944): 582.

problems that have "hitherto been insoluble" (p. 246). It would be the height of imprudence to suggest that the remarkable events of the late 1980s and early 1990 have rendered those problems nugatory. On the other hand, Christian thought about world politics — indeed, all prudent thought about these issues — must avoid the sort of easy cynicism that obscures the possibilities that have been created by the communist breakup and the democratic revolution.

Extending and developing the Murray Project in the 1990s, then, will involve reopening the issue of "world order," not in a return to the Wilsonian and Rooseveltian illusions of the past but in terms of a genuine Christian realism that discerns in the present opportunities an occasion to advance the "moral imperative" of an international public life fit for men made in the image and likeness of God.

The Quality of the Conversation

In times such as our own, when the gyrations of the "McLaughlin Group" pass for serious political discourse, perhaps the greatest contribution that those who would extend and develop the Murray Project can make to American public life is to deepen the quality of the conversation at the crossroads where moral norms and political decision making meet.

John Courtney Murray, as others in this volume have indicated, had quite definite ideas about the nature and tone of good political debate. It should be "cool and dry, with the coolness and dryness that characterize good argument among informed and responsible men" (p. 19). This was, however, no mere aristocratic preference for the drawing room over the church basement, the labor hall, or the auditorium platform. No, political argument stood under a moral imperative to be cool and dry because political association, by its very nature, depends "for its permanent cohesiveness on argument among men" (p. 18). No argument, no polis — and, it should go without saying, no democracy.

If we would wonder at the source of the incohesiveness of our public life today, we need look no farther than the fact that "cool and dry" political argument has given way to politics as entertainment. This would be troublesome in the best of times, but it is positively dangerous in times such as our own, marked as they are by a *Kulturkampf* that touches virtually every area of our public life.

The American Catholic community, where one might have hoped to find a continuing dedication to Murray's style of argument, has not been immune from the politics of rhetorical passion — a failing in which it has been joined, in ecumenical concord, by its Protestant brethren in Christ. And this, perhaps more than the foolishness of this or that pronouncement, has been the singular failing of the "public Church" over the past generation: its failure to model a style of public discourse that is at once dedicated, informed, passionate, rational, and committed to democratic civility.

And as that has been the religious community's singular failure, one can argue that that should be the great test of the extension and development of the Murray Project: whether or not those committed to the Project incarnate, once again, the classic method of public moral argument about the right ordering of our common life. Doing so, or failing to do so, we can be sure, will have significant, indeed determinative, consequences for the future of the American experiment in ordered liberty.

About the Contributors

GERARD V. BRADLEY is a professor of law at Notre Dame Law School. He is the author of *Church-State Relationships in America* and is working on a new book on constitutional theory.

FRANCIS CANAVAN, S.J., is Professor Emeritus of Political Science at Fordham University in New York. His most recent books include *Freedom of Expression: Purpose as Limit* (1984) and *Edmund Burke: Prescription and Providence* (1987).

JOHN C. CORT is a contributing editor of the *New Oxford Review*. He has written numerous articles on the implications of Christian social and economic thought and is author of *Christian Socialism: An Informal History* (1988).

ROBERT F. CUERVO is an associate professor of political science at St. John's University, Staten Island, New York. His doctoral dissertation dealt with "Public Philosophy in a Democracy" (1980). His articles and reviews have appeared in *Presidential Studies Quarterly, Faith and Reason,* and the *Journal of Politics*.

KENNETH L. GRASSO is an assistant professor of political science at St. Peter's College in Jersey City, New Jersey. His articles and reviews have appeared in *Interpretation, Thought, Law and Justice, Crisis, Faith and Reason, Perspectives on Political Science,* and the *Journal of Law and Religion*.

ROBERT P. HUNT is an assistant professor of political science at Kean College of New Jersey. He has written on the political thought of Reinhold Niebuhr and John Courtney Murray and his articles have appeared in *Law and Justice, Thought,* and the *Journal of Law and Religion.*

PETER AUGUSTINE LAWLER is an associate professor of social science at Berry College in Rome, Georgia. He is the author of numerous articles on political philosophy, religion, and American politics. He has also edited *American Political Rhetoric: A Reader* (1982).

WILLIAM R. LUCKEY is chairman of the department of Political Science and Economics at Christendom College in Front Royal, Virginia. He teaches political philosophy and constitutional law and has just completed a volume on the political thought of G. K. Chesterton.

DAVID T. MASON teaches political philosophy at Mary Baldwin College in Staunton, Virginia. He is currently completing work on a new book entitled *Greek Political Ontology.*

RICHARD JOHN NEUHAUS is editor-in-chief of *First Things.* He has written extensively on religion and politics and is author of many books including *The Naked Public Square: Religion and Democracy in America* (1984) and *The Catholic Moment: The Paradox of the Church in the Postmodern World* (1987).

DAVID NOVAK is Professor of Religious Studies at the University of Virginia. His books include *The Image of the Non-Jew in Judaism* (1983) and *Jewish-Christian Dialogue: A Jewish Justification* (1989).

MARY C. SEGERS is an associate professor of political science at Rutgers University in Newark, New Jersey. She is co-author, with James C. Foster, of *Elusive Equality: Liberalism, Affirmative Action, and Social Change in America* (1983) and is editor of *Church Polity and American Politics: Issues in Contemporary Catholicism* (1990).

GEORGE WEIGEL is president of the Ethics and Public Policy Center in Washington, D.C. His books include *Tranquillitas Ordinis: The Present Failure and Future Promise of American Catholic Thought on War and Peace* (1987) and *Catholicism and the Renewal of American Democracy* (1989).